The Course
of German History

'Mr Taylor, by cutting down to a minimum the ballast of dates and names that so often encumbers historical writing, and concentrating on the fundamental trends and events, has achieved both brevity and lucidity.'

The Observer

'He is not only a brilliant but a profound historian.'

New Statesman

'The profound is mixed with the wisecrack. It has the shortcomings of its virtues. It will shock the scholarly reader but it must challenge him too.'

American Historical Review

'*The Course of German History* is vivid, exciting, openly partisan.'

Adam Sisman, A. J. P. Taylor: A Biography

'His first best-seller, *The Course of German History* was written in a "journalistic" rather than academic style and remains extremely readable.'

Kathleen Burk, Troublemaker: The Life and History of A. J. P. Taylor

Routledge Classics contains the very best of Routledge publishing over the past century or so, books that have, by popular consent, become established as classics in their field. Drawing on a fantastic heritage of innovative writing published by Routledge and its associated imprints, this series makes available in attractive, affordable form some of the most important works of modern times.

For a complete list of titles visit
www.routledgeclassics.com

A. J. P.
Taylor

The Course of German History

A survey of the development of
German history since 1815

With a new introduction by Chris Wrigley

 London and New York

First published 1945
by Hamish Hamilton Ltd
First published by Methuen & Co. Ltd 1961
First published by Routledge 1988

First published in Routledge Classics 2001
by Routledge
2 Park Square, Milton Park, Abingdon, Oxon OX14 4RN
270 Madison Ave, New York, NY 10016

Reprinted 2004, 2005, 2006, 2007

Transferred to Digital Printing 2008

Routledge is an imprint of the Taylor & Francis Group, an informa business

Introduction © 2001 Chris Wrigley

Typeset in Joanna by RefineCatch Limited, Bungay, Suffolk
Printed and bound in Great Britain by
TJI Digital, Padstow, Cornwall

British Library Cataloguing in Publication Data
A catalogue record for this book is available from the British Library

Library of Congress Cataloging in Publication Data
A catalog record for this book has been applied for

ISBN10 0–415–25558–9 (hbk)
ISBN10 0–415–25405–1 (pbk)
ISBN13 978–0–415–25558–5 (hbk)
ISBN13 978–0–415–25405–2 (pbk)

CONTENTS

MAPS

INTRODUCTION

by Chris Wrigley
Head of the School of History and Art History,
Nottingham University

The Course of German History is one of A.J.P. Taylor's best known books. It has rarely been out of print since it was first published in July 1945. It was very much a product of the Second World War, history with a moral for the victors in a second modern war against Germany. Its message was that there were continuities in German history and Hitler and the Nazis were not an aberration but only an extreme version of Germany's drive for mastery in at least central and eastern Europe.

Alan Taylor began his Preface to the first edition by observing,

> The book is a pièce d'occasion. It is meant to be serious history. All the same I should never have written it except for the events of the last five years and, still more, the need of some historical background to the political problems of the present.

It had begun as a chapter on the Weimar Republic era (1919–22) of German history for a government handbook for British troops. Alan Taylor had written it in for the Political Warfare Executive (PWE), which was attached to the Special Operations Executive, an important part of the British wartime intelligence service. It was the second historical piece he had written for the PWE, and was the second rejected by them as too controversial. The first had been a handbook on Hungary, which he wrote between May and October 1943, but this was rejected as too polemical on the advice of another Oxford academic, Professor C.A. Macartney.[1] The Weimar chapter was rejected on similar grounds on the advice of the refugee German scholar, F.L. Carsten.[2] Instead, the PWE turned to E.J. Passant for a text, which later was turned into his book, *Germany 1815–1945* (Cambridge, Cambridge University Press, 1959).

Alan Taylor's message that the Germans as a whole were guilty of expansionist policies was not 'on message'. Just as the Allies during the First World War had striven to emphasize that those guilty for causing the war were the Kaiser and the Prussian militarized elite, and all would be well with a democratic German people, so towards the end of the Second World War blame was apportioned to Hitler and the Nazis, not the ordinary German people. Alan Taylor took pains to emphasize that nearly all Germans had been committed to a Greater Germany. He was deliberately provocative in writing in *The Course of German History*.

> ... the rest of the world had to pay the penalty for the political incompetence and timidity of the German middle class. The failure of the 'good Germans', not the ranting of the 'bad' ones, was the real crime of Germany against European civilization. (1961 edn, p.166)

He asked in a published letter in October 1944, ' ... how many German refugees, living securely in this country, are prepared to recognise the full national independence of the east European peoples, and to renounce forever all prospects of a European system under German leadership?'[3]

Alan Taylor came to German history from a robust radical background and an expertise in Austrian history. Born on 25 March 1906 at Birkdale, Southport, Lancashire, Alan John Percivale Taylor grew up the only child in a wealthy middle-class family, his father making his money in the family cotton cloth exporting business. His was a nonconformist and radical background, his parents swinging from radical to advanced socialist views from the First World War. Alan Taylor himself joined the Independent Labour Party and was briefly (as an undergraduate at Oxford University, 1924–7) a member of the Communist

Party. However, his politics, although socialist, by the 1940s onwards, were more individualistic radical and even populist. His visits to Germany, especially once the Nazis were in power, added to his distrust of Germany as a Power which derived from his study of the published multi-volume documents on German foreign policy.

His own archival research was primarily based on research in 1928–30 in Vienna (supplemented by work in the French and British archives). Later, he went on to write a substantial study, *The Habsburg Monarchy 1815–1918* (London, Macmillan, 1941), very much revised as *The Habsburg Monarchy 1809–1918* (London, Hamish Hamilton, 1948). As a result he saw German history and politics from an Austrian perspective. His concern for national self-determination for the Slav nationalities in the old Austria–Hungary was carried through to *The Course of German History*, written between the two versions of his book on the Austro-Hungarian Empire. Thus, for example, Alan Taylor was explicit that Weimar politicians, before the advent to power of Hitler, were reverting to expansionist policies:

> Only if Germany made reparation; only if Germany remained disarmed; only if the German frontiers were final; only, above all, if the Germans accepted the Slav peoples as their equals, was there any chance of a stable, peaceful, civilized Germany. (1961 edn, p.242)

During the war Alan Taylor advocated the reconstruction of Czechoslovakia, with the removal of the German minority populations. In the case of Yugoslavia, he championed Trieste going to it, not to Italy.

The book also expressed his concerns arising from the Second World War. He was very much an apostle of the Anglo-Russian alliance. In the first edition the book reached its climax with a final paragraph, now the third from the end, with Churchill proclaiming the alliance of Britain and Russia. After the subsequent sentence, the book then concluded that paragraph with:

> The 'many great nations', whom Bismarck had dismissed with scorn, at last awoke. Germany owed her unity and success to the disunion of her neighbours. That was now at an end. There will be no German 'New Order' in Europe. Instead there will be a 'New Order' in Germany

> which will owe nothing to German efforts. It will be imposed by the
> united strength of England, Russia and the United States; and it will
> prove impermanent unless these three powers remain as united in
> peace as they have been in war. (First edn, pp.223–4)

Alan Taylor continued to press for Anglo-Soviet understanding during the early period of the Cold War. Shortly before The Course of German History was published he wrote in a letter, 'In the near future, say the next twenty years, the Soviet Union is our natural ally.'[4] However, by 1948 he was disillusioned with the Soviet Union, observing on the radio, 'I care for liberty above all other causes . . . .'.[5] From at least the early 1940s his fundamental political position was: 'Without democracy Socialism would be worth nothing, but democracy is worth a great deal even when it is not socialist.'[6]

Alan Taylor had no doubts that he was writing a polemical book with The Course of German History. Shortly before he completed it, he informed a BBC producer that the book 'is as hot as can be – a good thing that it doesn't have to pass your censorship'.[7] He was later to criticize it as his 'unfavourite' book, being 'too clever and showy'.[8] This was the main negative note sounded by reviewers when it was published. In the American Historical Review it was observed, 'Grandiose in style, it often overshoots its mark. The profound is mixed with the wisecrack.' But Sigmund Neumann, the reviewer did praise it as,

> . . . a challenging essay, packed with substantial summaries and
> spiced with brilliant observations, reflecting his scholarly maturity,
> his lucid mind and his Vienna training . . . An answer to an impor-
> tant query, it is an impatient book, vivid and tempestuous, pointed
> and pugnacious, concise and over-zealous, severe and sarcastic,
> ambitious and angry.

R. Birley in International Affairs mostly praised it but felt that it was facile in its attempt to find continuities in German history and that in making the Nazis seem 'a normal development, quite to be expected, of German history, Mr Taylor nearly succeeds in making them respectable'.[9] Alan Taylor was to be severely criticized for this tendency in his later The Origins of the Second World War (London, Hamish Hamilton, 1961).

Lewis Namier in the *Times Literary Supplement*, who also found much to praise, observed that 'the book should prove of high value in the study of the German problem'.[10] However, this presumption that there was a long-running 'German problem' was to make *The Course of German History* seem dated. By the early 1970s it was deemed by one historian to be almost a caricature of anti-German history.[11] More generally, it was seen as one of several books of the war period which tried to explain the rise of the Nazis as due to some peculiarity of the German character.[12]

Alan Taylor was appalled by the atrocities of the Nazi era. When in Florence in April 1973, he wrote to Eva Haraszti of elderly German tourists,

> They looked so orderly, civilized, restrained. Yet they must have been in the prime of life under Hitler and most of them must have been Nazis. You think one man is a quite distinguished scholar; perhaps he was once a German officer, massacring prisoners-of-war in Russia. And that grey-haired lady. She was no doubt a Hitler Mädchen and after that a guard in a concentration camp. How could such ordinary people have been so surpassingly barbarous? It is beyond my understanding.[13]

Taylor was not alone in having such concerns. There was a major debate aroused by Daniel Goldhagen's *Hitler's Willing Executioners* (New York, Knopf, 1996).[14] Earlier, there were controversies over Fritz Fishcher's *Germany's Aims in the First World War* (German publication, 1961; English translation, 1967), which argued the Kaiser and his advisers had sought to dominate much of Europe both during and before the First World War, and over the uniqueness of the Holocaust (the *Historikerstreit*, 1986). Given these controversies, Alan Taylor's *The Course of German History* appears to be less out on a limb than once seemed to be the case. Nevertheless, it still remains a strong statement of the view that German history is exceptional. This is expressed vigorously at the very start of the book: 'The History of the Germans is a history of extremes. It contains everything except moderation . . .'.

Yet Alan Taylor was trying to write more than an anti-German tract. When he came to write a new preface to the 1951 edition of *The Course* of *German History* he argued that the study of international relations since 1848 had been dominated by German scholars or by those unduly influenced by the published German documents. He continued,

> Sooner or later we shall have to escape from the German version of the events of the last hundred years. I myself am halfway through a history of the relations of the Great Powers between the revolutions of 1848 and the collapse of the European system in 1918. If I can ever snatch leisure from the time-consuming life of a College tutor and complete it, this present book will appear more sensible.

This he did, the resulting book – *The Struggle for Mastery in Europe 1848–1918* (Oxford, Oxford University Press, 1954) – proving to be a classic of diplomatic history. He also went on to publish a brief biography of Bismarck – *Bismarck: The Man and the Statesman* (New York, Knopf, 1955). In writing the biography, he reversed his earlier distaste for Bismarck, observing later, 'Now I found Bismarck's personality fascinating . . . and he became one of the few I should like to recall from the dead.'[15] Even so, Bismarck came off relatively lightly in *The Course of German History*, being judged 'a barbarian of genius' (First edn, p.96).

Although very much a work of its time, *The Course of German History* remains a lively, if polemical, short history written by one of the twentieth century's greatest historians.

REFERENCES

1   Attila Pók, 'British Manual on Hungary in 1944', in A. Pók, *The Fabric of Modern Europe* (Nottingham, Astra Press, 1999, pp.201–7).
2   Kathleen Burk, *Troublemaker: The Life and History of A.J.P. Taylor* (New Haven and London, Yale University Press, 2000, p.181).
3   Letter by AJPT to *New Statesman and Nation*, 28 October 1944, p.285.
4   AJPT to Trevor Blewitt, 12 April 1945, BBC archives.
5   Radio broadcast on the BBC radio European Service, 7 July 1948; published in *The Listener*, 40, 1016, 15 July 1948, pp.92–3.
6   Review of John Strachey, 'A Faith to Fight For', *Manchester Guardian*, 7 March 1941, p.7.
7   AJPT to Trevor Blewitt, 23 August 1944, BBC archives.
8   AJPT to Eva Haraszti, 4 December 1970; A.J.P. Taylor in E. Haraszti Taylor (ed.) *Letters to Eva, 1969–83: A.J.P. Taylor* (London, Century, 1991, p.25).

9 Chris Wrigley, *A.J.P. Taylor: A Complete Bibliography* (Brighton, Harvester Press, 1980, pp.72–5).

10 *Times Literary Supplement*, 29 September 1945, pp.457–9; reprinted in L.B. Namier, *Facing East* (London, Hamish Hamilton, 1947, pp.25–40).

11 Robert Cole, *A.J.P. Taylor: The Traitor Within the Gates* (London, Macmilllan, 1993, p.102).

12 Another example was R.D. Butler, *The Roots of National Socialism* (London, Macmillan, 1941). For critiques of such approaches see, for example, D. Blackbourn and G. Eley, *The Peculiarities of German History* (Oxford, Blackwell, 1984), and R.J. Evans, *Rethinking German History* (London, Harper Collins, 1987).

13 AJPT to Eva Haraszti, 22 April 1973, in *Letters to Eva, op. cit.*, p.124.

14 R.H. Shandley (ed.) *Unwilling Germans? The Goldhagen Debate* (Minneapolis, University of Minnesota Press, 1998).

15 A.J.P. Taylor, *A Personal History* (London, Hamish Hamilton, 1983, p.207).

Nottingham, January 2001

PREFACE [1961]

This book was written in the last days of the Second World War. It had a curious origin. The chapter on the Weimar republic was written as a separate piece to be included in one of the many compilations which were being put together in order to explain to the conquerors what sort of country they were conquering. My piece proved unacceptable; it was, I learnt, too depressing. The Germans were enthusiastic for a demagogic dictator and engaged on a war for the domination of Europe. But I ought to have shown that this was a bit of bad luck, and that all Germans other than a few wicked men were bubbling over with enthusiasm for democracy or for Christianity or for some other noble cause which would turn them into acceptable allies once we had liberated them from their tyrants. This seemed to me unlikely. I therefore went further back into German history to see whether it confirmed the argument of my rejected chapter; and this book was the result. It was an attempt to plot the course of German history; and it shows that it was no more a mistake for the German people to end up with Hitler than it is an accident when a river flows into the sea, though the process is, I daresay, unpleasant for the fresh water. Nothing, it seems to me, has happened since to disturb the conclusions at which I then arrived.

When the book appeared, some reviewers expostulated that it

'indicted' a nation and that no country's history could survive such hostile scrutiny. I made no indictment; the facts made it for themselves. Indeed I left many of the worst facts out of the reckoning. There is little in my book about the Nazi terror, and nothing about the policy of mass extermination which brought death to some seventeen million innocent people during the second World war. Far from treating the Germans as barbarians or eternal aggressors, I was anxious to discover why a nation so highly civilized in most ways should have failed to develop political balance. On almost every test of civilization – philosophy, music, science, local government – the Germans come out at the top of the list; only the art of political behaviour has been beyond them. English writers give little help towards explaining this mystery. They have never recovered from the shock of learning that the victory of German nationalism was not followed by the beneficent results which were expected in the middle of the nineteenth century. German writers have been of more use; and my book, far from being unsympathetic towards Germany, is derived almost entirely from criticisms formulated by Germans themselves. Meinecke, for instance, once an admirer of Bismarck, confessed towards the end of his life that civilized Germans had been too passive about public affairs; they assumed that civilized life and the rule of law would be automatically provided for them by their irresponsible rulers without effort on their side. Rosenberg has claimed, perhaps even with some exaggeration, that the German working-classes abandoned the struggle for social democracy, once they were given economic security.

These writers, however critical, have one great handicap. They see the German problem as something wholly internal and are hardly aware that Germany's greatest problem has been to find a settled place in Europe. It is an advantage, and a rare one, for a writer on German history to be an Englishman, not educated in Germany; this advantage at any rate I possess. The key to Germany's past is to be found in her relations with her neighbours – predominantly defensive towards the west, always aggressive towards the east. For the last fifty years or more we in the west have seen only the formidable bulk and unity of the seventy or eighty million Germans, and have failed to realize how they would be overshadowed when the two hundred and fifty million Slavs stood on their own feet, economically and politically. The Germans have appreciated this cloud in the east, more and more vividly, during the course of the last century; this fear underlay their plans for conquest and extermination. No German of political consequence thought of accepting the Slavs as equals and living at peace with them; nor does the revisionist campaign against Czechoslovakia and Poland in western Germany suggest that their outlook has changed. Of course many Germans never think about the Slavs at all. These are the 'good Germans' who obtrude into every discussion of the German question, their 'goodness' being synonymous with ineffectiveness. The historian cannot deal with the politically impotent except in so far as their dead weight is thrown into the scales by more agile and positive forces. This book deals with what happened in Germany. It cannot therefore deal, except by implication, with those Germans who regretted what was happening, and – having regretted – participated. There were, and I daresay are, many millions of well-meaning kindly Germans; but what have they added up to politically?

This book attempts to answer the historian's question – how did this state of things come about? It does not pretend to answer the politician's question – how can this state be remedied? The historian does not deal in remedies. He thinks of the next stage in a process of conflicting forces, not of a 'solution'. At best he can record that certain 'solutions' have been tried and have succeeded or failed; this is useful though not decisive evidence that they might succeed or fail in the future. The German problem has two sides. How can the peoples of Europe be secured against repeated bouts of German aggression? And, how can the Germans discover a settled, peaceful form of political existence? The first problem revolves round the behaviour of others, not of the Germans; and is capable of solution. Germany is in the centre of Europe and has scored repeated successes by playing off her neighbours to east and west. If these neighbours are united, or even on reasonably good terms, the Germans will not be able to harm us or even themselves. The friendship between east and west did not long survive the second World war. All the same we have had a stroke of luck. The former allies remained in occupation of the parts of Germany which they had respectively conquered; and we reverted by accident to the old device of a divided Germany which saved Europe trouble over many centuries. It is not a good solution, and it is unlikely to be permanent; but it is better than none at all. The partitioning Powers profess to regret the division of Germany, and even claim to be working for her reunion; but I suspect that they encourage each other's obstinacy behind the scenes, appreciating that things could be much worse. Of course nowadays we officially deplore any suggestion that precautions against a new German aggression are necessary, or ever will be, and the German problem is posed in a different form: how can we build up Germany as a Great Power and use her as an ally against the Soviet Union without risk to ourselves? The answer is simple: it is not possible, and those who attempt the impossible will sooner or later pay the price. Preserving the present situation is the kindest policy towards the Germans themselves. For only a divided Germany can be a free Germany. A reunited Germany would cease to be free: either it would become a militaristic state in order to resume the march towards European domination, or its power would be compulsorily reduced by foreign interference, if the former allies had the sense to come together again in time. The flourishing state of Germany at present, particularly in the west, is evidence that disunion does not bring decay; on the contrary, disunion is the cause of Germany's prosperity. The victorious allies have done much better for Germany, despite their quarrels, after the second World war than after the first. Fifteen years after their first defeat the Germans were taking the hat round from one European capital to another; fifteen years after their second the Germans are casually considering whether to bestow a fraction of their charity on the Americans.

There was a great pother after the war about how we should educate the Germans in democracy. I never understood how this should be done. Democracy is learnt by practice, not by sitting on forms at a political finishing-school. Our only contribution should have been to ensure that the Germans did not 'solve' their problem at the expense of others; and the Western Powers would have done more for German democracy if they had given a firm recognition to the Oder–Neisse frontier with Poland than they did with all their political admonitions. However the general prosperity of the western world has been another stroke of luck for us; and maybe the Germans will forget their imperialist dreams so long as they remain prosperous also. I have almost reached the point of believing that I shall not live to see a third German war; but events have an awkward trick of running in the wrong direction, just when you least expect it.

This book deals predominantly with the German *Reich* in its narrower sense – the Little Germany which Bismarck set up in 1871. This is lopsided. Austria did not cease to be part of the German question when she was excluded from the political system of Germany in 1866. The survival of the Habsburg monarchy; support for it in war; the relations of the German and Austrian republics in 1918; and the efforts both to promote and to resist the *Anschluss* which was achieved in 1938; all were an intrinsic part of the German question. The conflict between Czechs and Germans in Bohemia shaped German history almost as much as the conflict between Poles and Germans in eastern Prussia. My excuse for passing over these things is that I published a history of the Habsburg Monarchy in 1949. It and the present book are complimentary, one not to be understood without the other. I have also written abruptly and somewhat cryptically about German foreign relations, particularly in the later years. Here, too, I can only offer as excuse other books of mine on international relations: *The Struggle for Mastery in Europe 1848–1918*, and *The Origins of the Second World War*. The observant reader will detect that my views have changed here and there; but, unlike many fire-eaters of the second World war, I have not gone so far as to stand on my head.

The manuscript of this book was completed in September 1944. It was published in England in July 1945. The last two paragraphs were added later so as to carry the record to what is still, surprisingly enough, the end of the story. I have put a few mistakes right for this present edition, and benefited here and there from later information. Substantially the book remains unchanged.

A. J. P. TAYLOR

1

DIVIDED GERMANY: THE LEGACY OF THE HOLY ROMAN EMPIRE

The history of the Germans is a history of extremes. It contains every-thing except moderation, and in the course of a thousand years the Germans have experienced everything except normality. They have dominated Europe, and they have been the helpless victims of the domination of others; they have enjoyed liberties unparalleled in Europe and they have fallen victim to despotisms equally without paral-lel; they have produced the most transcendental philosophers, the most spiritual musicians, and the most ruthless and unscrupulous politi-cians. 'German' has meant at one moment a being so sentimental, so trusting, so pious, as to be too good for this world; and at another a being so brutal, so unprincipled, so degraded, as to be not fit to live. Both descriptions are true: both types of German have existed not only at the same epoch, but in the same person. Only the normal person, not particularly good, not particularly bad, healthy, sane, moderate – he has never set his stamp on German history. Geographically the people of the centre, the Germans have never found a middle way of life, either in their thought or least of all in their politics. One looks in vain in their history for *juste milieu*, for common sense –. the two qualities which have distinguished France and England. Nothing is normal in German history except violent oscillations.

Certain permanent factors have, indeed, influenced German history, since the time when Charlemagne, by establishing the Holy Roman Empire, advanced German history from the stage of tribal legends. First was their geographic position. The Germans are the peoples of the north European plain, the people without a defined natural frontier. Without the sharp limit of mountain ranges, except at the Alps and the Bohemian mountains, the great plain is intersected by four great rivers (Rhine, Elbe, Oder, Vistula), dividing lines sharp enough to split the German people up among themselves, not rigid enough to confine them within settled frontiers. There is no determined geographic point for German expansion, equally none for German contraction; and, in the course of a thousand years, geographic Germany has gone out and in like a concertina. At times Germany has been confined within the Rhine and the Elbe; at others it has blown itself out to the Pyrenees and to the Caucasus. Every German frontier is artificial, therefore impermanent; that is the permanence of German geography.

Enduring too for a thousand years has been their ethnographical position. Here too the Germans have been the people of the middle; always they have had two neighbours and have shown two faces. To their west was the Roman Empire and its heir, French civilization; to their east, the Slavs, new barbarians pressing on the Germans as the Germans pressed on Rome. To the west therefore the Germans have always appeared as barbarians, but the most civilized of barbarians, eager to learn, anxious to imitate; and the record of German civilization is a story of sedulous and exaggerated imitation of the established order in the west – an imitation which began with Charlemagne's apeing of Caesar and has ended in Hitler's apeing of Napoleon. To the Slavs of the east, however, the Germans have made a very different appearance: ostensibly the defenders of civilization, they have defended it as barbarians, employing the technical means of civilization, but not its spirit. For a thousand years, again from Charlemagne to Hitler, the Germans have been 'converting' the Slavs from paganism, from Ortho-dox Christianity, from Bolshevism, or merely from being Slavs; their weapons have varied, their method has always been the same – extermination. Most of the peoples of Europe have, at one time or another, been exterminators. The French exterminated the Albigen-sians in the thirteenth century and the Huguenots in the seventeenth; the Spaniards exterminated the Moors; the English exterminated the North-American Indians and attempted in the seventeenth century to exterminate the Irish. But no other people has pursued extermination as a permanent policy from generation to generation for a thousand years; and it is foolish to suppose that they have done so without adding something permanent to their national tradition. No one can understand the Germans who does not appreciate their anxiety to learn from, and to imitate, the West; but equally no one can understand Germans who does not appreciate their determination to exterminate the East.

It may seem a platitude to count the German people as the third permanent factor in German history; but it is a platitude which is often overlooked. The German national state is new; but the consciousness of German national existence is old, certainly older than the conscious-ness of Spanish national existence, perhaps older than that of England or France. The Germans have been, for more than a thousand years, unmistakably a people; though that does not imply that they have always been the same sort of people. A political community has a way of life like a school or a trade union; and the individuals, so far as they are members of the community, are shaped by that way of life, even while they are helping to change it. 'National character' is the short-hand which the historian must use in order to express the effect on a community of geographical, political, and social surroundings. There has been a German 'national character' for more than a thousand years, a character not strictly identical, but recognizably the same. By the time of Charlemagne the Germans had settled down: from then on they were shaped by unchanging geographical circumstances, and by the political neighbourhood of the French on the one side and the Slavs on the other. The area of German settlement has been expanded, but never radically moved. There was never such a revolution as, in English his-tory, the change from a small island off the coast of Europe to the centre of a great world empire. When, late in their history, the Ger-mans talked of world empire, it was no more than a new version of the empire of Charlemagne. This routine has given to German history a pattern almost monotonous; of them, more truly than of most people, it may be said that there is nothing new under the sun. If a natural cataclysm had placed a broad sea between the Germans and the French, the German character would not have been dominated by militarism. If – a more conceivable possibility – the Germans had succeeded in exterminating their Slav neighbours, as the Anglo-Saxons in North America succeeded in exterminating the Indians, the effect would have been what it has been on the Americans: the Germans would have become advocates of brotherly love and international reconciliation. Constant surroundings shaped a German national character strong enough to withstand the increasing changes in social circumstance which occurred in Germany in modern times.

For a thousand years also Germany has had a political form. The *Reich*, the political expression of the German people, is the oldest political organization in Europe, older than England, France, Hungary, or Poland; and therefore older by far than any other European state. Since the moment when Charlemagne founded the Reich in 800, there has never been a time when the Germans were without the framework of a political organization. For even when the old Reich was dissolved in 1806, its place was taken first by the Confederation of the Rhine and then by the German Confederation in 1815. The continuity of the Reich is obscured by a twofold paradox. First, at no time before 1933 did the political energies of the German people find their sole outlet in the Reich; for most of its thousand years more political energy went into maintaining German states independent of the Reich, or even hostile to it, than into the Reich itself. Secondly, at no time did the Reich coincide with the national existence of the German people; it has always either carried its frontiers far beyond the German national area or failed to include all Germans within its limits. A history of the French state would be, by and large, a political history of the French people; a history of the English state would certainly be a political history of the English people. But a history of the Reich would not coincide with a political history of the German people. In the early period it would bring too much in; in the later period it would shut too much out. Yet, apart from the Reich, the Germans have no continuous political history. The historian is presented with a problem of presentation almost impossible of solution.

The Empire which Charlemagne founded set the tone for German history from the beginning. It was not intended as a German national state; it claimed to be a universal Empire, a revival of the Empire of the Caesars. The revival did not come from the inhabitants of Rome, of Paris, or of Naples; it came from barbarians, whose only connection with the real empire was that their ancestors had helped to destroy it. The history of the Germans as a civilized people thus began with the deliberate, planned imitation of an institution which had never been theirs. The Empire claimed to be universal. Here too the Germans struck the same note from the beginning. Unlike other peoples, they did not start from their own national state and gradually advance claims to domination: they demanded everything from the beginning. Most typical of all, this Empire – ostensibly the bulwark of Christian civilization and often accepted as such by the peoples of the West both then and since – inaugurated at once the policy of exterminating the Slav peoples of the East. Universalism, apeing of foreign traditions, ruthlessness towards the Slav peoples, these three things were to form the pattern of the Reich for more than a thousand years, and to compose the 'national character' of the German people. There was nothing innate or mysterious in this. The German character was determined by their geographical position: they were the barbarians on the edge of a great civilization. Hence their anxiety both to master this civilization and to imitate it; hence their barbaric ruthlessness towards the peoples who were pressing on them from behind. They were the people of the middle: dualism was dictated to them.

Charlemagne's Empire claimed to be universal, and the Reich maintained the claim sometimes more and sometimes less resolutely for six hundred years thereafter. But from the first it was unmistakably a German institution, and became progressively more so. By the fifteenth century it had acquired the almost official title of the 'Holy Roman Empire of the German Nation' – a contradiction in terms which confesses the failure to become either universal or a German national state. It both gave and denied to the Germans a national existence. The Reich was the greatest of feudal organizations, and the 'German Nation' of its title included only the great feudatories, the secular and ecclesiastical princes and the Free Cities. The Emperors, in the intervals of pursuing their universalist ambitions, made spasmodic efforts for centuries to reduce the great feudatories to obedience; but their efforts never succeeded, and each failure left the feudal magnates a little nearer independence than they had been before. In particular, the universalist aims of the Emperor always brought him up against the Pope, with his more truly universal position; and the Pope in self-defence stirred up feudal insubordination in the Emperor's rear. The position of Emperor remained theoretically elective, though certain great families established a hereditary series; and the greatest of these, the Hohenstaufen, might well have established a real monarchical power in Germany, had it not been for the distraction of their Italian adventures and the resultant conflicts with the Papacy.

At the beginning of the fifteenth century the prestige of the Emperors was at its lowest ebb; and one of a family which had dropped out of the Imperial running two hundred years before, the Habsburgs, was elected Emperor by the princes almost as a gesture of contempt – he was to be the despised holder of an empty title. But the Habsburgs were the greatest wielders in history of the strange political weapon of marriage; and within a century their successful marriages surrounded princely Germany on every side. Charles V, who was elected Emperor in 1519, hemmed Germany in with his family possessions – the Netherlands on the north-west, the Burgundian lands on the west, Milan on the south, and the reversion to Bohemia and Hungary to the south-east. In addition he was King of Spain, and so could draw on the wealth of the Indies for the subduing of the German princes. The moment for the decisive struggle against feudalism seemed to have come. Within Germany, everything called for a national king. The peoples both to the east and west of Germany, challenged by Imperial claims, had in answer created their own national states with unrestricted sovereignty: France and England on the one side, Poland, Hungary, and even Bohemia on the other, proclaimed the end of the middle ages and so spurred the Germans on to achieve their unification. In fact the task seemed easier for the Germans than for any other people. Everywhere the national states which overthrew the feudal order depended on the support of the urban trading classes; where, as in Poland, the trading classes were weak, the evolution was incomplete. Germany was at this time the life-line of European commerce, and her towns towered above all others in prosperity. Indeed the national monarchies in other countries sprang even more from resistance to the German commercial supremacy than from resistance to the Emperor. The trade of all Europe was poured by Venice into the funnel of the Rhine; and then was poured out from the great cities along the coast of the North Sea and the Baltic. These cities of the Rhine and of the Hanseatic League were 'Germany' – the Germany which had invented 'burgher' civilization and which led the world in all the arts of commerce. This Germany, proudly conscious of its national existence, now seemed eager to range itself behind a national king for the destruction of feudalism and the establishment of a national state.

Two great upheavals, one economic, one spiritual, abruptly ended these high hopes. The great geographic discoveries ruined Germany almost overnight and destroyed the confidence of the German burghers; the Reformation, failing to conquer all Germany, created a lasting religious division. The opening of the Cape route to India caused an economic collapse in Germany, the effects of which lasted for three hundred years. From being the centre of world commerce, Germany became within a generation an economic backwater. Her markets outside Germany passed to others. The wealth of her great burghers vanished away. Her great trading towns dwindled in size, shrinking ever more meanly within the medieval walls which they had formerly outgrown. Every trading community experiences the ups and downs attendant on the world market; but no trading community in modern Europe has ever experienced such a profound and lasting disaster as did the German middle classes just at the moment when their financial power was at its greatest and their national consciousness fully asserted – just at the moment, indeed, when they might have been expected to become the dominating political force, as they were already the dominating economic force, in central Europe.

Germany of the first two decades of the sixteenth century was a Germany of great wealth, of high culture, assertively self-confident, standard-bearer of the Renaissance. High-water mark of Germany's great age was the assertion of a national and reformed religion, expressed in the enthusiasm for Luther which swept all parts and all classes of Germany in 1519 and 1520. This was the decisive moment of German history. Napoleon once said that if the Emperor Charles V had put himself at the head of German Protestantism in 1520 he would have created a united German nation and solved the German question.

But the failure was more than personal: if German development had continued at its previous rate it would have created a united nation even against the Emperor and his universalist ideas. But the German impulse flagged with disastrous suddenness, and in none more rapidly than in Luther himself. From a resolute and irresistible popular leader, Luther suddenly became a timid mystic repudiating all connection with worldly affairs. The change was forced on Luther by the Peasants' Revolt of 1525. Luther had hastily to decide whether by the 'German nation' to which he had appealed he meant the German people or merely established authority, the princes. He decided in favour of the princes and became the wild, unrestrained advocate of a policy of absolutism and of ruthless repression. Here, as in all that he did, Luther reflected the spirit of the German people: he showed the lack of confidence in them which they felt themselves. The Luther who howled against the peasants spoke for a Germany whose markets had crumbled away.

No man has ever been so representative of the German spirit, and no man has had such a deep and lasting effect on German history. Germany is the Germany of Luther to this day. He was a man of great intellectual and of supreme literary ability, with a readiness to maintain his convictions to the death. But he turned with repugnance from all the values of Western civilization. He owed his breach with Catholicism to a visit to Rome, when he had seen, and rejected, the greatest glories of the Renaissance. He hated art, culture, intellect, and sought an escape into an imagined Germany of the past, romantic, irrational, non-European. In Luther was implicit the emotionalism of the Romantic movement, the German nationalist sense of being different, above all the elevation of feeling over thinking which is characteristic of modem Germany. In Luther, German sentiment first asserted itself, and it asserted itself against reason, against civilization, against the West. In the rest of Europe, religious reform implied going forward; with Luther it meant going back, repudiating everything which was carrying civilized life beyond barbarism. As once the German conquerors of Rome had prided themselves on being simpler, purer, than the heirs of Cicero and Virgil, so now Luther set himself up against Michelangelo and Raphael. Even the technical occasion of his breach with Rome was symbolic: he objected to the sale of indulgences in order to raise money for the building of St Peter's – if it had been for the purpose of massacring German peasants, Luther might never have become a Protestant.

In nothing was Luther more typical than in his attitude to the princes. Here, more than in any other aspect, did he represent the despair in themselves which had overcome the German middle classes. When, in 1521, Luther went to the Diet at Worms to defend his doctrines, he went under the protection of and as the spokesman of a united and enthusiastic people; never has there been a more tumultuous journey through Germany. The enthusiasm vanished overnight, and Luther crept under the wing of the princes of northern Germany, who became Protestant not as the most advanced, but as the most backward, section of German society – for them Lutheranism was merely a weapon against the political interference either of the Emperor or of the trading classes. Lutheranism, at first a movement of Reform, became, and remained, the most conservative of religions; though it preached the absolute supremacy of the individual conscience within, it preached an equally absolute supremacy for the territorial power without. Luther gave to Germany a consciousness of national existence and, through his translation of the Bible, a national tongue; but he also gave to Germany the Divine Right of Kings, or rather the Divine Right of any established authority. Obedience was the first, and last, duty of the Christian man. The State can do no wrong; therefore, whatever the State orders, that the Christian man can do without danger to his conscience, and, indeed, the more devout the individual, the more eager he will be to carry out the most violent and unscrupulous orders of the prince, God's mouthpiece. In the general decline which was overcoming Germany, the princes represented the one point of stability and order, and the German middle classes, speaking through Luther, surrendered to the princes without reserve. The movement against Rome which Luther personified had sprung from a national resentment against the Papacy, which, by its co-operation with the great feudatories against the Emperor, had prevented national unity. Lutheranism certainly destroyed Papal influence in north Germany, but, lacking confidence in itself, fell into the arms of the princes and thus actually strengthened, indeed made triumphant, the particularism which it had begun by attacking. So the first great expression of the

German national spirit repudiated the universalism of the middle ages, only to fall into a particularism which made German unification impossible for centuries.

Not only in its devotion to the authorities did Lutheranism increase German disunity. It failed to become the national religion of all Germans; in fact it carried with it little more than half the German people. Most of the nations of Europe were left, as a result of the Reformation, with dissenting minorities, whether of Roman Catholics or Protestants; but in every case, except that of Germany, they were unmistakable minorities, excluded from political life and in some cases eliminated later altogether. In Germany the division was permanent, and another element was added to the existing categories of German dualism. The backward, impoverished princes of the north-east and the trading cities of the North Sea and Baltic, devastated by the economic catastrophe, became Lutheran; the wealthier, more civilized princes of the south-west and even to some extent the inland cities of the Rhine, which had still some Continental trade to keep them alive, remained Roman Catholic. Both developments were a retreat from the flourishing days of the Renaissance, which had embraced all Germany: but while Lutheranism was the outcome of total surrender and collapse, Roman Catholicism represented the defence and maintenance of a real though limited prosperity. Hence the paradox of the ensuing centuries that, though Lutheranism was originally the expression of a middle-class national feeling, Lutheran Germany was both rigidly absolutist and utterly non-national; while Roman Catholicism, the enemy of nationalism, produced in Germany a genuinely German culture and even a genuinely German policy. Roman Catholic Germany produced the great works of Baroque art and developed the musical tradition which culminated in Haydn, Mozart, and Beethoven; Lutheran Germany, barren in all else, had also its musical tradition, the quietist withdrawal from the world, which came to a dead end with Bach – after Bach, Lutheran Germany had no cultural existence. In the world of affairs, the Roman Catholic Emperors, despite their universalist inheritance, struggled, however ineffectively, to defend Germany against foreign invasion; the Lutheran princes, concerned solely with their own existence, allied themselves with every invader of Germany who presented himself.

Such was the strange work of Luther. He made Germany a nation, but a nation divided against itself. He gave the Germans a spiritual individualism and destroyed for centuries their political independence. He broke with the medieval dream of universalism, only to lead Germany into the nightmare of particularism. He taught the Germans to believe in Liberty, but he taught them also that liberty is to be found only in the service of the prince. He created the German language, and he used his creation for attacking reason, for expressing hysteria. Like the Germans of a thousand years before and of four hundred years after, Luther was the barbarian who looks over the Rhine, at once the most profound expression and the most decisive creator of German dualism.

The first years of Charles V were the moment of Goethe's phrase which, once lost, eternity will never give back. The moment for making a national middle-class Germany was lost in 1521 perhaps for ever, certainly for centuries. By 1525 it was evident that the period of national awakening had passed, and there began from that moment a steady advance of absolutism and authority which continued uninterruptedly for more than two hundred and fifty years. There could be no further question of national unification; the only question was whether the Emperor could succeed in unifying Germany, without popular support, solely by means of military conquest. Thus at the very beginning of modern history Germany was offered the chance of unity, not on the basis of common effort, but only after a common experience of defeat. For thirty years Charles V struggled to establish Imperial authority over the German princes, not in alliance with any German feeling, but solely with non-German military resources; Germany was to be conquered, not united. Charles V failed. As his attempt had been purely military, the reasons for his failure were purely military too: he had to fight too many enemies at once; he was distracted by the Turkish attacks on the south-east and of France in the west; above all, the communications and organization of the day made it impossible either to create, or, if created, to maintain a Spanish army large enough to hold down all Germany. In 1555 came the compromise: Germany was to be divided permanently in religion according to the whim of each prince; the Emperor was to remain as the most powerful prince in Germany; but the less powerful princes were to remain as princes too, each prince absolute and untrammelled, however modest his resources; only the people of Germany were not permitted to have any political existence. This settlement of the Treaty of Augsburg is sometimes represented as a triumph of liberty and tolerance: a triumph indeed for the liberty of the princes, but in religion intolerance run mad, for henceforth even the Roman Catholic princes asserted that Roman Catholicism was true only if the territorial ruler maintained it.

The Treaty of Augsburg was the end of a long story: the end of the universal empire, the end even of the Holy Roman Empire of the German Nation. But as there was nothing new to take its place, the old Empire, itself the ghost of Rome, continued, ever more ghostlike, to haunt Germany for another two hundred years. In the early seventeenth century there was even an epilogue, a posthumous effort to assert the power of the Emperor in central Europe. After the abdication of Charles V in 1555, the Habsburg princes, titular Emperors, followed the example of the other princes and concentrated their attention on their hereditary lands, sapping the privileges of the estates and striving to establish the normal princely absolutism. In 1618, conflict with the most powerful of these estates, the Diet of Bohemia, became so grave that the Habsburg dynasty was threatened with destruction. But the Emperor managed to rally and, in the effort of rallying, not only established his absolute rule in Bohemia, but within ten years overran all Germany. For, though Imperial power had been declining ever since the Peace of Augsburg, the power of the princes, which had been just strong enough to defeat Charles V, had been declining even more; until by now no German prince was strong enough to withstand an Emperor who, a few years before, had been almost chased out of his capital by a few rebellious Bohemian gentry. In the first decade of the Thirty Years' War an utterly feeble Emperor was able to carry Imperial arms to the shores of the Baltic and to enforce Imperial decrees to an extent unknown for centuries. In 1629 was achieved a sort of German unity, a unity of exhaustion and reaction.

But while Germany had stood still, or rather slipped back, her neighbours had grown in strength, and the new military monarchs of France and Sweden would not tolerate a Germany subordinated to the Emperor. Hence the landing of Gustavus Adolphus in Germany in 1629; hence the interventions of both France and Sweden which continued for over twenty years. This long, confused period of conflict, the

Thirty Years' War, in fact contained two distinct themes: first, the Imperial conquest of the German princes, and then, the defeat of the Emperor by Sweden and France. The outcome was the Peace of Westphalia in 1648, a peace which regulated the political life of Germany for the ensuing hundred and fifty years. Westphalia was the charter of German liberties – that is, of the liberties of the German princes. These princes, who had been unable to defend themselves and who cared nothing for Germany, were secured in their independence by the arms of France and Sweden. The project of uniting Germany by means of a Habsburg conquest, never very likely, was made impossible. The Reich was artificially stabilized at a medieval level of confusion and weakness. Within the framework of Westphalia, the Emperor could never become more than a titulary dignitary. On the other hand, the Peace of Westphalia marked a great victory for the house of Habsburg in their family possession: the Emperor was recognized as a great European power, not in virtue of his overlordship in Germany, but as ruler of the Austrian lands, of Bohemia, and of Hungary. Westphalia was the first international act to admit that the Habsburgs had something great, apart from their high title: in other words, it recognized the existence (though not the name) of 'Austria' as something distinct from Germany and so added a new element to the tangles of the German problem.

The Thirty Years' War and Westphalia, its outcome, was no doubt the lowest point of German decline and humiliation. Still, it was not quite what it has been subsequently painted. It was not the cause of German decline and weakness, but rather the result. The impoverishment, the dwindling of the cities, the decay of cultural and material standards, all these had been proceeding for a century before the Thirty Years' War broke out. By 1618, German life had reached such a low ebb that any sort of violence and upheaval became tolerable; had it not been for the utter feebleness of the Germans, neither the victories of the Emperor nor the later victories of the Swedes and French would have been possible. The Thirty Years' War was not fought by the German people, least of all was it fought for religious reasons. It was fought by and against the German princes. The defenders of princely liberties, the majority of whom were Roman Catholic, called themselves Protestant; the protagonists of Imperial authority called themselves Roman

Catholics, although Wallenstein, the greatest of them, was an unbeliever. In every age rulers, fighting for their survival or for the extension of their power, have to talk the claptrap of the time: in the seventeenth century the claptrap happened to be religious.

Westphalia was imposed on Germany by foreign powers; but without the intervention of these foreign powers the state of Germany would have been still worse. Habsburg strength could never have maintained the position of 1629. New rivals would have arisen, and the wars between the princes would have continued until Germany was utterly destroyed. Sweden and France imposed peace on Germany, by no means a glorious peace, but a peace which gave Germany long years of modest quiet. The only alternative in 1648 was not less foreign interference, but more – the continuance of the war until most of Germany was actually partitioned between Sweden, France, and the Habsburgs. For that outcome none of the combatants was powerful enough: therefore they compromised on a peace which preserved in Germany a system of rule by princes who were quite incapable of surviving by their own strength. Westphalia was the result of the Habsburg-Bourbon balance of power; and the only German contribution was negative – the inability to look after itself. The princes were not only weak; they were artificial. German territories had been ceaselessly shuffled around for a century and more; and now there was hardly a dynasty with deep historical roots in the lands over which it happened to rule.

The outcome of the Westphalia system was therefore strange indeed. The German princes owed their existence to an artificial international order, not at all to the support of their peoples – not even to the support of the aristocratic section of their peoples – and they had no serious historical recollections to confine their course. Therefore, though altogether negligible in international affairs, they were less restrained in internal affairs than the greatest princes of Europe. Even Louis XIV had to consider the feelings of the great French nobles and was bound by the historical and legal differences between the provinces. But the most contemptible Margrave was limited by nothing: he had no sympathy with the local patriotism of his subjects and no patience with the antiquated rights of the estates. In fact, in the course of the hundred years after Westphalia the German princes attained without effort to the unchecked absolutism which in France needed a great revolution for its accomplishment. Westphalia was conservative only in the sense that it preserved the rule of the princes; it did not protect the rights or privileges of any other section of the community. So far as there were political traditions in Germany, Westphalia helped to destroy them and substituted complete subjection to dynasties without roots or substance. In the great age of reform at the end of the fifteenth and beginning of the sixteenth centuries, the German people had secured liberty in large measure. The Free Cities, which were subordinate only to the Emperor, had become almost sovereign states; but as well the towns within the secular principalities had established their autonomy. In the country, the peasants, never so completely reduced to servitude as in England and France, had still further reduced the burdens of feudalism, so that German liberties had for a while outstripped all Europe. This development ended abruptly with the failure of Lutheranism as a popular movement; and after Westphalia the current ran relentlessly in the opposite direction. Serfdom was reintroduced, often introduced into districts where it had not previously existed. It had now no longer a scrap of social justification; there was no pretence that the lord, in return for the peasant's services, gave protection – it was a system of naked exploitation, the rule of the strong over the weak. Similarly, the towns lost their self-government and were forced into the feudal mould of the countryside. Authority (*die Obrigkeit*), deified by Luther, indeed took on the divine character of omnipotence; and the German princes, impotent in the great world of states, found consolation in conquering their own subjects. By the end of the eighteenth century, a harsh inescapable feudalism held most of Germany in its grasp: the people exploited by and subjected to the lords, the lords gratefully subservient to the absolute prince. This feudalism was decked out with a medieval appearance and rigmarole; in fact it was of recent application and therefore all the more crushing and systematic. The rationalism of the enlightenment, elsewhere humane and progressive, was used in Germany to screw up the efficiency of a sham-traditional system of exploitation; and once again the greatest achievements of the human mind were perverted to the improvement of methods of barbarism.

Exceptions to this neo-feudalism, however, still remained in eighteenth-century Germany. The rule of the princes did not cover all Germany. The compromise which had been made by the Treaty of Augsburg and then perpetuated at Westphalia had established a balance between the Emperor and the princes. Imperial Germany, the tantalizing fragment, as it were, of the Germany which might have been, was the Germany of the ecclesiastical states and of the Free Cities. The ecclesiastical states, under the impact of eighteenth-century enlightenment, had lost most of their spiritual character, and became almost indistinguishable from the secular states except in the method of appointing the princes. Still, even at their worst the prince-bishops had a certain culture and a certain awareness of the great world; they could hardly escape knowing that the systematic robbing of his people did not exhaust the duties of a ruler. But only the Free Cities in their decline kept alive a feeble German culture and even a feeble consciousness of German unity. An inhabitant of Bavaria or of Hanover might wonder (if he were allowed to think at all) whether he was anything besides a Bavarian or a Hanoverian; an inhabitant of Frankfurt or of Hamburg could never be in doubt that, as well as being a 'burgher', he was a German. German nationalism survived in the Free Cities, but with curious results. The German 'burgher' owed his nationalism to his being free from princely rule; therefore he identified his national sense not with some authority, but with absence of authority – particularism and patriotism seemed synonymous, and, so far as there was any national tradition in Germany, it was a tradition which favoured German weakness and disunion. This was the political balance of the eighteenth century: authority, so far as it existed, had no sympathy with national sentiment; national sentiment, so far as it existed, was opposed to authority. Germany, it was clear, could not find within herself the impulse to overthrow the artificial structure; its destruction could come only from outside, from some decisive change in the factors whose balance had brought the elaborate compromise of Westphalia into being.

These factors were three: the princes, the Emperor, and France (Sweden, the other intervening foreign state, having now fallen out of the ranks of great powers). First, the princes had imposed upon the Emperor the compromise of the Peace of Augsburg in 1555; and when the princes could maintain themselves no longer, France had perpetuated the compromise in 1648. Though the system of Westphalia lasted a hundred and fifty years, there was never a moment when each party to the compromise was not seeking to increase his power in order to alter the bargain in his favour. The German princes, despite their international triviality, were consumed with land hunger, and most of the leading princes attempted at some time or another to transform themselves into real powers. The most obvious way would have been for the greater princes to eat up their lesser neighbours inside Germany; but this way was barred – neither the Emperor nor France nor the other princes would tolerate it. This doomed the ambitions of the Elector of Bavaria, who was surrounded either by German or by Habsburg lands and could acquire neither. In 1742 the Elector managed to win election as Emperor, the Habsburgs ousted from the Imperial dignity for the only time in modern history. But it was a barren success, due only to French intrigue and Habsburg weakness; and, on the death of the Bavarian Emperor Charles VII in 1745, the house of Bavaria was glad to sink back into obscurity.

This Bavarian episode pointed a clear moral – that a German prince, to become powerful, must seek sources of power outside Germany. This idea influenced the Elector of Hanover when he agreed to become King of England in 1714; but the results were disappointing. English jealousy of Continental entanglements and the British constitutional system made it altogether impossible for the Electors of Hanover to conquer Germany with British aid. The British connection made Hanover more important as a German state than it deserved to be, nothing more. The same idea guided the Elector of Saxony when he sought election as King of Poland; but here again results were disappointing. Far from being a source of strength, aristocratic, faction-ridden Poland was a source of weakness; and Poland in decline pulled Saxony down along with her, so that in the final disaster Saxony too almost vanished.

The Electors of Saxony and Bavaria had been among the greatest of the German princes; Dresden and Munich, their capitals, had long been centres of art and culture. Politically both failed; the most backward and despised of the Electors succeeded. Brandenburg, a frontier state in the sandy wastes of north-eastern Germany, its capital, Berlin, an overgrown military camp – till the eighteenth century not even overgrown – had little place in German history; remote and obscure, it hardly seemed to belong to Germany at all. Lying east of the Elbe on lands reconquered from the Slavs since the eleventh century, its people were mainly converted Slavs, and even the names of the great nobles often betrayed a Slav origin. The dynasty, the Hohenzollerns, had nothing great in their past, and no long-standing connection with the Electorate they had acquired; they were ruthless, unprincipled military adventurers. Towards the close of the fifteenth century, a Hohenzollern had been elected also as Grand Master of the Teutonic Knights, a crusading order, which by conversion or extermination – usually the latter – had pressed back the Slav peoples along the Baltic coast and carved out for itself a feudal domain. The Hohenzollern Grand Master secularized the Order, appropriated it, and amalgamated it with the Electorate, thus adding to the Hohenzollern possessions a great stretch of territory beyond the frontier of the Reich, the territory of East Prussia. This was true 'colonial' land, where the lords could practise unrestrained exploitation of the Polish peasants and would accept in return an equally unrestrained absolutism of the prince. Being outside the Empire, it was not affected by the Imperial law which forbade any royal title except that of the Emperor; and in 1703 the Elector of Brandenburg became 'King in Prussia'[1] – a title which was an intrinsic part of his power and not a mere personal union like the King of Poland or the King of England.

At the beginning of the eighteenth century, Prussia, though not a great power, was strong enough to be a useful member of the Grand Alliance against France and strong enough to give her ambitious rulers a vision of what being a great power would involve. The resources of Prussia were contemptibly small: no industrial areas, no important cities, no outlet to the sea, the land barren and unyielding, the nobility poor and ignorant, cultural life virtually non-existent. Prussia was, in fact, true march land, excelling in nothing but savagery and conquest. Fortunately for civilized communities, the wild keepers of the borders are usually too barbarous to organize their strength; but occasionally the marcher lord is a barbarian of genius, with incalculable results.

[1] Technically not King of Prussia until West Prussia was acquired in the partitions of Poland; but the incorrect title was generally used from quite early in the eighteenth century.

Frederick II, King of Prussia from 1740 to 1786, was a sport of this type, utterly savage in his aims and methods, civilized to the highest degree in his capacity for organization and for concentrating his resources on a given object. Frederick's aim was to force Prussia into the ranks of the great powers, to screw Prussia up, in fact, far above her true level. This was no 'growth of Prussia', for it sprang from nothing inside Prussia except the King's will; it was a planned 'making of Prussia', as artificial as the making of a canal. Prussia represented no popular force, stood for no idea, hardly even belonged to Germany either geographically or spiritually. Her only asset was the ruthlessness learnt in long years of oppression of the Slav peoples. Prussia was itself a conquered land; all the more suited therefore to become now the conqueror of others.

Frederick II was not, of course, alone in unscrupulousness among the statesmen of the eighteenth century. Indeed they first set him the example and then sought to emulate him. But in every other country there was some limit of tradition or some distraction of cultural life; Frederick II alone could concentrate on his aim. Therefore he achieved it. He jockeyed Prussia up into the ranks of the great powers. His success depended partly on territorial gains: the seizure of Silesia from the Habsburg Maria Theresa in 1740 first gave Prussia an industrial region, and the share in the first partition of Poland in 1772 linked up Brandenburg with East Prussia and brought more Polish peasants to be exploited. But his success depended still more on policy: on the cunning and adaptability of his diplomacy; on the harsh discipline of his army; on his own skill as a general; and on the oppressive efficiency of the administration. For all practical purposes, the army was the State; nothing else existed: the system of civil administration was a sub-department of the military organization, and practically all the resources of the State (five-sixths in 1740; three-quarters in 1786; five-sevenths in 1806) went on the upkeep of the army. Everything in Prussia was tense, strained, keyed up to the limit and often beyond it; a sort of political face-lifting carried almost beyond all bearing. Hence the violence, the extremism, the hysteria, which came to distinguish the Prussian governing class even in the eighteenth century, and of which Bismarck's screams and tears and breaking of jugs are a later example. Prussia was set a task almost beyond her strength; therefore she was always on the verge of a breakdown. Frederick the Great started Prussia on a path from which there was no turning back: she had to become ever greater or collapse altogether.

The making of Prussia was the work of the Hohenzollern rulers, almost of one Hohenzollern ruler. Still it could not have been accomplished without the existence of a unique landed class, the Junkers of eastern Germany. No factor is more important in the history of modern Germany, and no factor is less understood. The Junkers were landowners, lords of great estates. But they had nothing else in common with the French nobles or the Whig aristocrats, the landowners of western Europe. The French and English nobles were a leisured class, the French depending on feudal dues, the English on rents from their tenants. Both spent most of their time away from their estates, the French at court, the English in London. The one produced the French civilization of the eighteenth century, the other the British constitution; the greatest political work of man. The Junkers, however, were not a leisured class, drawing tribute from others. They were, for the most part, without tenants and worked their estates themselves, for they were the owners of colonial lands. The landowners of western Europe were part of a settled community, in which even serfs and copyholders had some legal existence, but the Junkers had no obligations to the conquered Slav peoples whose land they owned; these peoples had been utterly expropriated and had been degraded not even into tied serfs, but into landless labourers. The Junker estates were never feudal; they were capitalist undertakings, which closely resembled the great capitalist farms of the American prairie – also the result of a colonial expropriation of the American Indians. The Junkers were hardworking estate managers, thinking of their estates solely in terms of profits and efficiency, neither more nor less than agrarian capitalists.[1]

[1] The term 'Prussian Junker' has been often misunderstood, even in Germany. They were 'Prussian' as subjects of the King of Prussia, not especially as inhabitants of East or West Prussia, the provinces from which the King took his name. The confusion would not have arisen if the law of the Holy Roman Empire had allowed the Hohenzollern ruler to take his true title of 'King of Brandenburg'. Junker estates predominated in all the Prussian provinces east of the Elbe, in fact predominated more in Brandenburg, Silesia, and Pomerania than in East Prussia. For East Prussia the pagan 'Prussian' inhabitants were exterminated by the Teutonic Knights, and their land given to free German

This economic characteristic had a unique political result. Everywhere in Europe the Crown was striving to make the organization of the State more efficient; therefore, despite the King's personal preference for the manners and culture of the nobility, he had to turn for political backing to the capitalist middle classes, who alone possessed the virtues of efficiency and hard work. But these were the very virtues possessed by the Junkers and not possessed to the same degree by the German burghers of the eighteenth century. The German trading classes had abandoned all attempt to keep up with the capitalist triumphs of England, Holland, or even France. Instead they prided themselves on their civic liberties and on the high level of their culture as citizens of the world. These were not assets likely to appeal to Frederick II. But the Hohenzollerns had long ago stamped out the last flickers of aristocratic liberties; and the Junkers had neither the leisure nor the ability to develop a taste for culture – to go to Berlin was merely to leave the threshing floor for the barrack-room. Thus in Prussia alone in Europe, a reforming Crown could carry out its reforms through the agency of great landowners; and the greater the efficiency of the Prussian State, the more it needed the services of the Prussian Junkers. It was no paradox, but an inevitable development, that Frederick, the most efficient of the Hohenzollerns, first made absolute the Junker monopoly of civilian and military office. The State created by Frederick II combined two qualities which were elsewhere opposites. It had, on the one hand, the unscrupulous authoritarianism, the disregard both of humanity and of principle, everywhere characteristic of rule by a privileged upper class; on the other hand, a striving after efficiency and improvement, a rigid devotion to the balancing of accounts, elsewhere associated with the rule of a reforming middle class. The Prussian Junkers, one might say, were politically in the Stone Age; economically and administratively they looked forward to the age of steel and

---

colonists, who remained independent farmers; in the Brandenburg lands there was less extermination and the inhabitants were transformed into serfs. This explains the apparent paradox that, in the nineteenth century, the most strenuous liberal opposition to Junker methods of government came from the representatives of East Prussia, who had all the colonial farmer's dislike of aristocrats. The rural districts of East Prussia were the backbone of Prussian liberalism until the desire for agrarian protection brought great estate owners and small farmers together in the eighteen-eighties.

electricity. They were barbarians who had learnt to handle a rifle and, still more, bookkeeping by double entry. Ruthless exploiters of conquered land, they were untouched by European civilization and yet could master every technical improvement which Europe produced. Of course their achievement was not perfect or unbroken. Just as an individual Junker might neglect his estate for culture, or from laziness, and so paid the penalty in bankruptcy, so the Junker governing class sometimes failed to keep up with the times in organization, in military equipment, or even in political pretence. The great disasters of 1807, of 1848, and of 1918, warned them that the anachronism of their survival could be preserved only by ceaseless efficiency; and in each case the lesson was learnt. If the Junkers had owned fat acres instead of sand, if Prussia had ever enjoyed a long period of secure repose in Europe, the habits of leisure and inefficiency would have been too strong to overcome, and eventually at some crisis both Prussian Junkers and Prussian state would have collapsed. But both lived always on the edge of danger and bankruptcy; this bound them together and preserved them.

Frederick II forced Prussia into the ranks of the Great Powers. So far as Germany was concerned, his work produced little change in the established order. Even at his most ambitious, he never thought of uniting Germany under Prussia nor even of conquering any large part of German territory. He made Prussia a European power and so asserted his equality with the Emperor. But this was the height of his ambition. When he talked, as he did at the end of his life, of 'defending the liberties of Germany', he meant only the liberties of the German princes; in other words, the continuance of the balance of Westphalia under Prussian guarantee. He never hesitated to ally himself with foreign powers against the Emperor, never admitted a common German cause, never recognized the existence of a German people. Indeed, German territory conquered by Prussia was virtually lost to the German nation and condemned to slavery for the sake of the Prussian army. The top-heavy increase of Prussian power was to have extraordinary results in the following century; but, in the time of Frederick II, those few who were conscious of a common German loyalty regarded the victories of Prussia as a disaster. The greatness of Prussia was a still further assurance of German disunity.

The real effort to revive Germany in the eighteenth century still came from the Imperial side. After the settlement of Westphalia, the Habsburgs had despaired of the Reich and had turned more and more exclusively to their hereditary lands. By the end of the seventeenth century, the greatest of these possessions, Hungary, had been reconquered from the Turks; and the Habsburgs even dreamt of becoming the heirs of the Ottoman Sultans in the Balkans. This visionary project remained a dream: the Habsburg frontier was never permanently carried beyond the limits of the Kingdom of Hungary. Maria Theresa, who succeeded to the Habsburg lands in 1740, was hard pressed to defend her inheritance and had no sympathy with dreams and visions. Besides, being a woman, she could not be Emperor; she secured the election of her husband to the empty dignity merely to console him for his lack of real power. In her reign, the Habsburg lands were given a unified organization and character, which spared only Hungary: 'Austria' and even 'Austria-Hungary' had come into existence. Joseph II, elected Emperor in succession to his father in 1765 and succeeding Maria Theresa as ruler of the Habsburg lands in 1780, was impatient with his mother's caution and good sense. Intoxicated with the limitless rationalism of the Enlightenment, he returned to the ambitions which had distracted his ancestors, seeking both Balkan gains and the revival of Imperial power in Germany. Like Frederick II, whom he admired and attempted to imitate, Joseph II was a reformer on the throne: but, unlike Frederick II, Joseph could not carry out reforms through the agency of the landed nobility. The territorial magnates of the Habsburg lands were no Junkers; but aristocrats in the Western style – cultured, spendthrift, incompetent. Joseph needed middle-class agents to operate his reforms and, owing to the peculiar relationship between economics and nationalism in eastern Europe, he could attract middle-class support only by reasserting the Habsburg connection with the German Reich.

The German thrust to the east against the Slav peoples, which was in continuous operation from the eleventh century, had two distinct characters. One was the way of military conquest which created Brandenburg-Prussia: the Slavs were conquered, and in their place came not the German people, but Junker oppressors with no national sentiment, with indeed as great a contempt for German burghers as for their own Slav labourers. The other which was far more widespread was the way of economic penetration by means of the German trading class. In the great days of German prosperity, German traders from the Rhine had easily dominated the markets of all eastern Europe; when those great days were past, the markets of eastern Europe alone were safe from English and Dutch rivalry. Far beyond the area of German settlement on the land, the towns in eastern Europe had a predominantly German character; and where the Germans did not penetrate directly their influence was carried by the Jews, refugees from the Rhineland who continued to speak Yiddish, a medieval Rhenish dialect. These German colonists were of course 'subjects' of the territorial prince, as, for that matter, they would have been subjects of some German prince had they remained on the Rhine; but never for one moment did they regard themselves as sharing the destinies of the people in the surrounding countryside. In Budapest they were not Hungarians; in Riga they were not Russians; in Danzig they were not Poles. Everywhere they were consciously Germans; and moreover anyone from the surrounding country who entered the town and set up as a merchant or shopkeeper automatically became German also. In eastern Europe, it is not too much to say, German was an economic term, meaning anyone who lived by trade, by handicraft, by shopkeeping or by small industry. These people had no concrete 'national home' and little expected one; but they were unmistakably German.

It was to German sentiment and to German culture that Joseph II appealed when he attempted to make the Habsburg lands a centralized absolutist state. Joseph spoke of himself as 'Emperor of the German Reich' and assumed that his Habsburg empire would possess a unified German character. But he appreciated that this German-dominated 'Austria' had, in Vienna and the neighbouring Alpine provinces, too slender a basis; to be really German Emperor, Joseph needed a larger nucleus of German subjects. This was the motive for his long-pursued plan of acquiring Bavaria in exchange for the distant and non-German Austrian Netherlands. Had this plan succeeded, the whole future of Germany would have been different: the majority of Habsburg subjects would have been Germans, and the majority of Germans would have been Habsburg subjects. Habsburg power would speedily have extended to the Main, and Prussia would have been fortunate to survive even in north Germany. But Joseph's plan, though it looked forward to the days of public opinion and of national sentiment, was executed in the old way, by secret bargaining with the Elector of Bavaria and by attempts to juggle the Balance of Power. It was also opposed in the old way by Frederick II, first by an inconclusive war in 1778, then by a coalition of German princes in 1786. The plan was defeated and the artificial structure of Westphalia preserved, defended now not only by the Prussian army but by a new guarantor – in 1778 Russia was a party to the Peace of Teschen which ended the Austro-Prussian War and so became one of the guardians of German disunity. Thus Germany stagnated under the absolute rule of her petty princes, and the two real powers in Germany maintained against each other an uneasy balance. German sentiment was confined to the worlds of philosophy and literature; it had no political outlet. The existing order in Germany was too firm to be overthrown by diplomatic intrigues and by the movements of professional armies. It needed an earthquake to overthrow it, an earthquake which the German people were altogether incapable of producing. Once more the fate of Germany was determined by events outside Germany; once more the Germans were passive victims and passive beneficiaries. For the great upheaval which ended the old Reich and prepared the way for the new occurred beyond the Rhine; it was the upheaval of the French Revolution.

2

THE ASCENDANCY OF FRANCE, 1792–1814

The French Revolution altered Germany only less profoundly than it altered France: the old political order and in some parts of Germany the old social order were changed beyond recognition. But these great changes were brought about in fundamentally different ways. In France the revolution was the work of the French people: their sufferings and their efforts taught them the basic lesson of politics, the lesson of power. Not the moral or intellectual superiority of its ideas, but the *levée en masse* and the organizing genius of the Jacobins, caused the revolution to triumph; above all the need for mass support compelled the middle-class liberals to form with the peasants and town workers a united radical front, never thereafter totally dissolved. In Germany those who desired liberal reforms did nothing to promote their own cause; they waited passively, though querulously, to be liberated by the French, and the force which gave Germany the career open to the talents was not the force of the German peasants, but the force of the French peasants in its organized form of the French Army. The German liberals had no agrarian programme and no sympathy with the propertyless masses, whom they despised as obscurantist and reactionary; nor had they any feeling that liberal institutions needed to be fought for and defended – they expected them to be bestowed from above. In the twenty years between 1794 and 1814, the years of French victory, most of western Germany received the benefits of the French Revolution – freedom of enterprise, equality before the law, security of property and of the Individual, cheap efficient administration. But the Germans received these benefits without any exertion of their own; and every liberal institution actually increased their dependence upon 'authority'.

These great reforms were liberal, but they were French. A startling consequence followed. French interference in Germany stirred into patriotism the natural resentment against the interference of strangers. Most educated Germans (themselves a tiny class) welcomed the benefits imposed by the French; a few, however, began to parade a German nationalism, the sole quality of which was hostility to French rule. But French rule was synonymous with liberal reform. Therefore German nationalism took on from the start an anti-liberal character. To desire the career open to the talents or a rational and ordered system of government was to be pro-French and therefore unpatriotic. All the evils of the old order, the drill sergeant and the Junker, came to be regarded as essentially German. The Jacobins of Mainz who, in 1792, opened the gates of the city to the French soldiers were held up to Germany for a hundred years as the stock example of traitors; and German patriotism expressed itself in the defence of Prussia and Austria, the two despotic and half-Slav states, to whose existence Germany owed in fact her lack both of unity and of freedom. Thus, by an astonishing paradox, the French Revolution, by destroying the old order in Germany, not merely cleared the way for German unification, but actually ensured that unification would take place for the benefit of the Hohenzollern dynasty and of the great landowners east of the Elbe.

The influence of the French Revolution in Germany was of two distinct kinds: by increasing the military power of France it upset the balance of Westphalia, and by increasing the political influence of France it promoted in Germany great social and political changes. The French revolutionaries, in their early Utopian days, had nothing which could be called a foreign, still less a German, policy. They thought that wars were caused by the wickedness of kings and that the peoples everywhere were strong enough to restrain, if not to overthrow, their rulers. If France therefore made a solemn renunciation of wars of conquest and reduced her armed forces, war would automatically cease, and France would establish a hegemony in Europe based on moral superiority alone. This idealistic view did not survive the counter-revolutionary intervention launched against France by the Emperor and the King of Prussia in 1792; and as soon as the invading armies had been driven out, the French sought for some war aim more concrete than the universal propagation of the Rights of Man. They found this aim in the plausible doctrine of the natural frontiers: the Rhine was decreed to France by natural reason. The left bank of the Rhine was incorporated into France, and the main aim of French policy became for twenty years the maintenance of the 'France of the hundred departments'. French success gave the death-blow to the system of the Treaty of Westphalia. Instead of a balance between France, the Emperor, and the princes, France was now the predominant power in Germany, flushed with revolutionary strength and determined to destroy any hostile combination. The Directors and, subsequently, Napoleon were ready to arrange a temporary partition of Germany with Prussia and Austria; but ultimately they intended to destroy the independent existence of Prussia and Austria as well. Thus France, the principal architect of Westphalia, gave the signal for its end.

Prussia was the first to abandon the defence of Germany against the French. The King of Prussia joined but feebly in the original intervention of 1792, and withdrew his armies almost before serious fighting began; acquisition of territory at the second and third partitions of Poland was his real concern. In 1795 he made peace with the French republic on the sole condition of being left undisturbed to digest his Polish gains – so little did Prussia earn her later reputation as the national champion. The Emperor took longer to convince. But a long series of French victories, beginning with Bonaparte's Italian campaign of 1796–7 and culminating in Marengo and Hohenlinden (1800), reinforced the lesson of Joseph II's failure to restore Habsburg power in Germany; and first hesitatingly in 1797 and then more decisively in 1801, the Emperor Francis II gave up the Imperial, German cause and decided to concentrate on the extension of his family lands. The princes of Germany, still less the people of Germany, were not consulted; and the princes were lucky to be allowed to survive. If Napoleon had decreed their disappearance, they would have disappeared; for they possessed no armed strength of their own, still less any loyalty in the hearts of their subjects. Their very artificiality saved them. Napoleon needed agents in Germany who would be dependent on his will, and the German princes, in their helplessness, satisfied this need. The larger princes of Germany were aggrandized by Napoleon in order the more effectively to subordinate Germany to himself.

The princes, with their doctrines of State absolutism and their efficient enlightened administration, fitted easily into the Napoleonic system; for the French Revolution and Napoleon had only carried further what the enlightened despots had begun. But the ecclesiastical states and the Free Cities could not be squared with the rationalism of the revolution. They were the survivors of a medieval order, traditional, mystical, privileged – the one looking back to the days of priestly power, the other to the days of feudal 'liberties'. Napoleon and his agents did what Joseph II had failed to do: they 'rationalized' Germany. A glorified estate office was set up in Paris under the control of Talleyrand, and by its means all the ecclesiastical states and Free Cities, with a few exceptions, were distributed among the secular princes in the course of 1803. This was the great reduction from three hundred states to thirty so often wrongly ascribed to the Congress of Vienna. It was Napoleon, not the Allies, who ended medieval Germany. The ecclesiastical princes and the Free Cities had been essential to the survival of the Holy Roman Empire: they had been the sole balance against the secular princes, the outposts of a feeble Imperial power. When they vanished, the Empire was bound to vanish too. In 1806, after a further war with the Emperor, Napoleon decreed its end: the Emperor Francis II became Emperor Francis I of Austria, a secular prince like any other, and the leading German princes were created kings by the grace of the French Revolution. A slender thread of family tradition linked the Habsburg ruler with the old idea of a German Reich and with the still older idea, inherited from Charlemagne, of a Reich which should dominate all Europe. Apart from this, Napoleon's actions ended the political traditions of Germany as abruptly and as decisively as the execution of Louis XVI ended the political traditions of France. The position of the German rulers was as revolutionary in its origin as the position of Napoleon himself; the subjection of all Germany to princely absolutism, suspended since 1648, was now completed; and the Germans received the career open to the talents and the freeing of the peasants from feudal dues as they had once received the reformed religion – by order of 'authority'.

There had long been two distinct Germanies – the Germany of the two real powers, Austria and Prussia, and the Germany of the unreal princes. This distinction was now underlined. All Germany outside Prussia and Austria was organized into the Confederation of the Rhine under the presidency of Napoleon and, like the rest of Napoleon's empire, had imposed upon it a common social and political pattern. Each state received, by order of Napoleon, a formal constitution, modelled upon that of Imperial France; each state adopted, or imitated, the French code of laws. The privileges of the landed aristocracy were ended, the lands of the Church confiscated. The Jews were emancipated; the restrictions on enterprise were removed. The civil liberties which the revolution had given to France, Napoleon gave to Germany; all that was lacking was the inspiration which in France made the revolution greater than its greatest achievements. The German middle classes received their new freedom without enthusiasm, certainly without gratitude. There was no reason why they should be grateful to a ruler who was merely carrying out the orders of Napoleon. The professional and commercial bourgeoisie were drawn mainly from the former Free Cities and ecclesiastical territories; they did not care in the slightest whether they were subjects of the King of Bavaria or of the King of Wurtemberg so long as their king gave them efficient Napoleonic government. After all, a citizen of Augsburg or of Nuremberg was not likely, after long centuries of proud existence, to call himself a 'Bavarian' and so put himself on a level with the ignorant backward peasants of the surrounding countryside. The Napoleonic reorganization of Germany increased the territory of the secular princes, but it did not increase their power: loyalty to the prince, where it existed at all, became a purely rural sentiment, on a level with local fertility superstitions or a harvest festival.

The Free Cities were thick on the ground throughout all western Germany and set the tone for middle-class thought even in the towns which had never enjoyed 'liberties'. There lingered round them a faint recollection of their great past, but they were now decayed, of no economic importance and tiny in population. At the beginning of the nineteenth century the total population of all the Free Cities and university towns in Germany was less than the population of Paris. These towns and cities contained all the literate, thinking part of the German people. Their inhabitants were remote from real life, dependent, for their existence, on state employment or on a university chair. Their politics were intense but abstract, more like the politics of a college common-room than of a popular movement. They talked a great deal about Germany, but they meant by that only a few thousands like themselves; and though they kept alive the 'German' idea, they thought of it as an idea quite divorced from power. They had a sincere liberal faith, but assumed from the start that their faith must be ineffective; in fact they soon made the further assumption that power was, by its very nature, illiberal and unprogressive. To achieve power for themselves never entered into their calculations; and in view of the economic backwardness of the German bourgeoisie this omission was no doubt inevitable. But they wished to see their ideas succeed and so arrived at the comforting conclusion that, in time, liberal ideas would triumph not by acquiring power, but merely by their innate virtue. The belief in the victory of ideas, without the foundation of an effective political organization or of a coherent class backing, was to be the ultimate ruin of German liberalism; and, though it had many sources, its most important origin lay in the days of Napoleonic rule, when the men of liberal ideas saw their ideas established in Germany without any effort of their own. Napoleon is often accused of having enslaved the Germans. His real fault lay in emancipating them. He did for the German liberals what they were never afterwards able to do for themselves.

The Napoleonic revolution not only created in Germany the basis for German liberalism. It cleared the way for another force, which was afterwards to play an even more decisive role in German politics, the force of German clericalism. So long as the ecclesiastical states existed, Roman Catholicism could be no more than a factor in the manœuvres of the princes. It was impossible to feel enthusiasm, still less devotion, for a prince-bishop of Salzburg or of Mainz. But the moment the ecclesiastical principalities were destroyed, the bishops became once more religious leaders; and Roman Catholics were no longer subjects of a particular sort of prince, but adherents of a particular religion.

Many of the former subjects of prince-bishops became now the subjects of Protestant princes; but whether the secular prince was Protestant or Roman Catholic it was possible, and often necessary, to assert Roman Catholic teaching and practice against him in a way that had been altogether impossible, even when necessary, against an ecclesiastical ruler. Just as the burghers of the Free Cities did not transfer their loyalty to their new rulers, but became instead vaguely devoted to the 'German' idea, so the inhabitants of the ecclesiastical states, too, cared nothing for their new rulers and gradually became associated in a common 'German' cause – the defence of German Roman Catholicism. This is perhaps the strangest of all the many paradoxical outcomes of Napoleon's interference in Germany: by applying without limit the rationalist principle of secular sovereignty, he made possible the growth of a strong political party the only purpose of which was resistance to rationalism and to the limitless sovereignty of the State.

Directly, in the Germany under his rule, Napoleon produced German liberalism and German clericalism; indirectly, in the Germany beyond the frontiers of his Empire, he produced their opposite, German nationalism. Within Napoleonic Germany, there was little resentment against French rule: the articulate classes, the professional and commercial middle class, were in far better circumstances than they had ever been. The only complaints against French rule came from the classes who had lost by the destruction of feudalism – the feudal landowners, especially the Imperial knights who had held directly of the Emperor – and from the utterly feckless who would never benefit from any change of system; and these classes could not hope for support within the area of Napoleonic rule. But the Napoleonic order did not extend to all Germany; instead it added to the existing dualisms – the Germany that had been under Rome and the Germany that had not, Protestant Germany and Roman Catholic Germany, Hohenzollern Germany and Habsburg Germany – a new dualism: Napoleonic Germany and the Germany of the two independent dynasties. Austria and Prussia both suffered defeat at the hands of Napoleon, but both continued to exist, though the Prussian state after Jena was only on the margin of existence. In both, the ruling classes added to the normal 'feudal' dislike of revolution resentment at defeat. But the defeat of Austria was not crushing and the resentment at it therefore limited; the defeat of Prussia was complete and Prussian resentment therefore beyond all bounds. Both dynasties desired the defeat of Napoleon; but the Hohenzollerns, having nothing more to lose, were ready to bid *va banque* – the Habsburgs were not. Neither, however, thought in terms of 'liberating' Germany: their only object was their own preservation and recovery.

Of the two, Francis I, the Habsburg Emperor, represented the more 'German' cause. So far as any sentiment for the Reich existed, it centred still on the last Holy Roman Emperor; and those political writers, such as Gentz, who cared for the 'German way of life' with its old order of ecclesiastical states and Free Cities, looked to Francis I to emancipate Germany from French rule and French innovations. Despite the popular myth to the contrary, far more German patriots from outside either of the two monarchies entered the service of Austria than of Prussia during the years of Napoleonic domination; but they suffered a fate common in history – having chosen the losing side even their existence was denied. The Habsburg cause was, too, the only cause in Germany to receive some popular support in the literal sense of support by the masses rather than of support by journalists and academic lecturers. The rising of the German peasants of Tyrol under Andreas Hofer in favour of Habsburg rule was the only genuinely popular movement in Germany in the Napoleonic period. Prussian history can show nothing of that kind.

The supporters of the Habsburg cause desired to preserve, or to revive, the old, pre-revolutionary order; but that was not really the wish of the Habsburgs themselves. Francis I was the successor of Joseph II as well as the heir of Habsburg traditionalism; his policy was absolutist, rather than reactionary, and he expected his followers to show a devotion which he did nothing to merit. His medievalism was limited to the building of a sham medieval castle at Laxenburg (for the embellishing of which he characteristically pillaged all the great Austrian monasteries); in real life, he was a plain autocrat, not an enlightened one, and he was quite as shocked as Napoleon at the rising of the Tyrolese peasants – even though the rising was in his favour. Experience seemed to confirm the scepticism of Francis I in his own cause. In 1809 he was persuaded by the romantic nationalism of his advisers to launch a crusade for the emancipation of Germany. The attempt failed;

Napoleon was once more victorious. But even in 1809 the Austrian Empire, though diminished, was still a considerable state: the Emperor was still an important, though hardly an independent ruler, and the territorial magnates of Austria had hardly felt the impact of Napoleonic rule at all – they were not discredited, and certainly not impoverished by defeat. Thus the victories of Napoleon were just enough to prevent Austria's reviving her claim to the leadership of Germany, not great enough to drive Austria to desperate courses.

With Prussia it was different. Great Prussia had been no slow natural growth, but the artificial creation of Frederick II. Its existence was precarious, and without logic. The Prussian motives for withdrawing from the war with France in 1795 were typical of the contradictions of Prussian history: fears for the collapse of the Prussian state mingled with projects of ever greater Polish gains. Frederick William III, narrow-minded, commonplace, autocratic, was incompetent to maintain Prussia's greatness, but too obstinate to abandon it. He refused to join the coalitions against Napoleon which offered a chance of success, yet, in 1806, engaged alone against the French Empire. The Prussian state collapsed almost before the first blow; the Prussian armies melted away in a disintegration unparalleled in the history of modern Europe. Great Prussia ceased to exist; and Napoleon intended that Prussia should cease to exist entirely. Only the sentimental devotion of the Tsar Alexander I to a brother monarch saved Prussia from obliteration. At the meeting at Tilsit in 1807, Napoleon and Alexander partitioned Europe, but each encroached a little on the other's sphere. Napoleon made the Grand Duchy of Warsaw, pale shadow of old Poland, out of Prussia's Polish lands; in retaliation Alexander insisted on the survival of the rest of Prussia as an independent state. Great Prussia had been built on the spoils of Poland; yet, by a strange paradox, the restoration of a fragment of Poland saved Prussia from extinction. But it was a Prussia reduced almost beyond recognition: only five million left of her former ten million subjects, a heavy indemnity imposed, and the army strictly limited to 42,000 men.

Frederick William himself was quite incapable of seeing any way out of the disaster; but his ear was caught by those who argued that the only way to defeat France was to imitate her. He had no faith in these advisers; but his kingdom was in such utter confusion that it was not worth opposing their advice. Curiously enough, the most thorough-going of the reformers, Stein, who subsequently became the first hero of anti-French German nationalists, was actually imposed upon Freder-ick William by Napoleon, in furtherance of his usual policy of extend-ing French power by extending French institutions. Stein was not a Prussian subject, but an Imperial knight from the Rhineland, whose stock-in-trade was hatred of the French who had dispossessed him. 'I hate the French,' he said, 'as much as it is allowed to a Christian to hate' – and he did not trouble much about the limitation. His hatred was an intellectual, class hatred, consciously formed, though he him-self always wrote to his wife in French and spoke French for choice. Only resentment at his loss made him go to the people, to become 'German'; German nationalist feeling was to be raised against the French in a jacquerie organized from above. Stein had no sympathy with the Hohenzollern dynasty and hated the selfish, un-German Prus-sian state; but Frederick William III was the only German prince who might be resentful enough to follow an extreme course. Stein planned to turn the Prussian state from a Junker state into a state of all the people: the peasants were to be won by agrarian reform which would arouse their enthusiasm as the Jacobins had aroused the enthusiasm of the peasants in France, and the urban middle classes were to be stirred from their long lethargy by local self-government. These projects would not save the Prussian state. They would capture the Prussian state for Germany, and Prussia would become the starting-point of a free Germany, in which it would disappear, Frederick William alone of the German princes surviving as a constitutional king. Prussianism was invited to revenge its humiliation at the hands of Napoleon by committing suicide.

Even in utter defeat neither the dynasty nor the Junkers could accept Stein's programme; and Frederick William from the moment of appointing him thought only of how to shake him off again. Stein lasted a little over a year. Then he was denounced to Napoleon as an enemy of France and dismissed on Napoleon's orders. He fled to Rus-sia, where he found in Alexander I a more sincere liberal and a more effective liberator of Germany. In Prussia the work which he had begun was arrested and remained unaccomplished. But the Junkers learnt from this alarming episode. They resolved to use Stein's weapons, the reforms of the French Revolution, not to strengthen Germany, but to strengthen themselves: they would remain Junkers, but now Jacobins as well. The peasants were still to be emancipated, but they were to be freed not only from feudal burdens, but freed altogether from the land. In the hands of these Junker reformers, emancipation was no longer a means of creating a free national peasantry, but a 'clearance' (*Bauernliegen* – laying the peasants flat – was the German term), comparable to the clearing of the Scottish Highlands or to the English enclosures of the eighteenth century. Emancipation benefited only the highest class of peasants, who were already rich independent farmers. All below them lost their remaining scraps of security: they were compelled to surrender some of their land to their lords and to sell more, and, in the absence of industrial towns to which they could escape, they remained dependent on their lords, impoverished, helpless agricultural labourers. All that remained of Stein's programme was fine words, to mislead not the peasants of the time, but the historians of future generations.

Stein's constitutional policy was jettisoned altogether. Nothing more was heard of local autonomy: the towns continued to be ruled by the agents of the central government, and the countryside by the Junkers' manorial courts. Hardenberg, who had been an associate of Stein's and became the leading minister on Stein's dismissal, was also a reformer, but not of a dangerous character. Administrative efficiency was his sole concern. His reforms produced a stronger government machine, therefore made the Crown more powerful than before. Hardenberg was quite willing to work with and through the Junkers if they would act as efficient instruments; and this condition the Junkers could fulfil. Jena had put them on their mettle. As so often in their history, the threat of destruction taught them how to avoid destruction and warned them that they must be laborious and competent servants of the State if they were to survive at all. Thus Prussia came out of the 'years of reform' not freer than before, but with a government harsher, more extensive, and more absolute than ever.

Hardenberg's plans were not complete, however, with administrative reform. Ultimately he too, though for an opposite reason from Stein's, desired a Prussian parliament, a 'constitution'. Stein had looked forward to a united Germany; Hardenberg wished to preserve the efficient Prussian state and feared German national sentiment, particularly at the moment of liberation from Napoleon. He had no desire to see Prussia swept away into a liberal, national Germany. Therefore he urged on the King the establishment of a Prussian parliament, which, without diminishing the powers of the Crown, would assert Prussian unity and mark it off from the rest of Germany. Sham constitutionalism would be a barrier against German unification. The idea was too daring for Frederick William and his Junker circle. Hardenberg's constitution was never drafted, still less issued. Only at the moment of greatest excitement, in 1814, the year of liberation, Frederick William stirred a little. He promised that he would grant his people a constitution at some time in the future. That was the sole reward which the subjects of the King of Prussia received for their efforts and sacrifices in the great war. Hardenberg's idea was set aside. But it remained latent in the minds of the Junkers; and in 1848, at the hour of their greatest danger, a Prussian parliament was at last set up – to save Prussia from national Germany.

The greatest 'reform' of the years of reform did not originate as part of a thought-out plan. It followed inevitably from the rigid limit which Napoleon had imposed on the size of the Prussian army. A great army could be built up only by the rapid training of reserves. Scharnhorst and Gneisenau, the Prussian military organizers, had to abandon willy-nilly the accepted idea of a professional army distinct from the people and to organize instead a system of general military service on a short-term basis. This was a revolutionary measure, and its authors, not surprisingly, talked of it in the democratic phrases they had learnt from Stein. Instead of an army there was now 'the people in arms'; instead of professional officers, leaders, not necessarily of aristocratic birth, chosen by the localities. In reality the new system was evidence not of the liberalism of the army chiefs, but of the subservience of the Prussian subjects: they could be relied on to answer to the sergeant's bark from the first day. The admission of a few middle-class officers did not mean that professional efficiency became more valued than social rank; it meant only that even the middle classes valued high rank as much as its possessors themselves. In other countries the revolution gave the people universal suffrage; in Prussia it gave them universal military service. In the original scheme there was one genuinely popular element. As the male population could only be gradually passed through the training of the regular army, the rest of the men were brought together in a Home Guard, the *Landsturm*, unequipped and ill-trained, which was supposed to rise in popular fury at the moment of liberation. In 1813, when the time came the *Landsturm*, in the few places where it was tried, was an utter failure; unconditional obedience and democratic initiative could not flourish side by side. After 1815 the *Landsturm* was pushed aside and, later, abolished altogether. It was an alien conception from a strange world.

The military system of Scharnhorst and Gneisenau rested not on liberalizing the Prussian state, but on militarizing the Prussian people. From it there followed a consequence of the first magnitude, perhaps the greatest single factor in shaping the destinies of modern Germany. The militarism of the Prussian people could not be left to chance; it had to be formed as deliberately as supplies were accumulated in the arsenals. Therefore the Prussian state had to busy itself in the education of its subjects: the schoolmaster had to make up for the time missed on the barrack square. Prussian education, first: for the middle classes, later for the masses, was the wonder of nineteenth-century Europe; but few outside Germany understood its purpose. The elementary school-teacher, the secondary schoolmaster, the university professor, were all servants of the Prussian state, performing with enthusiasm a task only second in importance to that of the army chiefs. In performing this task they were given a wide-freedom, just as Prussian generals were given a wide freedom in the field. But it was 'academic freedom' to achieve a purpose, the most flagrant example of the German adaptation of the weapons of civilization for uncivilized ends. Prussian, and later German, education was a gigantic engine of conquest, the more effective in that it was conducted by volunteers.

The great Prussian reforms of 1807–12 were thus not merely imposed from above, as even Stein had planned; they were all designed to strengthen authority and to make the subjects of the King of Prussia more subject than ever. But the reforms were accompanied by a cloud, or a smoke screen, of liberating, if not liberal, phrases and ideas. For the first time, German national enthusiasm began to focus on Prussia as well as on the Emperor; and it was an enthusiasm of a different kind. Pro-Habsburg and pro-Prussian German nationalism both sprang from resentment at French supremacy in Germany; but they followed different courses. Those who looked to Francis I to liberate Germany from the French and to establish the Reich anew had a wider sentiment than merely hatred of the French. They had a conception, romantic indeed and muddled, of the old Germany with its flourishing Free Cities, with its 'liberties' and with its rich diversity, the Germany which had withered in the time of Luther and the Peasants' Revolt. They were seeking to follow and to restore German tradition, and to redeem Germany not merely from foreign domination, but from the domination of foreign ideas. Though their starting-point was nationalist, they were soon transformed into conservatives and pushed their nationalism into the romantic background, so that by 1815 the German political writers who looked to Vienna disliked German nationalism almost as much as they disliked Napoleon.

The German nationalists who found their spiritual home in Berlin took the opposite course. Their very choice revealed a harsher, more realistic, attitude of mind. No one outside Prussia (and they were all non-Prussians) could be devoted to the King of Prussia as any German might be devoted to the Emperor of Austria, heir of the old Reich. But the King of Prussia, being more humiliated, was more likely to favour war to the death against the French; therefore these German nationalists preferred him – Prussia was merely the instrument of German liberation, not a cause in itself. Prussia could not claim any share of the German tradition. For whatever might be disputed about medieval Germany, one thing was certain: in the middle ages Prussia did not exist. Even the most conservative Prussian, even the Hohenzollern dynasty, had to be in some sort revolutionary. German nationalism as preached at Berlin could not appeal to history or to tradition; it could only rely upon an unreasoning assertion of the superiority of everything German. After all, it was difficult to think of any reason why Germans should prefer to be ruled by Frederick William III instead of by Napoleon, except that Frederick William was German and Napoleon was not. The argument soon went further: if Frederick William was superior to Napoleon merely by being German, there was no reason why his rule should be limited to Germans – it was also desirable that he should rule over the French and, indeed, over all the other peoples of Europe. Fichte, the greatest exponent of this doctrine, arrived quite early at this conclusion: the Germans (of course under Prussian leadership) were 'to serve Europe' by bringing it under their rule. Fichte, like the other theorists of Prussian freedom, was in origin an admirer of the French Revolution and a perfect representative of the trend of German liberalism. These middle-class liberals, academic and remote, were without political force of their own. First they had expected to be liberated by the French; and now, disliking the French rule which was the price of liberation, they not only asked to be 'liberated' by the King of Prussia, but hoped to console themselves by thrusting the same 'liberation' on the other peoples of Europe.

Fichte was the great figure at the newly founded University of Berlin in these years; and his teaching is often regarded as evidence of the rising self-confidence of the German people. In fact his every word was an expression of confidence only in the Prussian army. Fichte's mission of liberation was not to the taste either of the King or of the Prussian generals; but his lectures were a harmless gesture against the French, and French officers, connoisseurs of rhetoric, often formed the most admiring part of his audience. Fichte inspired not a German uprising against Napoleon, for there was none, but a myth of profound significance for the future: the myth that German liberty and Prussian self-preservation were the same and that liberation was to be found not in social and political changes within Germany, but in union with the most backward elements in Germany against the foreigner. Service in the Prussian army was the German version of service in the cause of liberty, and the defeat of the French at the battle of Leipzig the German substitute for the fall of the Bastille. Where the French youth of 1789 had founded the great political clubs and so prepared the way for the triumph of the Jacobins, the patriotic Germans of 1813 organized gymnastic societies under the bruiser-poet Jahn and displayed their enthusiasm not in rhetoric, but in Swedish drill.

On the outbreak of war in 1813, Fichte dramatically suspended his lectures 'until the liberation of the fatherland'. But his only contribution to this liberation was to retire to his study, there to experience sensations of enthusiasm; and the only contribution of German nationalism was to give the battle of Leipzig the romantic name of the 'battle of the nations'. In fact, no nations fought at Leipzig, only the professional armies of the old order on one side and the polyglot conscripts of the French Emperor on the other. The Russian and Austrian armies were composed of drill-hardened peasants, not a man of whom had an inkling of any national cause. In the Prussian army of 300,000 men there were 10,000 volunteers; these, and two solitary battalions from the rest of Germany, were the sum total of the national movement. This handful of volunteers came from the academic middle class. Of any movement of the masses against the French there was no trace at all. The French were never troubled in Germany, as they had been in Spain and in Russia, by guerrillas. French couriers travelled across Germany without escort, and Napoleon received his regular post from Paris even on the day of the battle of Leipzig. French civil officials were unquestioningly obeyed until the moment when they handed over their authority to the agents of the advancing Allies. The absence of any popular movement is not surprising. Men will rise to defend old and cherished institutions or to further new and inspiring ideas. In Germany there was neither one nor the other. In the three hundred years since the time of Luther, the German princes had deprived Germany of all her traditions; there was nothing left to call forth a stubborn conservative rejection of foreign ways such as roused the Spanish peasants. Germany had been levelled too much to produce a Vendée. But the levelling had come from above. Germany was not stirred by the ideas of liberty which had evoked the *levée en masse* in 1791. In the world of politics, the Germans knew nothing but authority, *die Obrigkeit*; and the war of liberation could only remove one authority and substitute another.

The myth of the national uprising against Napoleon was later fostered by the German intellectuals who had been present at Leipzig in the same sense as George IV was present at Waterloo. But the originator of the myth was none other than Napoleon himself, ashamed to admit that he owed his defeat to his own blunders and to the strength of the three eastern powers whom he had despised and humiliated. To be defeated by an elemental upheaval of the peoples of Europe was less disgraceful, indeed almost noble. In fact, Germany turned against Napoleon only in the sense that the German princes sensed the coming storm and changed sides. The King of Prussia, too timid to break with Napoleon even after the Moscow campaign, was driven into war, but not by the Prussian people. War was thrust upon him by General Yorck, most reactionary of Prussian officers, who made a military agreement against orders with the Tsar. This was a strange 'revolutionary war', imposed on the King by soldiers whose only concern was to redeem their professional reputation, tarnished in 1806. The other German princes were not even driven over to the Allied side by patriotic officers. They admired and regretted Napoleon, who had increased their territories and enhanced their titles, and they adopted the cause of 'liberation' from diplomatic calculation and only just in time. The Bavarian army, for example, set out to fight for Napoleon, but was 'converted' by the preliminaries of the battle of Leipzig, news of which fortunately reached it on the way. Only the King of Saxony jumped too late and arrived at the Allied camp as a prisoner, to the embarrassment of his jailers, all of whom had been dependents of Napoleon a few days or weeks before. Thus Germany passively endured the war of liberation, just as previously it had endured conquest by the French and before that the balance of the system of Westphalia. The Allies defeated the French, but they could not undo the effects of French rule; and they had to devise a new system for Germany which would serve the interests of Europe, as previously the Napoleonic system had served the interests of France. The people of Germany were not consulted. They could not be consulted. As a political force they did not exist.

3

THE GERMAN CONFEDERATION: THE YEARS OF AUSTRO-PRUSSIAN PARTNERSHIP, 1815–48

In 1815 the victorious Allies, meeting at the Congress of Vienna, gave Germany a new political form: but they could not treat Germany as a clean slate. The war against Napoleon had been fought in the name of the independence of the European states; and the princes of Germany had as much right to exist as any other. They were, no doubt, the creation of Napoleon, but they had been accepted as allies, and their existence was an accomplished fact. There was little territorial shuffling within Germany in 1815; the great remodelling had been done in 1803. The King of Saxony lost nearly half his kingdom, as a penalty for having delayed too long his change of sides; and the kingdom of West-phalia, a Napoleonic appanage, was broken up – some of it restored to the King of Hanover (who was also King of England), the rest allotted to Prussia.

The one serious territorial problem was that of the lands on the left bank of the Rhine which had been part of France for the preceding twenty years and, before that, a tangle of ecclesiastical states. A secular

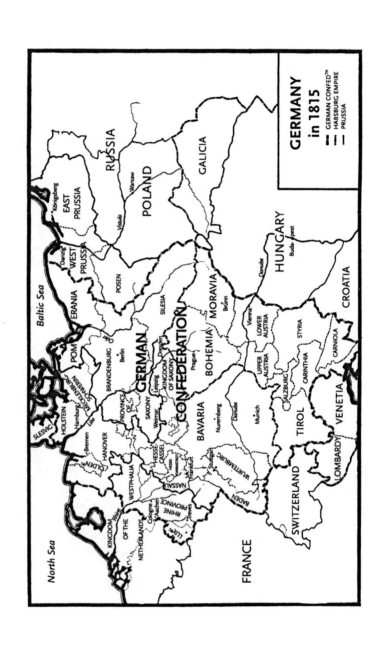

GERMANY in 1815

━━━ GERMAN CONFED^{TN}
┅┅┅ HABSBURG EMPIRE
──── PRUSSIA

North Sea

Baltic Sea

RUSSIA

EAST PRUSSIA

Königsberg

WEST PRUSSIA

Danzig

Vistula

POLAND

Warsaw

GALICIA

HUNGARY

Buda-Pest

CROATIA

Danube

POSEN

SILESIA

MORAVIA

Brünn

Vienna

LOWER AUSTRIA

STYRIA

CARNIOLA

POMERANIA

BRANDENBURG

Berlin

BOHEMIA

Prague

UPPER AUSTRIA

CARINTHIA

MECKLENBURG-SCHWERIN

PROVINCE OF SAXONY

GERMAN

KINGDOM OF SAXONY

Leipzig

Dresden

CONFEDERATION

SALZBURG

TIROL

VENETIA

HOLSTEIN

SLESVIG

Hamburg

Bremen

Elbe

Weimar

BAVARIA

Nuremberg

Munich

Danube

LOMBARDY

OLDENBURG

HANOVER

HESSE-CASSEL

Frankfurt

NASSAU

WÜRTEMBURG

Stuttgart

SWITZERLAND

WESTPHALIA

KINGDOM OF THE NETHERLANDS

RHINE PROVINCE

Cologne

Aachen

Treves

Rhine

LUX.

BADEN

FRANCE

ruler had now to be found for them. They were not a tempting prop-
osition: strategically exposed to French invasion, they were aggrieved at
being separated from France and hankered after French rule. They were
almost entirely Roman Catholic and, if they were to have a German
ruler, hoped for the Emperor of Austria. But Francis I, and still more the
Austrian generals, refused to resume the traditional role of defender of
Germany, which had caused the Habsburgs so much barren effort. By a
strange chance, these lands found themselves in Prussia, an outcome
most undesired both by themselves and by Frederick William III. Prussia was entitled to territorial gains enough to restore her to the extent
of 1805. But the Tsar Alexander dreamt of a liberal kingdom of Poland
under his sovereignty and therefore denied to Prussia the greater part
of the Polish lands of which Napoleon had deprived her to compose
the Grand Duchy of Warsaw. All that Prussia recovered was the 'Grand
Duchy of Posen', a strip of territory connecting West Prussia and
Silesia. The Prussians then proposed as compensation to annex Saxony,
but this was denied them by Austria and England. As a last resort they
were fobbed off with the left bank of the Rhine, which became Rhenish Prussia, geographically and spiritually without connection with the
rest of the kingdom. Prussia had imposed on her the task of defending
the Rhine against the French and shouldered it most unwillingly; it
was, as it were, a practical joke played by the Great Powers on the
weakest of their numbers. Prussia lost, or rather failed to recover, three
million Poles, and acquired three million Germans. The Prussian governing class thought nothing of this; they knew only that they had lost
three million amenable serfs and had acquired three million free peasants and burghers, all influenced by Roman Catholicism or by French
liberalism. They lamented the empty acres of the Vistula; neither they
nor anyone else had an inkling that they had acquired what was to be
within a century the greatest industrial region in the world. The same
Polish factors which had kept Prussia in existence in 1807 compelled
Prussia in 1814 to become the leading Germanic power.

More difficult than these territorial questions was that of the German order. The Confederation of the Rhine had been a dependency of
Napoleon; the new Confederation had to be a dependency of the Allies,
but with a different aim. Napoleon sought to mobilize the resources of
Germany for his further plans of conquest; the Allies wished merely to

prevent a new French aggression. The German Confederation which they created was a negative organization, seeking to keep the lesser German states out of the way while the two Great Powers resisted France – Prussia on the Rhine and Austria on the Po. It was a new version of the system of Westphalia, with some pretence of making the German states assist in their own survival. The Great Powers who determined the constitution of the German Confederation tried to combine two contradictory ideas: on the one hand they wished to respect and to consolidate the independence of the German states; on the other to promote in Germany, by voluntary agreement, the measures of united action which Napoleon had imposed by force. The Federal Act, therefore, not only provided for a federal organization of defence; it declared in favour of constitutions in the member states and authorized the Federal Diet to promote a common system of weights and measures, a common code of law, and – most far-reaching of all – a German customs union. But the Federal Diet had no power to compel co-operation; each state retained its complete sovereignty, and a single state could wreck any proposal by its refusal.

The German Confederation anticipated, on a smaller scale, the attempt of the League of Nations to square the circle of common action and absolute sovereignty, and, like the League of Nations, was doomed to a hopeless task. Just as the League of Nations rested, in fact, on the strength of two Great Powers, England and France, so the German Confederation was, in fact, protected by Austria and Prussia; and the lesser states of Germany, like the members of the League of Nations, played at being sovereign states without making any exertions to preserve their existence. The analogy is a little unfair to the League, in that a few of its smaller members would have made sacrifices for the cause of collective security if they had been given any encouragement to do so, whereas no German state ever bestirred itself. The German rulers preferred to devote their revenues to their own pleasures or, at best, to the promotion of culture (just as the peoples of the democratic countries preferred to devote their resources to the improvement of social conditions). Only a strong public opinion could have driven the German princes into fulfilling their duties, and this public opinion did not exist. Such public opinion as there was in the states of western Germany demanded constitutional liberties, not a more national policy; and the greater the degree of liberalism, the less willingness to risk this liberalism for the national cause.

The German Confederation was assigned, without much reflection, the boundary of the old Reich. But the old Reich had been the remnants of a universal Empire, with a national element added almost as an afterthought; the Confederation was, by definition, a national association. Taking over the old frontiers created two problems for the future. On the one hand, it excluded East Prussia and the territories acquired by Prussia in the partitions of Poland – West Prussia, that is, and the Duchy of Posen; East Prussia was mainly, and the Polish lands partly, inhabited by Germans, and the extension of German predominance was a burning issue both during the revolution of 1848 and in the politics of Bismarckian Germany. On the other hand, the Confederation included Bohemia. In the old Reich, Bohemia had occupied an anomalous position. The King of Bohemia had been an 'elector', but he had never been obliged to follow the Emperor in war and, alone of the princes, had enjoyed the title of King of an Imperial land. He was, in fact, rather a sovereign associate of the Reich than a feudal dependant Since 1526, when the crown of Bohemia passed to the head of the house of Habsburg, these questions of feudal law had lost their practical importance; but Bohemia remained in a distinct position, rather more like the independent Kingdom of Hungary (which also had the Habsburg ruler as king) than a full member of the Reich. In 1815 this decayed feudal tradition was ignored. The Czech people, who made up the majority of the inhabitants of Bohemia, had been for two hundred years without a national culture or a territorial upper class; they were a people lost to history, and it was easy to assume that the German inhabitants of Prague or Brünn made up Bohemia. The Czechs had once been willing to be part of a universal Reich; but they could never consent to be members of a national Confederation, and conflict was inevitable as soon as they recovered their national consciousness. Thus, embedded in the federal act, there lay concealed the Czech question and the Polish question, the two problems which define the limits of German power.

The scheme devised by the Great Powers at Vienna was criticized from two sides. On the one hand, some conservatives, swayed by the enthusiasm for tradition which was so marked an aspect of the romantic movement, desired to revive the old Reich and to restore the glories of the medieval Empire. Twenty-one German princes urged Francis I to resume the Imperial crown. Sentimentalism, not reality, inspired this offer. The abolition of the ecclesiastical states and of the Free Cities had destroyed the balance of the old order, and no secular prince was willing to disgorge the spoils which he had received from Napoleon. In any case, no one could seriously wish to revive the Reich as it had existed in 1792, on the outbreak of the wars with France; and to put back the clock of history a thousand years was beyond even a German conservative. Francis would not accept an empty dignity and saw that it could be made effective only by appealing to revolutionary nationalism against the princes. He replied to the offer: 'Only a Jacobin could accept this crown.' The Austrian representative was to preside at the meetings of the Federal Diet; that was the last relic of the old Reich.

Conservative criticism was vain nostalgia rather than the offer of an alternative. The criticism from the other side offered an alternative, but one which did not yet exist. The exponents of German nationalism who had applauded the victory of the Allies from the wings now called on the Allies to create a German national state. They expected the Great Powers to dethrone not only the German princes, but two of their own number, the King of Prussia and the Emperor of Austria, as well. Some national enthusiasts even supported the offer of the Imperial crown to Francis I in the hope that he might turn out to be a Jacobin after all. Stein, the most ruthless and impatient of them, looked instead to the Tsar. Stein had acted as administrator for the German lands which the Russians had taken over from the French during their advance; and he proposed that these territories should remain under an Imperial commissioner as the starting-point of national Germany. Stein's scheme was decked out with an impressive national phraseology; its practical sense was that Germany should be made national by grace of Alexander I, just as it had been made liberal (to Stein's indignation) by grace of Napoleon. Alexander was visionary enough to listen to Stein's advocacy; but even he could not contemplate taking over, indeed surpassing, Napoleon's performance. Stein's speciality was to allot himself impossible tasks. First, he had set out to turn Frederick William III into a German liberal; and now he tried to lure Alexander I into becoming a German nationalist. His plans were impracticable, but they revealed, in the last resort, his soundness of judgement: he never thought of employing the efforts of the Germans themselves. A national Germany established by Alexander was absurd but not impossible; a national Germany established in 1815 by the Germans was never contemplated by anyone.

The handful of German nationalists were active and vocal after 1815. What they expressed was not a determination to succeed but regret and resentment at their impotence. The patriotic associations of students, which had played no part against Napoleon, now wished to acquire, by boasting, a sort of posthumous importance. Jahn's gymnastic societies paraded round the university towns with all the airs of the conquerors of Napoleon; and romantic secret societies, the *Burschenschaften* (associations of hobbledehoys), sprang up to prepare for the coming radical Germany. The excitement and turmoil of a great war had made the students reluctant to return to their libraries and lecture rooms. They wanted the excitement and turmoil to continue; and as the real enemy, Napoleon, had disappeared, they had to create some imaginary foe, a turnip ghost, who would justify their sham uniforms, their displays of violence, their anti-Semitism, and their verbal pugnaciousness. Germany after 1815 was distracted by their staged radicalism, of which the most striking was a symbolical 'burning of the books' in 1817. Why books should be burnt or what it symbolized these 'students' never explained – for students to burn books was somehow a gesture of the great new era of romantic freedom which ought to have been created by the fall of Napoleon. These undergraduate follies were not evidence of a nationalist movement in Germany. They were student disturbances, which could become significant only in a country without serious political life. If they had been ignored, they would have faded away with the fading of the excitement of the great war; for student generations are short. But the nerves of the ruling classes too were on edge. Strained and exhausted after the great struggle, they treated the student agitation as a real political affair and so gave it an undeserved place in history.

No one could foresee in 1815 that the Hundred Days marked the end for ever of the French plans of European dominion. For more than a generation, the policies of the Great Powers were shaped by the apprehension of a new Napoleonic war; and their precautions became meaningless only when this apprehension lost its force. Italy and western Germany, disunited, without strength of their own, sentimentally attracted towards France, were the weak spots of this system of security; and the responsibility for both fell on Austria. Metternich, the Austrian Chancellor, was doubtful of Austria's resources and weighed down by the size of his task. Hence he reacted with exaggerated alarm to every breath of disruptive radicalism or of pro-French feeling. He, too, was an eighteenth-century rationalist with no faith in the traditions which he defended; he regarded the victory of the 'revolution' as inevitable and himself doomed to the defence of a losing cause. With all his acuteness of personal judgement and mastery of diplomatic technique, he lacked any real political sense; he flattered the German students by taking them seriously and set all Europe astir to control a few dozen undergraduate societies.

The corner-stone of Metternich's German policy was co-operation with Prussia. There was nothing far-fetched or Machiavellian in this. Prussia, too, was a conservative military monarchy, without national unity or constitutional life. Frederick William III had experienced at the hands of Napoleon defeat and humiliation; therefore he was even more apprehensive than Metternich of any whisper of liberalism or of pro-French feeling and indeed looked pathetically to Metternich for guidance and protection. Moreover the principles of German nationalism seemed to menace Hohenzollern, far more than Habsburg, existence. Many nationalists had imagined the Habsburg Emperor as head of a new Germany; hardly any supposed that the King of Prussia would survive in a national Germany, let alone lead it. It was well known, too, that the Kingdom of Prussia included over a million Poles; therefore the establishment of the national principle would involve, at the very least, the disruption of the Prussian Kingdom. No one, on the other hand, had the slightest appreciation that Bohemia was not German and even the Habsburgs themselves treated Hungary as a separate unit, so that the Habsburg lands could be incorporated in a national Germany almost in their existing form. The Austrian statesmen disliked the radical nature of the nationalist agitation and feared for their social position; still, they expected, in the last resort, to bargain with German nationalism, as they had bargained with so many dangers in the past. But, for a whole generation after 1815, no compromise seemed

possible between German nationalism and a great independent Kingdom of Prussia. The conflict between Prussia and the national principle
appeared irremediable, far deeper than Austria's conflict. This would be
so obvious as to require no labouring had not the history of Germany
between the Congress of Vienna and the revolutions of 1848 been
obscured and perverted by the genius of a great historian. Treitschke, a
Saxon liberal of Czech origin, became after 1866 a convert to the cause
of Prussian domination in Germany. Not only did he persuade himself
that in embracing this cause he had not abandoned his earlier liberal
principles; he set out to prove that Prussia had always been the nucleus
of national Germany and that Prussia had aimed at the unification of
Germany ever since 1815. This proof needed five long volumes, *German
History in the Nineteenth Century*, a work of the greatest literary power,
which has naturally bewitched every subsequent writer on this period.
Treitschke was faced at the outset with a complete contradiction of his
theory: the fact that Frederick William III was utterly dependent on
Metternich and sought his protection from the nationalist agitation in
Germany. His explanation was puerile: Frederick William, innocent,
indeed simple-minded, was entangled, or rather hypnotized, by the
subtleties of Metternich's argument. Once abandon Treitschke's
hypothesis and all the difficulties disappear. Frederick William III had
never recovered from the experiences of 1806. The student buffooner-
ies in Germany after 1815 drove his anxiety beyond all bounds; and he
importuned Metternich for some firm action, some counter-
demonstration of the 'forces of order'. Metternich, though not so anxious, was apprehensive too. Just as the statesmen of Europe after 1919
personified in 'the Bolshevik peril' all the problems created by the First
World War and by their own incapacity, so the rulers of Prussia and
Austria, conscious of mounting difficulties, saw them incorporated in
'the radical movement'. The event which in 1819 touched off their
fears into action was the murder by a romantic student of Kotzebue, a
minor dramatist who added to his income by writing a news-letter to
the Tsar. It was a fitting symbol of the academic nature of the radical
movement that a futile journalist should be its only victim.

Prussia and Austria took action on a grand scale. Metternich met
Hardenberg, the Prussian Chancellor, secretly in Bohemia; drafted a
series of decrees providing for federal inquiry into the universities and

for federal standards of political censorship; and forced these decrees on the other German states at a meeting at Karlsbad almost as conspiratorial as the meetings of the *Burschenschaft*. This was Austro-Prussian dualism in action, and for a repressive purpose. The Karlsbad decrees were the only positive activity of the Federal Diet; they became the great example of Metternich's repressive policy; and the Confederation was discredited once and for all by its police task. The Karlsbad decrees were blamed for the disappearance of the radical movement which followed at once; in fact they merely gave a halo of martyrdom to a movement which was already practically extinct. The League of Nations might easily have been led, in the first year or two of its existence, into promoting measures against Bolshevism (and was indeed so accused by the Comintern); in that case the decay of the Communist movements after 1923 would have been wrongly attributed to the 'Geneva decrees'. The radical movement in Germany needed no decrees to bring it to an end. It was a movement of university students, and the life of a student generation is four years. By 1819 the young men who had defeated Napoleon by proxy were taking their degrees and looking round for bureaucratic positions in the lesser states; their successors never developed the same craving for excitement and wearied of Swedish drill with 'Father Jahn'. The commission of inquiry into the universities set up by the Karlsbad decrees sat for interminable years and ultimately produced a wordy, high-sounding report on the misdeeds of students who had long ceased to be students and on professors long since dead. But in its eight years of activity it managed to identify only 107 subversive individuals in the whole of Germany; these 107 alone experienced any practical effect of the Karlsbad decrees.

There was a more serious reason for the fading of the liberal movement in Germany after 1820. The wars against Napoleon were followed not merely by political excitement, but by material prosperity as well. Austria and Prussia had received large English subsidies, some of the lesser states smaller ones. The Germans, as it were, exported their man-power to the battlefield and obtained English gold in return; but man-power was their sole article of export. After 1815 the English gold passed into circulation, and there was a brief period of heady misleading activity. By 1820 the gold had been exhausted, used up in buying

English manufactured goods and colonial products. All over central Europe prices collapsed, the artificial briskness ended, and German life fell back into a duller, humbler air. For the Germany of 1815 was almost entirely an agricultural country without flourishing industries or an independent prosperous merchant or manufacturing class. Only a quarter of the population lived in the towns, though any place with more than 2,000 inhabitants was dignified with that name; the entire town population of Germany was only half as much again as the population of Paris; and most towns had, if anything, dwindled since the sixteenth century. Germany had no industries in the modern sense of the term: no serious coal production, no steam engines, no large factories. She had old-established handicrafts: the weaving of Silesia, the cutlery of Solingen, the making of clocks and toys in the Black Forest. These industries employed the leisure hours of peasants; they could not be the foundation of a middle class. The intellectual life of Germany was remote, suspended from reality. The writers wrote for each other or sought the patronage of some prince. There was no German 'public' and therefore there were no political movements, only the disputes of academic politicians. Goethe was the greatest of all German writers, but he could not live by the sale of his books; he had to become first manager of the Court theatre and then general administrator in the petty state of Weimar. Thus there began in 1820 what German historians call the 'quiet years', the dead period when the Napoleonic storm had blown over and when the new forces which were to disrupt Germany had not established themselves, the long calm which lasted until the war crisis which coincided with the accession of Frederick William IV of Prussia in 1840 and until the new outburst of the romantic movement both in literature and politics which was the prelude to the revolutions of 1848.

The 'quiet years' silenced liberalism without benefiting conservatism. The precarious balance was indefinitely prolonged. The conservative theorists, Gentz at their head, wished to bring Germany back to her traditions; to transform the parliaments of the lesser states into feudal Estates; and to breathe new life into the decaying provinces of the two Great Powers. Even Metternich, in his cynical, abstract fashion, was caught for this romantic programme and lectured the German princes on the merits of consulting their Estates. But the Western states had not undergone the levelling of their absolutist rulers and of the French revolution for nothing. There was no elaborate system of rank, no assortment of privileges, to provide the variety which Estates needed. There was not even a returned *émigré* nobility such as gave France for a few years a misleading air of feudal fashions. The lesser German states were all indisputably 'liberal'. That is, they had a social and political uniformity: no class privileges, a middle-class bureaucracy, and representative Chambers with legislative powers, but unable to do more than criticize the administration in a carping, negative way. These German constitutions followed the lines of the Charter which the French bourgeoisie had imposed upon Louis XVIII in 1814; and in the same way gave the administrative middle class a public voice but no power. The Chambers were representative of the 'people' only in the sense that they represented wealth and education; rigidly based on limited suffrage, the last thing they desired was to represent the uninstructed masses. The Conservative programme of transforming the unhistorical Chambers into pseudo-historical Estates (for no real tradition of Estates existed) would have substituted for the monopoly of middle-class bureaucracy a partnership of landed nobility and loyal peasants – a programme unwelcome not only to the middle-class bureaucrats but just as much to the lesser princes who had no desire to revive the power of their landed nobles. Advocacy of Estates was the only attempt made by the Confederation to put into effect the constitutional promises of 1815; and it made the liberal bureaucrats more distrustful of the Confederation than ever. They refused to admit that there was anything positive in conservative ideas and so identified both Metternich and the Confederation, his instrument, with barren repression. In theory they were mistaken; in practice things worked out much as they imagined, for Metternich's dry rationalism made him sceptical and ineffective even in regard to his own plans.

The 'quiet years' were therefore the heyday of constitutionalism in the separate states, though they stifled liberalism as a German movement. This constitutionalism was strangely abstract, doctrinaire. The creed almost exclusively of bureaucrats, it thought solely in terms of legal procedure; precision and rule, not freedom or achievement, were its aims. In the absence of an independent capitalistic middle class, constitutional life was a game played by the servants of the state among themselves. Only the officials and the professional men, themselves dependent on court patronage for their livelihood, had votes; and even the leaders of the opposition in the various Chambers were civil servants on leave. On one thing all agreed: fear of the central power and a conviction that a national Germany would be the doom of their precious 'liberal' existence; united distrust therefore of the masses, through whom national sentiment could alone become dangerous, and united resolution to exclude the masses from political life. Thus was completed the trend by which German constitutionalism associated itself both with particularism and with an attitude of hostility to democracy. The German princes, without real existence, became the patrons of a constitutional liberalism which was also without roots or popular support; strange alliance of two artificial entities, brought together by a common helplessness. Both denounced the Vienna settlement; yet both could survive only so long as the balance created in Vienna continued to operate.

The Vienna balance shook a little as a result of the French Revolution of 1830. Liberal excitement spread, for a moment, beyond bureaucratic circles; and the possibility of French intervention in Belgium raised the danger of a European war. The war scare lasted just long enough to reveal the complete disorder and unpreparedness of the Federal machinery of defence, but not long enough to promote a demand for reform. There was liberal bustle in most of the petty states; and some of the princes, such as the Duke of Brunswick, who exceeded the normal princely level in eccentric violence or plain lunacy, were chased off their thrones. But there were no serious constitutional changes and little hint of any new national feeling. However, radical students and journalists finally managed to screw themselves up to the point of a monster rally at Hambach in the Bavarian Palatinate in 1832, the first feast of nationalist oratory on a large scale since the days of the burning of the books and other feats of emancipation in 1817. Two years later, fifty students of a more practical turn of mind attempted to seize the Town Hall in Frankfurt and proclaim the German republic. They were dispersed by the Town Guard.

Metternich, though without much conviction, staged a new radical peril; and in 1834 persuaded the German states to revive the machinery of the Karlsbad decrees. His real anxiety was the ineffectiveness of the Confederation; and he hoped by means of the radical body to induce the German princes to surrender some of their sovereignty to the central authority. In a curiously detached despairing way Metternich actually wanted a Confederation with some powers; but he would not compel agreement and his bogy was not frightening. Sole outcome of the discussions at Vienna was a Federal Court to arbitrate between the states; and the Court never met. Metternich, all through his life, flattered himself that his diplomacy, rather than the superior strength of the Allies, had defeated Napoleon; and he could never rid himself of the delusion, so closely echoed at Geneva a century later, that the ineffective Confederation could be made effective by some additional article, some unobserved constitutional twist. But the defect of the Confederation was inherent in its composition. The lesser states, with their artificial sovereignty, feared the two great members of the Confederation more than they feared France; and therefore even those princes, such as the King of Bavaria and the King of Hanover, who had respectable armies of some size, planned to keep them out of a French war so as to preserve their independence thereafter. Austria and Prussia could be counted on to resist France for the sake of their position as Great Powers; and the lesser princes could safely devote all their ingenuity to avoiding the burden of federal obligations.

The Confederation was as a result an empty farce. The federal army was not organized; the federal fortresses were not garrisoned; even the federal dues were not paid and throughout its fifty years of life the Federal Diet conducted its business on stationery borrowed from the Austrian Chancellery. In 1840 there was a new war scare, an alarm that France, baulked in the Near East, might renew the programme of the natural frontiers. There was a rather febrile revival of the 'spirit of 1813', with rather better poems and even less practical results. The full failure of the Confederation was now obvious: Austria had her hands full in Italy, and only the Prussian army garrisoned the Rhine. Prussia had become unwittingly the defender of Germany, and the associations between Prussia and German nationalism were renewed for the first time since 1813. The alarm blew over; and after it there was much mutual reproach and high talk. Most of the states actually paid their federal contributions. But it was impossible to agree what use should be made of these subscriptions, and the fund remained intact in the hands of the Rothschilds at Frankfurt.

The story of the German federal organization was thus one of unbroken failure. Failure in the military sphere, failure in the constitutional sphere. Failure, too, in the other tasks envisaged by the Final Act. Nothing was done to promote a uniform code of law or a uniform standard of weights and measures; nothing was done through the Confederation to lower the tariff barriers within Germany. It is usual to blame the two Great Powers for this failure: but in at any rate some spheres they would have welcomed federal achievement and were defeated by the veto of the small states. Both, for instance, desired a federal system of defence; both made proposals for a German code of law; and Austria at least would have welcomed tariff co-operation. But only force would lead the petty princes to abate a scrap of their absolute sovereignty. The subjects of the petty princes had no force, and Austria and Prussia were debarred by their monarchical principles from using any. From 1815 to 1848, a political generation, no advance was made, and the stagnation which had followed Westphalia seemed to be renewed. But in that generation great changes took place, changes in the economic and spiritual life of Germany, changes above all in the balance of the two German powers.

In 1815 Austria was indisputably the greater of the two Powers, Prussia still shattered and exhausted by the disasters of 1806. In the following thirty years Austria's lead was greatly lessened, though it probably still remained at the end. For Austria this was the 'Metternich era', the period when all attempt at a constructive policy was abandoned, when 'administration took the place of government' and when even administration was mainly concerned with the exclusion of liberalism. The experiences of the eighteenth century had shown that reforms could not be carried through merely by Imperial will, but must rest on a reforming class. In the Austrian Empire there was no competent reforming class, and, in the reign of Francis I, not even a reforming Imperial will. Each year the finances grew worse and the bureaucratic confusion more inextricable; the equipment, the organization, and the effective strength of the army steadily declined. Moreover, from the point of view of German standing, the most constructive part of Metternich's policy had a weakening result. In 1815 the impression made by the Germanizing policy of Joseph II still remained, and it was generally supposed, in a vague way, that the Austrian Empire was a German state. Metternich set himself to remove this impression. He feared the development of German nationalism as part of the liberal danger; he feared that German nationalism would look sympathetically on the claims of national Italy and so help to deprive the Habsburgs of their rich Italian possessions; and, further, his trumped-up devotion to tradition made him seek to revive the consciousness of the historic states and provinces into which the Austrian Empire was divided. In Hungary, Metternich gave up Joseph II's policy of co-operating with the German trading classes and, instead, breathed new life into the aristocratic constitution. His intention was to make aristocratic Hungary a barrier against bourgeois German nationalism; instead, the Hungarian nobles allied themselves with Magyar nationalism and transformed old Hungary into a liberal-national state. In Bohemia too, Metternich stirred the decayed Diet into a feeble revival and sought to promote a Czech national consciousness, though only in the cultural sphere. Even in the German lands of the house of Habsburg, Metternich gave the Estates a sham existence, in order to substitute provincial sentiment for a common German character, a policy which had little success except in Tyrol. Metternich's patronage of Hungarian, Czech, and Slovene sentiment perhaps served 'the strength which comes of diversity' in his favourite phrase; but it undoubtedly made the German inhabitants of the Austrian Empire conscious, as they had not been in 1815, both of their German nationality and of their minority position within the Empire. Metternich's cynical policy aimed at making the victory of German nationalism within the Austrian Empire impossible; but his policy stimulated, in the minds of both Austrian and non-Austrian Germans, the idea of the Austrian Empire as a half-German or even a non-German state. In 1815 no one could have imagined a Germany without Austria; by 1848 the position of Austria in Germany had become a problem without obvious or agreed solution.

The history of Prussia in these thirty-three years was the exact opposite: the efficiency of her government increased and its German character became more pronounced. The idea of a Prussian leadership of Germany, when consciously formulated in 1848, still came with a shock of surprise; but the way for it had been unwittingly prepared throughout the preceding generation. In 1815 the policy of Prussia was neither German nor liberal. Frederick William III had rashly promised a constitution to his subjects, but he was determined not to implement his promise; the last relic of the days of liberation was a further promise, given in 1820, that the state debt should not be increased without the consent of the Estates of the Kingdom. But for more than twenty years the King did not need to borrow, and Prussia remained therefore despotically ruled by the King's ministers and by the governors of the eight provinces into which the Kingdom was divided. Provincial Estates existed, but, lacking financial authority, they lacked all sense and provided merely an opportunity for meagre display and even more meagre speeches. The Prussian ministers, energetic men without interest in historic institutions, regarded the provincial Estates with contempt and distrust, and systematically reduced their importance. While Metternich was deliberately reviving the Austrian provinces, the Prussians were rather less deliberately reducing theirs, though both had the same hostility to liberalism and the popular will.

One Prussian province possessed a distinct character and was, for some time, given privileged treatment. This was Posen, the Polish territory recovered at the Congress of Vienna. Alexander I had conceived the romantic ambition of establishing a liberal-national Poland under his own sovereignty; and he had regretted having to restore to Prussia even a fraction of her former Polish territory. The Prussian rulers feared the attractive power of Alexander's Kingdom of Poland with its ostensibly liberal constitution and its national character. 'Congress Poland' aimed at winning the support of the Polish aristocracy; Prussian policy in reply aimed at winning over the lower ranks of the national classes. The Poles were told that their national character would be respected and preserved; the province was given, in a modified form, the Polish coat-of-arms and the high-sounding title of a Grand Duchy; most striking of all, Prussian agrarian policy, which elsewhere benefited the lord at the expense of the peasant, was here reversed in order to benefit the Polish peasant at the cost of the Polish lord. The Grand Duchy of Posen was for some years the freest and most Polish part of the partitioned lands, the centre of national feeling and the starting-point of the movements for liberation. But this strange situation did not last. There were continual complaints from the other Prussian provinces with

Polish subjects, especially West Prussia; and the widening breach between the Tsar and Polish feeling lessened the need for a pro-Polish policy in Posen. In 1830 the conflict between the Tsar and the Poles broke into an open Polish revolt; and, when this had been crushed in 1831, Congress Poland was ruled by Russian military force. In Posen too the period of Polish freedom ended. Prussian policy ceased to protect the Polish peasants and began instead an educational campaign for the spread of German. Much to their surprise the conservative Prussian bureaucrats found themselves, not for the last time, serving the revolutionary cause of German nationalism, which they disliked and feared.

This strange and unwelcome alliance was forced on Prussia also in another connection both in Posen and on the Rhine. The two great acquisitions of the Congress of Vienna; remote in everything else, had the one common characteristic of Roman Catholicism; and the possession of more than six million Roman Catholic subjects forced on the Prussian state for the first time the problem of its relations with an independent ecclesiastical authority. The Prussian state had always been, in religious matters, both totalitarian and tolerant: it cared nothing for belief so long as it exacted obedience. Now it would have cared nothing for the Roman Catholics if they had confined their religion to private life. But the Roman Catholic Church could not be accommodated in the Prussian system: itself intolerant, it would not be reduced to the authority of another. The challenge existed from the beginning and, after 1830, broke out into open conflict. The occasion was a dispute over mixed marriages: the Roman Catholic bishops attempting to forbid them except on prescribed conditions, the Prussian state resisting this interference with the secular law. But the real issue was whether the Prussian state must accept any limits other than its own will. By 1840 the Archbishop of Cologne was in prison, the Bishop of Treves forbidden to enter his see, and, on the other hand, the Archbishop of Posen, who had refused to take up the fight, forced to resign by Papal pressure. Poles and Roman Catholics were joined in an 'un-German' cause; and the agents of the Prussian government were applauded by Protestant German nationalists.

The religious conflict provided almost the only event in the long dreary years of the reign of Frederick William III. The real significance of these years could only be observed thereafter: the new efficiency learnt in the years of disaster was maintained in the years of peace. The Prussian monarchy and the Prussian ruling class never forgot their lesson and so outstripped their Austrian partners. Without a scrap of the culture which made the Austrian aristocracy patrons of music and the arts, the Prussian Junkers and officials excelled in the drab spheres of tax-collecting, the balancing of accounts, and the making of roads. Metternich tried to resist liberalism by manufacturing conservative ideas – the ideas of historic institutions, provincial diversity, religious obedience. The ideas of the Prussian landed and bureaucratic classes were little more than a feeble echo of Metternich's; their real answer to liberalism was the weapon of their administrative efficiency. The Prussian Junkers were too poor to afford the aristocratic luxury of unbalanced accounts; and they brought to the affairs of state the same competence as was demanded on their own estates. Of all the hereditary governing classes of Europe, the Prussians alone maintained their monopoly of political power into the twentieth century; and it was their application at the office desk which kept them afloat.

The 'quiet years' modified the character of Prussia in two separate spheres. The philosophy of Hegel first made of the advance of Prussia something inevitable; the Zollverein first made Prussia appear essential to Germany. The University of Berlin, founded in the days of humiliation after 1806, had been from the beginning an instrument of state policy; but the teaching of Fichte and his followers, though inspiring, had been more German than Prussian. Hegel, who succeeded Fichte in 1814, performed for the state, and especially for the Prussian state, the same service in political theory which centuries before Luther had performed in terms of theology. He argued that true freedom was to be found in working in line with the trend of history; that the Prussian state was the culmination of the historic process; and that therefore submission to the Prussian state should be the choice of every free man. This squaring of the circle was welcome gospel to all those who had found it hard to reconcile their German pride and the circumstances of everyday subjection; now they understood that in accepting subjection they were really free. Hegel remained the 'German philosopher' *par excellence*, even when his fashions of thought were a little outmoded. None could escape from the spell of his teaching. The extreme radicals, of whom Marx and Engels were the most outstanding, and who hated the Prussian monarchy, could only argue that the 'forces of history' were going elsewhere – in the direction of a radical republic – and so confessed that they understood human freedom as little as their master.

The Zollverein fitted in well with the doctrine of both Hegel and Marx. The Prussian territories of 1815 straggled across northern Germany from Aachen to Königsberg, held together neither by geography nor by a common past, a haphazard collection of separate provinces each with its distinct scale of tariffs and prohibitions. Prussia could not wait for the general German tariff which had been promised in the Federal Act. In 1818 there appeared a uniform Prussian tariff system, the first tariff system in all Europe conceived in a spirit of moderate protection and carried out to a conscious plan. Far from considering German needs, the tariff was typical of Prussian selfishness, disregarding the interests of other German states and making the Federal establishment of a common tariff system impossible. The prospect of Germany economically united by consent was killed by Prussian policy almost before it was born. Instead, the Prussian economic administrators conceived the plan of attacking the small neighbouring states piecemeal and forcing them one by one into the Prussian tariff system, a plan of economic conquest which they pursued for ten years with limited success. The states entirely surrounded by Prussian territory succumbed to Prussian pressure, but these states were few, and by 1828 the original Prussian plan was worn out. Then came the great and unexpected development. The lesser princes objected to any general German tariff union as a diminution of their sovereignty. On the other hand they were beginning to fear that the capitalist middle class which was at last developing in western Germany would regard the internal tariffs of the German states as an intolerable imposition and would turn in irritation and despair to the radical programme of a single German republic. The princes, in other words, reversed their position and actually favoured tariff unions as the sole means of winning the middle classes back from Jacobinism, and these unions, far from envisaging a united Germany, were created with the deliberate purpose of making a united Germany unnecessary. Two tariff unions came into being almost simultaneously in 1828; a Prussian agreement with

Hesse-Darmstadt and a union between Bavaria and Wurtemberg. There followed six years of economic threats and bargaining until in 1834 the various groups came together in a single union, the Zollverein, which embraced almost all the German states except Austria and a few economic dependencies of England, such as Hanover and Hamburg.

The Zollverein was almost the only serious event in the 'quiet years', and for this reason has come in for more than its due of interest. It was not a step towards the unification of Germany, but a device for making the unification of Germany less necessary; it was the price which the German princes, including the King of Prussia, paid for continuing to exist. Moreover it was an achievement of the princes, not of the peoples. The concessions which it involved were violently opposed in the Chambers of the lesser states; and if Prussia, who made the greatest financial concessions, had possessed a parliament, the Zollverein would never have been established. The Zollverein became, in time, a powerful instrument in Prussia's control of Germany. But the Prussian statesmen who made the Zollverein had not the slightest idea of its political consequences; they saw only the rambling, unworkable frontiers and desired to save money on their customs officers. Metternich, indeed, feared the political advantages which it would bring to Prussia; but in his usual despairing way he feared without being able to prevent. The Habsburgs had a more pressing problem – to remove the tariff barriers within their own territories; and even that they were unable to accomplish until after the revolution of 1848. To suppose that the entire Habsburg Empire could be economically united with non-Habsburg Germany was beyond the range of Metternich's hopeless spirit; for this would be to revive the conception of a central Europe dominated from Vienna which had been defeated in the Thirty Years' War. Thus the Zollverein presented to the German lands of Austria the alternative of going with the rest of Germany or with the other Habsburg lands – a choice between national sentiment and economic advantage, which was never fully made. On the other hand, while the lesser states certainly drifted away from Austria economically, they had no intention of subordinating themselves to Prussia; and all the members of the Zollverein, except those hemmed in by Prussian forces, fought against Prussia in 1866.

The Zollverein was in large part the result of Prussian determination, but like so many Prussian achievements it was a *tour de force* with unforeseen results. Its aim, so far as it expressed a deliberate policy, was to prevent economic union through the German Confederation, a protectionist union which would have been dominated by Austria and would have found its centre of gravity in the Danube valley to the political and economic ruin of Prussia. The Prussian Zollverein, in contrast, looked across the North Sea to the world market. Based upon the low Prussian tariff, it promoted German prosperity not by excluding foreign goods but by making trade between Germany and foreign countries easier. It was in origin essentially a consumer's scheme, catering for German industrial development only by accident. But the Zollverein, despite its anti-national origin, could not be maintained without an increasing appeal to national sentiment; and that sentiment moved in terms of conflict, not in terms of prosperity. Within a decade of the founding of the Zollverein, the great publicist, List, was arguing that the purpose of unity in economic, as in other, matters was to make Germany stronger for war – stronger, in the first place, for economic war, stronger ultimately for war pure and simple. The sensible Free Trade bureaucrats of Prussia who designed the Zollverein and at first controlled its workings loathed List's doctrines, but in the long run they lost and List won. They would have been appalled to know that the Zollverein, instead of promoting the exchange of goods between Prussia and the outer world, would ultimately prepare the way for a unified and exclusive central Europe; and that instead of drawing German trade down the Elbe and Rhine to the North Sea it would end by committing Prussia's military resources to the support of the Berlin to Baghdad railway.

Travailler pour le roi de Prusse had been a favourite saying of the eighteenth century. In the nineteenth century the Prussian governing class, conscious of its weakness, worked for causes which it hated and feared. Every success injured the traditional Prussian order, yet drove it further on its course, until the time when the Prussian rulers, aristocratic, particularist, limited in their aims, became the instruments of a demagogic German nationalism which recognized no bounds. At the beginning of the century the Prussian rulers had found Stein's programme of defeating the French by adopting the most extreme courses of the French revolution too wild for them. With the Zollverein they began to

follow the same line of policy towards the danger of German nationalism. The Zollverein was not evidence that the Prussian rulers aimed at
the leadership of united Germany. It was rather witness to the sacrifices
they would make to prevent a united Germany. But one step led on to
another. The Zollverein was an 'ersatz', an economic substitute for
national unification; as the danger grew greater, the Prussian rulers
were driven to offer in the Bismarckian Reich a political 'ersatz' as well.
The Zollverein of the eighteen-thirties and 'forties was not very
important economically: the railways and the application of science to
industry would have come even without the Zollverein, and would
have initiated the great industrial change. It was certainly not important
politically, for it neither created in Prussia a habit of leading nor in the
other states a habit of being led. But it was very important as a symbol
of the resourcefulness of the Prussian governing classes, of their readiness to appease and to exploit the new political forces. The classes that
ruled Prussia would dig their own graves provided that they retained a
monopoly of wielding the spade.

When, a generation later, most of Germany had been united under
Prussian rule, German writers, and others too, accepted the Hegelian
doctrine that the 'forces of history' had been working towards this end
in the thirty-three years which followed the Congress of Vienna. In
reality, Germany, protected from the domination of a single Great
Power by the mutual jealousy of three Great Powers, tended during
these years to break up, not to come together, and was less united in
1848 than in 1815. Then the intellectual classes, and to some extent
the military classes as well, had been brought together by the emotions
of the war of 'liberation'; in peace they fell apart. The lesser princes
were fearful of Austria and Prussia; Prussia and Austria, no longer
fearing France, were jealous of each other. The middle-class liberals of
the western and southern states boasted of their constitutional life, and,
though they desired a united Germany, it was a Germany in which the
Prussian and Austrian monarchies should play no part. The Austrian
liberals wanted both to liberalize Austria and to draw closer the links
with the rest of Germany; the Prussian liberals wanted to liberalize
Prussia, but not to be brought within Austria's sphere. The Austrian
governing classes wanted to keep things exactly as they were; the Prussian governing classes wished to improve Prussia's position, but not at

the price of surrendering to liberalism. And while middle-class reformers wanted a Germany which would resemble the France of the July monarchy, the radicals aspired to imitate the France of 1793. The explosion of 1848 occurred in the name of unity, but it had nothing of unity except the name. The rulers, the reformers, and the revolutionaries were divided both from each other and among themselves.

4

1848: THE YEAR OF GERMAN LIBERALISM

The statesmen of the Congress of Vienna had hoped to give Germany a stable existence. But their settlement was mechanical, an arbitrary arrangement without any anchorage of devotion or enthusiasm. It did not inspire the conservatives; it was hated by the liberals; it was passively accepted by the masses. The Confederation had been intended as a defensive association against France; but in the two alarms of 1830 and 1840 it had proved altogether ineffective. All that remained was the authority of Prussian and Austrian armed strength, negative and unconstructive. But this partnership was breaking up, losing both its moral conviction and its actual power. After the death of Francis I in 1835, the Austrian Empire was under the nominal rule of an imbecile, Ferdinand, actually administered by a jealous, despairing triumvirate – Metternich, Kolovrat, his rival, and the Archduke Lewis, youngest and feeblest brother of Francis I. Austria's policy became ever more hopeless, her finances ever more disordered, her armies ever weaker. The moral authority which Austria had once enjoyed existed no more; even the most conservative lost all faith in this 'European China'.

Prussia remained well administered, her finances in good order, her commercial policy enlightened and successful. But her ruling classes were drifting away from the narrow conservatism of the Holy Alliance. In the war crisis of 1840 Prussia had stood out alone as the defender of Germany, and nationalist enthusiasm had centred on Prussia for the first time since 1813. Before 1840 the rulers of Prussia had assumed that the unification of Germany would destroy Prussia; 1840 gave them the first glimpse of the idea that Prussia might exploit nationalist sentiment to conquer Germany. The more immediate cause of the change in Prussian policy was the character of Frederick William IV, who became King in 1840. German royal houses ran easily to eccentrics and lunatics. Ceaseless inbreeding, power territorially circumscribed but within these limits limitless, produced mad princes as a normal event. The mad King of Bavaria, the mad Duke of Brunswick, the mad Elector of Hesse, the imbecile Emperor – these phrases are the commonplace of German history; and of the utterly petty princes hardly one was sane. The house of Hohenzollern had been unique in its unbroken succession of sensible uninspired rulers (the exception was a genius, not a madman). Frederick William IV broke the long run. He was always eccentric, and he ended mad. Impulsive and romantic, his mind chock-a-block with contradictory ideas, he turned Prussian policy away from moderation and entangled Prussia so deeply in German affairs that she could never be disentangled again. The union of Junker Prussia and national Germany, this wedding of opposites, was perhaps inevitable; but it needed a madman to accomplish it.

Frederick William IV was not a liberal. His ideas, when he could sort them out, were medieval-revivalist, the Prussian political counterpart of the Oxford Movement. Hating liberal constitutions as much as his father had done, he yet dreamt of some rigmarole of feudal Estates. Hating revolutionary nationalism and devoted (in theory) to the traditional headship of the House of Habsburg, he yet dreamt of some resurrection of the old Reich, in which the Emperor should have the nominal superiority, but the King of Prussia the real power. These ideas were not confined to the secrecy of the closet. Frederick William was a great orator and poured out his intentions on every occasion. He was the first master of what became a speciality of German politics – the meaningless but inspiring phrase, the high-sounding roll of words in which that extraordinary language can turn dirty water into wine. Almost his first act was to call off the conflict with the Roman Catholic

Church which was disrupting the Rhineland and to project a vague scheme of Christian reunion. Nothing came of his scheme, but the conflict was not renewed; the deep-seated antagonism between the Prussian state and any rival authority was obscured, and there remained a vague impression that Prussia included without strain both Protestant and Roman Catholic Germans and so was more truly 'national' than Roman Catholic Austria. Frederick William's visionary Estates were not so easy to translate into practice. The Junker land-owners were willing to give themselves the airs of a feudal aristocracy, simulating a medieval reverence for a king who was divesting himself of his powers for their benefit. But a States General needs a third estate, unprivileged, humble, and dependent on the royal grace; and no such estate existed. In Prussia, as elsewhere in Germany, the third estate would be composed of liberal lawyers and bureaucrats, their minds set on a written constitution and on a parliament elected by a uniform suffrage. For, although the Kingdom of Prussia took its name from the land of Junker estates, in fact more than half its provinces lay west of the Elbe and were as much affected by the legacy of Napoleon as any of the lesser states.

As a result the constitutional projects of Frederick William IV remained empty phrases. Sole outcome was a meeting of committees of the provincial Diets in 1843; but the 'United Committees' too failed to devise a constitution which should have no meaning. Where impulsive romanticism failed, iron rails succeeded. In 1835 there had been opened in Bavaria the first railway in Germany, the five-mile line from Nuremberg to Fürth. By 1840 railways were working in Prussia, and soon railway construction was proceeding in all directions. Or rather, in all directions but one. No line ran east from Berlin to the 'colonial' lands of East and West Prussia, and it seemed as if the railways would pull Berlin, as it were, away from the Junker east over to the liberal and industrialist west. The Eastern Railway (Ostbahn) was essential for the Junker landowners. It was essential politically if they were to retain their connection with Berlin, and so their monopoly of political power; it was essential economically if the cornlands of eastern Germany were to establish a hold over the increasingly populous west. But private enterprise would not build the Ostbahn, even when offered a guarantee of interest by the Prussian state. Therefore the Ostbahn would have to

be undertaken by the state itself. The political consequences were paradoxical. In the first place, the Junkers identified state enterprise and
their own interest more than ever, so that – even before 1848 – Junker
writers talked a socialistic claptrap; some, to disguise their particular
interest in the *Ostbahn*, advocating the state ownership of all railways.
Secondly, some idealistic cover had to be devised to cloak the reality
that the wealthy western provinces were being asked to subsidize for
the benefit of the eastern provinces railways which would not pay their
way. The solution was simple: the *Ostbahn* was represented as the
standard-bearer of German culture in Polish lands, the greatest German
thrust into eastern Europe since the Teutonic Knights; it would free East
and West Prussia from the north–south line of the Vistula and attach it
to the east–west line of Prussia from Königsberg to Aachen. The private
benefit of the Prussian landowners was concealed in the promotion of
the German national cause.

In the third place, the *Ostbahn* made the landowners advocates of a
constitution. They had supported the King in his resistance to liberalism so long as a constitution was demanded on grounds of principle.
But Frederick William III had promised, in 1820, that the Prussian state
would not increase the state debt without the consent of a representative body. Only the daring and ruthless Junker, Bismarck, argued that, if
the state built an efficient railway, the promise need not be kept;
Bismarck was as yet unknown and the Junkers were for the most part
honourable and unenterprising. Frederick William IV was thus deserted by the very class on whom Prussian absolutism rested: the *Ostbahn*
drove the Junkers and the Junkers drove the King forward into constitutionalism. But the representative body was to be as unrepresentative
as possible, merely a general assembly of the provincial Diets with a
fine-sounding name, the 'United Diet'. The evil principle of direct
suffrage was still excluded from Prussian soil. But the United Diet,
when it met in April 1847, behaved as though it were a liberal parliament. It made the classical liberal demands: regular periodical meetings and no additional taxes without its consent Its demands were
rejected, and the Diet in return refused to sanction the loan for the
Ostbahn. Opposition came, naturally enough, from the Rhinelanders;
but the first and most determined in condemning the railway were
the members of the third estate from East Prussia, both in town and

country, whose long experience enabled them to recognize Junker self-interest under its disguise of service of the German cause. In June 1847 the United Diet broke up after an empty session. But not a vain one. The meeting of the United Diet and the debates which followed sapped the confidence of Prussian absolutism and, still more, its prestige. Frederick William could not undo what had happened, and prepared, during the following winter, to make the concessions which he had refused in June. The Junkers, on their side, could not nerve themselves to follow Bismarck's wild promptings; they succumbed morally to liberalism. The old Prussian order, like the old order in Austria, seemed in German eyes to be in dissolution. The two pillars of authority in Germany were undermined and it needed only a breath from outside to overthrow them. The way was clear for the year of revolutions.

1848 was the decisive year of German, and so of European, history: it recapitulated Germany's past and anticipated Germany's future. Echoes of the Holy Roman Empire merged into a prelude of the Nazi 'New Order'; the doctrines of Rousseau and the doctrines of Marx, the shade of Luther and the shadow of Hitler, jostled each other in bewildering succession. Never has there been a revolution so inspired by a limitless faith in the power of ideas; never has a revolution so discredited the power of ideas in its result. The success of the revolution discredited conservative ideas; the failure of the revolution discredited liberal ideas. After it, nothing remained but the idea of Force, and this idea stood at the helm of German history from then on. For the first time since 1521, the German people stepped on to the centre of the German stage only to miss their cues once more. German history reached its turning-point and failed to turn. This was the fateful essence of 1848.

The Germany of 1848 was still, for all practical purposes, the Germany which had experienced the Napoleonic wars, still, that is to say, a predominantly rural community. Since 1815 there had been a great and continuous rise in population: from twenty-four and a half million in 1816 to thirty-four million in 1846 (or if the Austrian lands in the Confederation are included from thirty-three to forty-five million).[1]

[1] These were not all Germans. There were two million, rising to three million, Slavs (Poles) in Prussia, and four and a half million, rising to six million, Slavs (Czechs and Slovenes) in Austria.

But the proportions of town and country had remained unchanged: in Prussia 73.5 per cent of the population was classed as rural in 1816 and 72 per cent in 1846. The towns were still small, still dominated by the professional and intellectual middle classes. Industrial capitalists, still less industrial workers, did not exist as a serious political force. Even the material basis for modern industrialization had hardly been laid: in 1846 London alone consumed more coal than all Prussia raised. The revolution of 1848 was not the explosion of new forces, but the belated triumph of the *Burschenschaft*, the students of the war of liberation who were now men in their fifties. Arndt, the writer of patriotic poems against Napoleon, and even 'gymnastic father' Jahn were as much the symbols of 1848 as they had been of 1813; but now their voices quavered as they sang of their youthful energy, and their muscles creaked as they displayed their youthful energy in Swedish drill.

The liberals who occupied the forefront of 1848 were the men of 1813, now sobered by the long empty years. They had learnt to be cautious, to be moderate, learnt, as they thought, worldly wisdom. They had sat in the parliaments of the lesser states and had come to believe that everything could be achieved by discussion and by peaceful persuasion. Themselves dependent on the princes for their salaries or pensions as civil servants, they put belief in the good faith of princes as the first article of their policy, and genuinely supposed that they could achieve their aims by converting their rulers. Behind them were the radicals, men of unknown names and without experience: members of the same intellectual middle class, but of a younger generation – the product of the Romantic Movement, the contemporaries of Liszt, of Paganini, and of Hoffmann. These radicals were not interested in practical results. For them revolution was an end in itself, and violence the only method of politics. Yet, though they appealed constantly to force, they possessed none. The radical attempts of 1848 – Hecker's proclamation of the German republic in April and Struve's rising in September – were not even damp squibs, merely bad theatre. The radicals appealed constantly to the people, and demanded universal suffrage and a People's Republic. But they had no connection with the people of Germany, no mass support, no contact with the masses, no understanding of their needs. Thus the revolution was played out on a carefully restricted stage: on the one side the ruling princes, on the other the educated middle class in its two aspects, liberal and radical. In the end the peasant masses cleared the stage; but these peasants were disciplined conscripts in the Prussian army.

Yet the unpropertied uneducated masses were discontented and restless both in town and country; and there was in 1848 an unconscious mass revolution as well as a conscious liberal one. The inexorable increase of population made the peasants of eastern Germany land-hungry and drove the peasants of western Germany into the grip of the moneylender. The intellectual talk of revolution filtered down to the peasants, just as the intellectual ferment of the Reformation had filtered down to them in the sixteenth century. In the early months of 1848 central Europe experienced a sporadic peasant stirring, pale image of the Peasants' Revolt of 1525. In the east peasants refused their services, even attacked castles, proclaimed their freedom by appearing with clean-shaven chins; in the west they expected the community of goods and assembled in the village market places to await the general division of all property. This universal movement was altogether ignored by the middle-class liberals, and even the most extreme radicals averted their eyes. The peasants were left leaderless and unorganized. Often they turned back to their 'natural leaders', the landowners. Elsewhere they accepted the directions of 'authority'. But everywhere the revolutionary impulse was lost. The revolution of 1848 had no agrarian programme.

The revolutionary leaders lived in the towns and therefore could not ignore so completely the movement of the urban masses. But they had no social programme, or, at best, one produced shamefacedly and *ad hoc*. The handicraft workers were being ruined by the competition of cheap mass-produced English goods; and in the winter of 1847 to 1848 the first general economic crisis devastated the larger German towns. The revolution of March 13th in Vienna and the revolution of March 18th in Berlin, which together cleared the way for the German revolution, were both glorified unemployed riots. Yet there was no connection between the political leaders and this movement of the unemployed. The town workers were given soup kitchens and relief on task work but not as part of a deliberate social policy. The liberals yielded against their economic principles in order to still the social disorder; the radicals seconded the demands of the masses not from conviction but in order to capture the masses for what they regarded as the real revolutionary aims – universal suffrage, trial by jury, election of army officers, cancelling of pensions to state officials, and so on. The liberals used the mass unrest to extract concessions from the princes. The National Guard, that universal liberal expedient, for instance, was everywhere advocated as the defender of social order. The radicals, more daring, whipped up the masses in order to frighten the princes still more. But not even the few extreme radicals such as Marx, who called themselves Socialists, had any real concern for the masses or any contact with them. In their eyes the masses were the cannon fodder of the revolution; and they had no words too harsh for the masses when they wearied of filling this role. Nothing could exceed Marx's horror and disgust when his friend Engels actually took an Irish factory girl as his mistress; and Marx's attitude was symbolical of the German revolutionaries.

This divorce between the revolutionaries and the people determined the happenings of 1848. The revolution had officers but no rank and file. The old forces, on which the system of 1815 rested, succumbed to their own weakness and confusion; but no new forces took their place. There followed instead the rule of ideas, and this rule ended as soon as the old forces recovered their nerve. The German Confederation of 1815 had depended not on its own strength, but on the triangular balance of France, Austria, and Prussia. In the early months of 1848 this balance was overthrown by the revolutions in Paris, Vienna, and Berlin. The citizens of Germany – quite literally the established inhabitants of the towns – suddenly found themselves free without effort of their own. The prison walls fell, the gaolers disappeared. The Germany of intellectual conception suddenly became the Germany of established fact. For this transformation the three revolutions on the circumference were all essential. Had a single centre of power remained the German revolution would never have taken place. To consider the causes of the failure of the German revolution is thus a barren speculation. The successful revolutions were in Paris, Vienna, and Berlin. There was no successful revolution in Germany; and therefore nothing to fail. There was merely a vacuum in which the liberals postured until the vacuum was filled.

The revolution of February 24th in Paris, which overthrew Louis Philippe, evoked in all western Germany the sort of response which had been evoked by the events of the great revolution of 1789, but this time on a wider scale. In almost every state there were long-standing disputes between ruler and people – some strictly constitutional, others purely personal, most a mixture of legal grievances and private misdemeanours on the part of the prince. Typical was the conflict in Bavaria where the King had become infatuated (to the shocked indignation of his people) with an Irish music-hall dancer who called herself Lola Montez (the same whom Swinburne immortalized as Dolores, Our Lady of Pain). Such absurdities do not cause revolutions; but they can become the critical incidents in a revolutionary situation. So, after the Paris revolution all the petty disputes which had been running on for years came to a head and were decided. In every state the existing ministers were jettisoned and more liberal ministers appointed; in every state the suffrage was extended; in some the ruler was changed, as in Bavaria where both Lola Montez and her royal admirer were driven into exile. Nowhere was there a real shifting of power; for there was no real power to shift. In 1791 and again in 1830 similar echoes of the French revolution had been stilled by the armed force of Austria and Prussia. In the early days of March 1848, Austro-Prussian interference was being again prepared; but before it could operate the power of the two military monarchies was itself shaken by the revolutions of Vienna and Berlin.

The revolution of March 13th in Vienna was a real revolution. The Metternich system was feeble without and rotten within. The administration, the finances, the army were in decay; the court was torn by disputes and faction) and the few energetic members of the Imperial family actually desired Metternich's fall. The movement of March 13th was a movement of all classes of the community. It ended old Austria for good and shattered the prestige of conservatism throughout Europe. A government of bewildered officials was hastily botched together and constantly changed under the impulse of new street demonstrations. For more than two months there was in Austria no real authority, and in Germany Austrian power vanished to nothing. Still, Austrian power had been only a secondary influence in Germany since 1815: the Austrian armies had always been centred in Italy, and Austria owed her position in Germany more to tradition and political skill than to actual strength. The really decisive event of 1848 was the revolution in Berlin; this alone made possible the brief career of German liberalism, and the ending of the Prussian revolution brought this career to a close.

Old Austria fell from deep-seated ineradicable causes which made the revolution inevitable. But the Prussian monarchy had none of the diseases which it needs a revolution to cure. Its administration was efficient, its finances in good order, the discipline of its army firm and the self-confidence of the army officers unshaken. The atmosphere of 1848 was certain to produce riots in Berlin. But according to all reasonable expectation the Prussian army was strong enough to restore order and to maintain absolutism. And so it did when the riots flared up into street fighting on March 18th. The rioters were pressed back, the streets cleared, the army was within sight of controlling all Berlin. The abnormal factor was the character of Frederick William IV. Disliking the army and hating the military traditions of his house, bewildered and depressed by the failure of his romantic ideas during the meeting of the United Diet, he could not go through with the conquest of his capital. Even on March 18th he had coupled force with exhortations. On the next day he lost his nerve altogether: promised first to withdraw the troops if the barricades were removed, and at length ordered the troops to withdraw unconditionally. By March 21st Berlin was, outwardly, in the hands of the revolution. A burgher guard patrolled the streets; the King drove through the streets wearing the revolutionary colours of national Germany; and ostensibly he embraced the revolutionary cause in the most famous of all his many phrases – 'Prussia merges into Germany.'

The victory of the Berlin revolution determined the course of events in Germany. Where the Prussian army had failed no prince could hope to succeed. The way was open for the liberal middle classes to put into practice their programme of a Germany united by consent. Radicalism, even if it had possessed more driving power, seemed unnecessary. After all, no one would choose the way of the barricades if the meeting of committees could achieve the same result. But the Berlin victory was illusory – hence all the disasters of the future. The Prussian army was not defeated: it was resentful, humiliated, but still confident. The army leaders were determined somehow to win back the King and to renew the struggle broken off on March 19th. Nor was Frederick William IV a convert to the liberal cause. His nerve had failed. He complained to Bismarck that he had been unable to sleep for worry. Bismarck replied roughly: 'A king must be able to sleep.' Short of going out of his mind (which did not happen until 1858) Frederick William would have a good night sooner or later; and thereupon Prussian policy would begin to recover its strength. Moreover Frederick William at his most distraught had all the cunning of the mentally unstable. Forced to agree to the meeting of a Prussian parliament, he tried to turn his surrender to advantage by suggesting that all Germany should send representatives to the Prussian parliament and so achieve German unification *ipso facto*. His readiness to sink Prussia in Germany was fraudulent, and the Germans were asked to entrust themselves to Frederick William's erratic impulses.

Frederick William's sham conversion was not without effect. It obscured at the decisive moment the essential ineradicable conflict between middle-class idealistic Germany and landowning conservative Prussia. If the Prussian army had emerged from the March struggles victorious, as it deserved to do, it might have gone on to conquer all Germany for the cause of order; but this development might well have provoked in Germany a real revolutionary effort and, in any case, would have estranged Prussia from national Germany for ever. As it was, Prussia slipped, almost unperceived, on to the liberal side; and when in the following year the liberal cause began to fail, the memory of the March days enabled the liberal leaders to delude themselves into taking Frederick William as their protector. In March 1848 Frederick William seemed to capitulate to the revolution; in the sequel the revolution capitulated to Frederick William in April 1849. At the time Frederick William's capitulation came a week too late. With the fall of Metternich on March 13th German liberalism felt able to do without a protector; and the military resistance in Berlin made Prussia appear, as was in fact the case, less liberal than Austria. No part of Germany responded to Frederick William's invitation. Indeed the German liberals opposed the meeting of a Prussian parliament at all. They would have preferred to limit Prussia to the separate provincial Diets, so as to prevent any rival to the German national parliament. The judgements of the German liberals were the judgements of lawyers. They recognized that the existence of Prussia was a menace to German unity; but they saw the existence incorporated in the Prussian constitution, not in the Prussian army. They supposed that Prussian militarism had been beaten for good and all, beaten so decisively that they could actually assist Frederick William without risk against his own parliament. Consistent in their legalistic outlook they had to pretend that the surrender of Frederick William on March 19th had been voluntary; had they once admitted that the barricades and bloodshed of Berlin had played a part in the birth of the German revolution their political philosophy would have been destroyed – much as the advocates of the League of Nations had to conceal the reality that its basis was the defeat of Germany in war.

Thus the revolutions of Vienna and Berlin allowed the Germans to determine their own destinies for the first time in their history. The expression of this freedom was the National Assembly at Frankfurt, concentration of the spirit of 1848. Its origin was symbolic. Not a seizure of power by revolutionaries, not a dictation of new principles from below, but a co-operation between intellectuals, self-appointed spokesmen of Germany, and the Federal Diet, still posturing as the mouthpiece of the princes, brought it into being. The learned world was, characteristically enough, caught unawares by the revolutionary situation. Fifty-one learned men were gathered at Heidelberg reading papers to each other, as learned men do, when the March storm broke. Suddenly and to their surprise their claims came true: they had to speak for Germany. They spoke with all the responsible solemnity peculiar to academic politicians, and conformed to the spirit of a non-existent constitution. Dissolving themselves as the fifty-one, they re-created themselves and their learned friends as the pre-parliament, academic ideal of a parliament by invitation. This strange nominated body conducted itself on the best parliamentary principles: held debates, passed resolutions, finally even made laws. It summoned a German Constituent Assembly, laid down the rules by which this should be elected, and then dispersed leaving a committee of fifty as the provisional government of Germany. Meanwhile the Federal Diet, abandoned by the protecting great powers, was trying to maintain its legal rights if only by giving them away. It invited the states to send new, and more liberal, representatives – the seventeen[1] – and these seventeen also devised a plan for a National Assembly, which was then amalgamated with the plan of the pre-parliament. Thus the National Assembly which met on May 18th began its career with a background of respectability and legality.

The elections for the National Assembly were variously conducted. In those states which already possessed constitutions it was elected on the existing suffrage; in the states without constitutions, which included both Prussia and Austria, by universal suffrage. But these variations did not matter. In the limited constitutional states of western Germany, still more in unconstitutional Austria and Prussia, only the wealthy and the educated, the lawyers and the civil servants, were known; and only the known can attract votes. The result therefore was an assembly of 'notables', as strictly confined to the upper middle class as if the voters had been the *pays légal* of the July monarchy. There was not a single working-man and only one peasant (a Pole from Silesia). Fifteen, mainly post-masters and customs officers (a way of getting known), ranked as lower middle class. All the rest were the well-to-do products of university education: 49 university professors; 57 high-school teachers; 157 magistrates; 66 lawyers; 20 mayors; 118 higher civil servants; 18 doctors; 43 writers; 16 Protestant pastors, 1 German Catholic and 16 Roman Catholic priests. One hundred and sixteen admitted to no profession, and among these were the few nobles; but even of the 116 far more were wealthy bourgeoisie – a few industrialists, rather more bankers and merchants. There were only sixteen army officers, and these from the liberal western states. Germany of the idea had taken on corporate life.

None of the members had experience of national politics (except a few who had sat in the Federal Diet); but most had been members of their state Chambers and all knew the technicalities of political procedure. Indeed Frankfurt suffered from too much experience rather than too little: too much calculation, too much foresight, too many

[1] The total membership of the Confederation was over thirty (thirty-nine in 1817, dwindling to thirty-three by amalgamation by 1866), but the smaller states were grouped in 'circles' to give an effective membership of seventeen. The plenum was to meet only to decide constitutional changes – and none was ever made.

elaborate combinations, too much statesmanship. Hardly a vote was taken for its own sake, always for the sake of some remote consequence. The members of the Assembly wanted to give Germany a constitution; but they also wanted to show that a liberal German government could defend social order at home and the interests of Germany abroad. Almost their first act was to create a Central German Power to exercise authority in its name. But a real shifting of power was beyond their imagination, and their utmost ambition was to convert the princes to liberalism, not to overthrow them. Therefore the Central Power had to be entrusted to a prince, though a prince of reliable liberal character; and he was found in the Austrian Archduke John, brother of the late Emperor and with genuine liberal sympathies. But the choice was hardly determined by his personal qualifications: it sprang mainly from the calculation that in June 1848, Austria was more submerged by the revolution than was Prussia and would therefore be more obedient to the directions of Frankfurt. Still, there was a deeper element – a survival of the traditional idea of the headship of the house of Habsburg and a belief that only under the Habsburgs could an all-embracing Germany be achieved. In June 1848, no one proposed the King of Prussia as head of Germany. To do so would have been a confession of weakness, a willingness to accept something less than complete unification. Prussia, it was assumed, would accept the overlordship of a Habsburg; but no one could suppose that the Habsburgs, even in defeat, would subordinate themselves to the King of Prussia.

The election of Archduke John was thus an expression both of the romantic Right and the radical Left; it revived the traditions of the Holy Roman Empire and at the same time asserted the democratic idea of Greater Germany. In June 1848 the confidence of German nationalism was still unbounded, and there seemed no limits, historical or geographic, to what it could achieve. John came to Frankfurt, established himself as Administrator of the Reich, appointed a full set of ministers. The Federal Diet abdicated into his hands. In fact the Central Power had all the qualities of a government except power. The Minister of Foreign Affairs was not recognized by any foreign State except revolutionary Hungary – which was recognized by nobody else; the Minister of War had no soldiers; the Minister of the Interior had no means of ensuring that the orders which he issued to the governments of the German states would be obeyed. The salaries of the ministers and of Archduke John were paid out of the funds collected in 1840 for federal defence, which had remained on deposit with the Rothschilds. No national taxes were levied. The only takings of the Central Power were the voluntary subscriptions raised throughout Germany for the creation of a German fleet; and the Minister of the Navy was unique in actually having money to spend. The German Navy – a couple of discarded ships bought as a job lot in Hamburg – was the most absurd and yet the most complete expression of the spirit of 1848, of the idea of achieving power by persuasion. Unable to contemplate the real task of challenging the armed forces of Austria and Prussia, the German liberals found a substitute for the struggle for power in buying a navy by street corner collections; and the two decaying ships at their Hamburg moorings alone obeyed the Central Power of the German nation.

The essence of Frankfurt was the idea of unity by persuasion. The Central Power had to show, by example, that it was fit to govern Germany and to be Germany in the eyes of foreign powers. Like a manager on trial, the Central Power produced samples of its governing capacity and, by means of orders to the princes, conducted a campaign against the unrest and disturbances in Germany. These orders the princes, gratifyingly enough, obeyed. But in achieving this success the Frankfurt liberals were sawing off the branch on which they sat: only the menace of new outbreaks kept the princes obedient to Frankfurt, yet Frankfurt was doing its best to bring these outbreaks to an end. The members of the Assembly could not but look forward with apprehension to the time when the princes felt secure once more and they devised a highly liberal solution: the princes were to retain their armies (of which only a real revolution would deprive them), but the soldiers were to take an oath of loyalty to the German constitution. Thus the liberals confessed by implication that they could not rely on the word of the princes – the only guarantee of Frankfurt's position – but their alternative was to trust the word of illiterate peasants. The device of the constitutional oath was not a success. The soldiers of the lesser states took the oath and later disregarded it; Frederick William refused to allow it to be given to the Prussian army, and the Assembly, itself meeting under the protection of Prussian soldiers, averted its eyes. The Frankfurt liberals were not actuated, as is sometimes supposed, by class interest. They were not capitalists or property owners; they were lawyers and professors. Disorder and revolution offended their principles and threatened their high ideal of creating a united Germany by consent. Nothing good, they believed, could come of the intrusion of the masses into politics; and they regarded the repressive activities of the armed forces as essential to the security of the liberal cause.

The refusal of Frankfurt to go with the masses, the failure to offer a social programme, was a decisive element in the failure of the German liberals. This refusal and this failure are the theme of *Germany: Revolution and Counter-Revolution*, the pamphlet which Engels wrote for Marx and which is still the best analysis of the events of 1848. But there was another, and even more important, cause of failure, a disastrous mistake which Marx, Engels, and most German radicals shared. The National Assembly had come into being when the armed power of Austria and Prussia collapsed; and its prestige waned as Austrian and Prussian armed power revived. These armies won new confidence, no doubt, in the repression of internal disorder. But the prime purpose of armies is foreign war, and it was in foreign war of a sort that Austrian and Prussian absolutism were reborn. Not the social conflict, but the conflict on the national frontiers – in Bohemia, in Poland, and in Sleswig and Holstein – determined the fate of German liberalism. In the struggle against the Czechs, against the Poles, against the Danes, the German liberals unhesitatingly supported the cause of the Prussian and Austrian armies and were then surprised when these weapons were turned against themselves. Liberalism was sacrificed to the national cause.

The conflict with Czech nationalism in Bohemia had been entirely unexpected. The well-meaning German professors had assumed that Bohemia, with its educated German minority, was part of national Germany: after all, they did not count the German peasants as members of the national community, so that still less did they count peasants of any other race. The committee of fifty actually invited Palacky, intellectual pioneer of the Czech rebirth, to swell their number; and the German liberals were shocked and astonished at his famous reply of April 11th, in which he declared himself a Czech and put forward the. Austrian Empire as the protector of the Slavs against either Tsarist or German rule. Palacky's letter was the most fateful document in the history of modern Germany. It asked the Germans to renounce the vast expanse of eastern Europe where they had long held cultural and economic supremacy and to accept as national Germany only those territories where the majority of the population was genuinely German. This demand was ridiculed by Germans of all shades of national opinion. To accept the national frontier would actually imply accepting something less than the frontier of the despised German Confederation; and the possession of Bohemia made all the difference between being a great and the greatest European Power. Without Bohemia Germany had but a tenuous link with the valley of the Danube and south-eastern Europe, especially before the coming of the railways; and moreover Bohemia was already one of the outstanding industrial areas of central Europe, all the more outstanding in that the industrial development of the Ruhr and Rhineland had hardly begun. But the German attitude was not determined solely by these selfish material considerations. The German nationalists of 1848 were inspired by a belief, none the less genuine for appearing to French or English judgement absurd, in the superiority of German civilization. They thought of themselves as missionaries of a great cultural cause and regarded any withdrawal in eastern Europe as a betrayal of the values of civilization. The most clear-sighted radicals, Marx and Engels above all, held rightly that industrialization and the growth of towns were the essential preliminary to political freedom, and they identified industrialization, as it had been identified historically, with German influence. In the programme of Palacky, still more in the Slav Congress which he organized at Prague in answer to the Frankfurt Assembly, the German liberals and radicals saw only a movement of peasants, attempting to preserve a reactionary feudal order.

The Czech claim to Bohemia threatened all the highest ambitions of German nationalism. Without Bohemia, Germany might be a respectable national state, but neither a new Empire of Charlemagne nor the Greater Germany of radical idealism. The Slav Congress, ineffective and tentative as it was, went still further: by asserting, however feebly, the rights of Slav peasants against German traders and artisans, it challenged German hegemony throughout eastern Europe. The Frankfurt Assembly inevitably supported the 'national' cause. But it had no weapons of defence. As always it had to proceed by political devices and to bless the weapons of others. The only material weapon in Bohemia was the Habsburg army; and within three months of the Habsburg defeat in Vienna, to which the Frankfurt Assembly owed its existence, the liberals of Frankfurt were calling for a Habsburg victory in Prague. They got their way. The Imperial court, dominated by fear of the Vienna revolution, at first welcomed and encouraged the Czech movement, but this soon became too democratic for their liking. On June 12th a few Czech radicals tried to seize power in Prague, apparently with the idea of proclaiming a Bohemian republic; and this gave Windischgrätz, the Austrian general, the opportunity to subdue Prague by military force – the first victory of the counter-revolution in central Europe. This was a victory for Habsburg militarism and therefore a step towards the defeat of German nationalism. Yet the German liberals, blinded by hatred and fear of the Czechs, put themselves on the Habsburg side and welcomed the victory of Windischgrätz as if it had been their own. They had always recognized the national claims of the Magyars, a people with a continuous history and a flourishing culture; and they believed that the victory of Windischgrätz had established the German character of the non-Hungarian provinces of the Austrian Empire. The German and Magyar nationalists both assumed that the Habsburg lands would be henceforward held together only by a personal link, and that Magyar-dominated Hungary and the Greater Germany into which the rest of the Austrian Empire would be incorporated would be united in a common anti-Slav policy. The German liberals were confident that the Habsburg power was, as it were, 'captured' for German nationalism, so confident that, instead of resisting the meeting of a central Austrian parliament at Vienna as the expression of the unity of the Habsburg lands, they welcomed and aided it, believing – quite wrongly – that it would be a further instrument for their national and liberal ends.

Events in Bohemia brought the Germans on to the side of the Habsburgs. Still they could plead that the Habsburg Empire now had a liberal parliament. Events in Prussian Poland, however, not merely brought the German liberals on to the side of the Hohenzollerns, but even led them to support the King of Prussia against the Prussian parliament. The Polish situation differed fundamentally from the Czech, in that the Poles were a historic nation whose existence could be neither disputed nor ignored. Polish liberty was an essential element in the radical creed. The extreme radicals believed that they could achieve their programme only by means of a revolutionary war; and they proposed to provoke a war with Russian Tsardom by fulfilling in the Grand Duchy of Posen the promises of constitutional freedom made both for Posen and the Russian Kingdom of Poland in the Treaty of Vienna. By a stroke of amateur Machiavellianism the German radicals who had denounced the 'Vienna system' for thirty years were now designing to conduct a war against Russia in its name. War with Russia, not love for the Poles, was the motive of their policy; they intended to renew German claims in Poland, once Russia was defeated. West Prussia was mainly inhabited by Poles, yet was excluded from the promises of 1815, since it had not been torn from the Kingdom of Prussia by Napoleon and so did not need to be restored by the Treaty of Vienna; as a result the radicals did not trouble themselves with the claims of the West Prussian Poles. On the other hand, the Grand Duchy of Posen, though indisputably part of the old Kingdom of Poland, had a considerable German minority; so that the radicals were proposing to establish Polish national rights in districts sometimes with but few Polish inhabitants.

In the first distracted days after the March rising the weak Prussian government of well-meaning liberals was swept along by the radical current and admitted in the Grand Duchy the autonomy promised in 1815. The Prussian army was withdrawn to barracks, a Polish force was brought into being, and the administration was put into the hands of the Poles. This produced a conflict of a character quite unexpected by the radical strategists. Tsar Nicholas I, wiser than the counter-revolutionaries of 1792, accepted the opinion of his Chancellor, Nesselrode, that the German revolution would disintegrate if left to itself, and decided against intervention. The Germans in Posen, refusing to be the victims of a political manoeuvre, resisted the Polish authorities and appealed to their fellow-Germans for support. This was the opportunity for the Prussian army chiefs. At the end of April the Prussian general in Posen disregarded the civil government, defeated the Polish forces, and expelled the Polish administrators. The Grand Duchy was to be split up: the larger part was declared to be German, and even in the fragment left to the Poles the Germans were to be especially privileged. No element of national equality remained. The radicals of Berlin, baulked of their war with Tsardom, and the Poles of Posen, denied their freedom, appealed to the National Assembly at Frankfurt to act on its pro-Polish phrases and to compel the Prussian government to keep its word.

It was an awkward demand for the Frankfurt liberals. They wished to appear all-powerful in Germany, yet knew that they were impotent to compel the Prussian government or any other. They wished to defend German rights; yet they dared not do so on the basis of nationality statistics (which justified some of the German claims), for these statistics would justify the claims of the Czechs in Bohemia. William Jordan, one of the most respected liberal leaders, solved the dilemma: the right of the stronger, he said, must decide, and 'healthy national egoism' demanded that the Grand Duchy of Posen should become German. In these phrases, welcomed by the liberal majority, the Frankfurt liberals delivered themselves to the Prussian army and, by an inevitable logic, delivered German liberalism first to Bismarck and later to Hitler. The right of the stronger which they evoked would then be turned against them, and 'healthy national egoism' would be translated into 'blood and iron'. On July 27th the Frankfurt Assembly rejected the radical complaints and bestowed its blessing on the Prussian army in Posen as it had already blessed the Austrian army in Bohemia.

There was a strange result. The Prussian parliament had been elected on the same day and with the same franchise as the National Assembly, but it was very differently composed. The wealthy, respectable candidate went to Frankfurt; the poorer, more impatient candidate made the shorter journey to Berlin. The Prussian parliament was dominated by radicals from East Prussia, who had learnt political reality in bitter struggles with the neighbouring Junkers. These radicals cared no more for Polish rights than did the Frankfurt liberals, but they were eager to force a breach between the Junkers and the Tsar, the Junkers' protector. In September the Prussian parliament rejected the partition of the Grand Duchy of Posen, and, a month later, demanded the execution of the promises of 1815. The Prussian radicals, hostile to the Tsar and jealous of Frankfurt, dreamt even of transforming the Prussian state into a Polish-German federation, aloof from national Germany. The estrangement between Frankfurt and Berlin was complete. The

Prussian parliament was offensive in itself to German nationalism, for it implied the existence of a Prussia distinct from Germany; but it became doubly offensive when it renounced the claims of 'healthy national egoism' in Posen. The Frankfurt liberals, who had applauded the victory of the Prussian army in Posen, were thus led on to desire a victory of the Prussian army in Berlin – despite the fact that the defeat of the Prussian army in Berlin had been the essential preliminary to the Frankfurt parliament.

In the autumn of 1848 there were yet more immediate reasons for Frankfurt's dependence on the Prussian army. The third and most deeply felt frontier issue of 1848 was the question of Sleswig and Holstein, two duchies which had long been under the sovereignty of the King of Denmark; Holstein inhabited entirely by Germans and a member of the German Confederation, Sleswig inhabited partly by Germans, partly by Danes, and outside the Confederation. The legal tangle – the relation of the Duchies with each other, with the German Confederation, with the King of Denmark, with Denmark, their position in the treaty structure of Europe, their laws of succession – provided endless material for controversy and confusion; but the essential question was clear. Did the principle of German national unity override treaty rights and international law? The number of Germans involved was not great – half a million at most – the theoretical challenge all the more marked. The problem of the two Duchies was the breaking-point of the traditional idea of personal sovereignty, for neither the Danes nor the Germans were prepared to leave the Duchies in their former position. In 1848 Denmark too had its constitutional revolution; and the Danish liberals were determined to incorporate Sleswig in the Danish constitutional state. Once Denmark abandoned personal union, there was something to be said for the German case, much more than for the German case in Bohemia or in Poland. All the more unexpected to the German liberals was the reaction of foreign opinion. These liberals were educated men of high culture, who attached great importance to the judgement of liberals in the western countries. Hitherto they had won foreign approval. German nationalists of all shades of opinion had recognized the claims of Hungary; foreign observers knew nothing of the Czech case in Bohemia and unanimously accepted the German version of a reactionary conspiracy; and the Frankfurt hostility to Polish claims was altogether dwarfed by the Tsarist repression in Russian Poland. But in the question of Sleswig and Holstein foreign liberals saw only the bullying of a small nation by a great one; English, French, Italian liberals united to condemn Germany. The German liberals were not shaken by this condemnation. They were too convinced of the rightness of their cause. Rather they concluded that there was a deliberate conspiracy against Germany; if western liberalism condemned German nationalism in Sleswig and Holstein, so much the worse for western liberalism. In fact, the question of Sleswig and Holstein made the first, not very marked, but yet decisive breach between the German nationalist movement and the liberals of western Europe, a breach in which the western liberals, ironically enough, were on the side of the 'Vienna settlement'.

The dispute between Denmark and the Duchies broke into open conflict as early as March 1848; and the pre-parliament had already set on foot a federal war against the Danes. But when it came to the point national Germany, so sensitive in its honour, so vast in its claims, had no forces with which to conduct a war even against Denmark. The only agent of national Germany was the Prussian army; the liberal ministry in Prussia responded to the appeal from Frankfurt, and the Prussian generals, still humiliated by the March days, obeyed the orders of the civilian ministers. During the early summer the Prussian army made easy headway against the Danes. But it soon became clear that Prussia would have to face more formidable opponents. Both England and Russia were resolved to uphold the settlement of 1815 and to keep the control of the entrance to the Baltic securely in harmless Danish hands. A European war threatened. Enthusiastic liberals from south Germany clamoured for 'sanctions' – federal execution was the current term – against Denmark, whatever the risk; but the risk would have to be borne by conservative Prussian officers. Prussia was faced with a war from which she could not possibly gain: she would probably be defeated, but even if she won, the advantage would go to the German liberals, who would thus be all the stronger to destroy Prussia's independence. Therefore at the end of August Prussia concluded an armistice with Denmark and left the national cause to fend for itself.

Prussia had thus openly defied the authority of the National Assembly and the Central Power. The German liberals were at last inescapably faced with the problem of power. Powerless to coerce Denmark, they yet had to coerce Prussia into renewing the war against Denmark or else to confess the impotence of the national idea on the strength of which they had based their political philosophy. The ministers of the Central Power realized that their orders carried no weight with the Prussian army; but a motley majority of the Assembly – national idealists, radical extremists, pro-Austrians eager to humiliate Prussia – broke away from their leadership and refused to acknowledge the armistice. The ministry resigned. But no new ministry, ready to take on an open conflict with Prussia, could be formed. The coalition of idealists and impossibilists dissolved. The Assembly was compelled to eat its own words and to approve the armistice which a week before it had rejected. A ministry openly favourable to the two Great Powers came into existence. This betrayal of the German cause was too much for the radicals who had been growing increasingly impatient with the moderation and statesmanship of the liberal majority. There were radical riots in many western German towns and, finally, on September 26th, in Frankfurt itself. The National Assembly, with no forces of its own, had to appeal to the King of Prussia, whom only a fortnight before it had solemnly condemned. Prussian troops restored order; and from the end of September the National Assembly and Central Power met under the protection of Prussian bayonets. In March 1848 national Germany had condescendingly tolerated the Prussian state. In October the Prussian state allowed national Germany to prolong its existence.

National Germany owed its temporary success to the defeat of the two military monarchies in March; yet, in order to defend the 'national' cause in Bohemia and in Posen, it had welcomed the reassertion of Austrian and Prussian military power. In the autumn of 1848 the reviving monarchies took up the struggle with their own capitals; but so far as national opinion was concerned, with opposite results. Habsburg victory over the October revolution in Vienna made Austria unpopular, Hohenzollern victory over the abortive November revolution in Berlin made Prussia popular in Germany. The conflict in Vienna was a conflict over the character of the Austrian Empire. Was it, as the Germans of Frankfurt and Vienna and the Magyars alike held, a union of two states, one German, the other Magyar? Or was it, as the Habsburg ministers, the Austrian aristocracy, and the Czechs and

Croats alike held, a single Empire in which no single nationality held a preponderant or privileged position? The Habsburg Court had recovered from the utter confusion and hopelessness of the spring. There was now an effective ministry, its outstanding personality, Bach, a pre-March radical, won over to the cause of a centralized and reformed Austrian Empire. This ministry, supported by a majority of the Austrian parliament – a majority partly non-German, but also composed of Germans who subordinated their nationality to the maintenance of the Empire – was determined to undo the concessions made to Hungary in the days of collapse and to reduce Hungary from an independent state to a province of the Empire. The success of their plan would be as much a defeat for German as for Hungarian nationalism; for no one imagined that national Hungary could be incorporated in the German national state, and the entire Austrian Empire would therefore stand aloof from Germany. Early in October the radicals of Vienna tried to prevent the sending of troops to Hungary; and on October 6th Vienna broke into revolution.

The October revolution was a revolution in favour of an independent Hungary and a national Germany; but neither came to its assistance. Hungary had an organized and equipped army, but failed to use it, partly from constitutional scruples against crossing the Austrian frontier, more from a reluctance to make sacrifices in what seemed to the Hungarians a foreign cause. National Germany had no forces and therefore fell back on the most disastrous of idealist weapons – it displayed moral sympathy. On October 27th, while the civil war in Austria was still being fought, the Frankfurt Assembly resolved that, where German and non-German lands were under the same ruler, they should be united only by a personal tie. Thus the Assembly committed itself to the programme of the partition of the Austrian Empire at the very moment when that programme was being shot to pieces on the Vienna barricades. Early in November the Austrian army conquered Vienna and so ended all hope of a Greater Germany. The imbecile Emperor Ferdinand was replaced by his young energetic nephew Francis Joseph; a new ministry was formed under Felix Schwarzenberg, ruthless, cynical advocate of the policy of military power. The first act of the new ministry was to execute Robert Blum, a radical member of the Frankfurt Assembly who had fought on the side of the Vienna revolution; its second to denounce the Frankfurt resolution in favour of the partition of Austria. The Austrian parliament, now purged of its German radicals, was left temporarily in being, occupying itself in futile constitution-making until its dissolution in the following March. But in liberal German eyes Austria reverted to despotism in November 1848, and to a despotism flagrantly anti-German. The dreamers and radicals still hoped for a miracle which would restore Austria to liberalism and to Germany; the moderates and realists abandoned Austria and consoled themselves by pretending that the inclusion of Austria in Germany had never been part of their national programme.

In Prussia too, militarism was victorious in the autumn of 1848, but victorious without violence and without a breach with Frankfurt. Here the struggle between King and Parliament was not national, but strictly constitutional. The Prussian parliament wished to enforce an oath of constitutional loyalty on the Prussian army. This demand did not inter-est Frankfurt, which – having failed with its own constitutional oath – was jealous that the Berlin parliament should not succeed. In fact, many Frankfurt liberals, regarding the Berlin parliament as a rival and more radical body, desired its defeat. Having backed the loser in Austria, they were the more eager to be on the winning side in Prussia and, by offering the King their moral support (threadbare as this was), to create the impression that they had contributed to his success. As one of the liberal leaders said: 'It is in the interests of the National Assembly that the Prussian Crown should be victorious over its parliament, but that it should achieve this victory with the help of the National Assembly.' Frederick William and his generals did not need this help, though Frankfurt tried to claim credit for offering it. In November, Frederick William appointed an openly reactionary ministry and broke with his parliament. It was first moved to a provincial town, and then dissolved; and the King issued a restricted constitution by decree. The parliamentary radicals attempted to resist. They refused to leave Berlin, held meetings of parliament in various halls and finally in cafés and beer cellars, they appealed to the inhabitants of Prussia to refuse to pay taxes. Nothing happened: taxes were paid, the radical deputies were chased home. There had been no real victory of the revolution in Berlin in March; therefore no real counter-revolution was necessary in November. The Prussian army and the Prussian governing class moved back into positions from which the King's erratic feebleness, not the strength of the revolution, had ejected them.

By the end of 1848 the power of the two German powers was restored; the Central Power therefore became utterly meaningless. The Frankfurt Assembly still debated. The idealists who had hoped to disregard both Great Powers and to build Germany on ideas were discredited. It was the turn of the moderate men – professors, determined as professors so often are, to demonstrate that they were men of the world, politicians from the petty states who wished to show their practical wisdom. The two German powers existed; therefore Germany should hitch herself to one of them, should, by her superior political cunning, 'capture' one of them for the German cause. It was futile to try to capture Austria: her November victory had been too emphatic, her anti-national policy too blatant. But it was possible to interpret the defeat of the Prussian parliament as a defeat for particularism, possible to believe that Frederick William still held to his romantic vision of a Prussia merged into Germany. Thus there came into being the party of Little Germany, the sensible men who would be content with something less than complete unification. Greater Germany was a creed, a conviction; Little Germany an expedient, a temporizing with reality. No national principle could underlie the programme of giving only some Germans national unity; and in fact all Little Germans were Greater Germans at heart – only they were prepared to postpone the realization of the full programme. No one at Frankfurt ever argued that Little Germany was better than Greater Germany. The Little Germans argued that Little Germany could be secured now and that it could be secured peacefully, without revolution. They were opposed by the idealists who would accept nothing less than the whole; by the radicals who were Greater Germans simply because this needed a revolution; by the Roman Catholics who feared Prussian rule; and by the friends and dependants of Austria. The Little German liberals devised a moderate monarchist constitution with limited suffrage and the King of Prussia as Emperor; but they could not carry this against the coalition of democrats, clericals, and pro-Austrians. To win over the democratic vote, they jettisoned all their liberal restrictions and moderation except the one item of the Emperor. An astonishing compromise resulted. On the one hand the Frankfurt Assembly excluded Austria from Germany and offered the Imperial Crown to Frederick William IV – the Little German programme. On the other hand it established in this Little Germany a centralized democratic constitution based on universal suffrage, which was only compatible with the victory of Greater German ideas. Thus even at the moment of its abject failure the Frankfurt Assembly postulated the ultimate destiny of Germany and of Prussia: Prussia could dominate Germany, but only on condition of serving the national German cause.

In April 1849, a deputation went from Frankfurt to offer the Imperial Crown to Frederick William IV. The offer had been expected in Berlin, and there had been long discussion between the King and his reactionary ministers. The Prussian ministers and generals would have nothing to do with national Germany. They were ready to use the opportunity of the confusion in Germany for some land-grabbing in the old Prussian style; but apart from this they wished to renew the conservative partnership with Austria. Frederick William, on the other hand, could not altogether resist the romantic prospect of the Imperial Crown if only it could be freed from its democratic associations. He would have liked to accept the Crown on condition that it was offered to him by the princes. Urgent and desperate promptings from his advisers only induced him to give this acceptance a negative form: he would not 'pick up a Crown from the gutter', would not accept the Crown unless it was offered to him by the princes. This answer he gave to the Frankfurt deputation on April 3rd. They heard only the refusal, for they knew by now that the princes would not voluntarily surrender their sovereignty. Prussia would not, Frankfurt could not, force the princes into unity. The liberal revolution had reached its term.

With the failure of the mission to Berlin the history of the Frankfurt Assembly was over. The moderate men, the men who shrank from violence, went home. Only the radical minority remained. Late in the day, with the revolutionary flood ebbing away to nothing, they tried to put into practice the revolutionary programme and to evoke a real revolution in Germany. They proclaimed that the German constitution had come into force, called for radical revolutions in the German states, and decreed the elections for the German parliament for July 15th. The elections never took place. Rhetoric could not change the practical fact that the only force in Germany was the Prussian army; and this army easily subdued the radical risings in Dresden, the Bavarian Palatinate, and Baden, which the Frankfurt appeal had provoked. The Assembly, or rather its radical rump, was chased by the Prussian army from Frankfurt to Stuttgart in Wurtemberg, and from Stuttgart it was chased out of existence. Sole remnant of national Germany was the Archduke John, still clinging to a theoretical Central Power in order to prevent a Prussian domination of Germany. In December he surrendered his title into the joint hands of Austria and Prussia. The German revolution was defeated, and liberal Germany never to be renewed.

As is usual after failure, every man drew the conclusion that the movement would have succeeded if his advice had been followed, and most despaired of the stupidity of their fellows. A few extreme radicals remained faithful to the revolutionary cause and hoped for a more violent revolution in the future. Next time, they believed, the masses must be drawn in; the cause of national union must be adorned with the attractions of Socialism. This was the programme of Marx and Engels to which they devoted the rest of their life, until their national starting-point was almost forgotten. They advocated Socialism so as to cause a revolution; only much later did their followers suppose that they had advocated revolution in order to accomplish Socialism. The radicals who did not despair of Germany were few. Far more accomplished their own revolution by emigrating to the freedom of the United States. German emigration had already begun on a big scale, more than a hundred thousand a year, in the early 'forties. It dwindled to fifty thousand in 1848, when it seemed that Germany might be at last a place worth living in. After 1848 it soared once more, running at a steady average of more than a quarter of a million a year throughout the eighteen-fifties. These emigrants were the best of their race – the adventurous, the independent, the men who might have made Germany a free and civilized country. They brought to the United States a contribution of inestimable value, but they were lost to Germany. They, the best Germans, showed their opinion of Germany by leaving it for ever.

Like the radical emigrants, most liberals too were disillusioned by their experience of practical politics. Many withdrew to academic studies or served Germany by applying science to practical needs. Some turned from politics to industry and finance. So Hansemann, most liberal of the Prussian ministers of 1848, founded the Discontogesell-schaft, one of the greatest of German banks. The liberal politicians who remained politicians resolved to be more moderate and practical than ever. Their faith in the strength of their idea was destroyed; therefore they believed that liberal Germany must be achieved by subtlety and guile. But it would be wrong to suppose that the liberals of Germany vanished or that liberal convictions counted for nothing in Germany after 1848. The professors, the lawyers, the civil servants of the lesser states, remained predominantly liberal: they were still liberal in 1890 and even, for the most part, in 1930. But in 1848 they were a serious and respected political force. After 1848 they counted for less and less and, at last, for nothing at all.

The real significance of the revolution of 1848 was not so much its failure at the time, but the effect of its failure in the future. After 1850 there began in Germany a period of industrial development, after 1871 an industrial revolution. Economic power passed within a generation into the hands of industrial capitalists, Industrial capitalists, it is commonly held, are in politics liberal; but this view is an abbreviation of the real course of events. Industrial capitalists, like all business men, judge everything by the standard of success. A good business man is one who succeeds; a bad business man is one who 'fails'. When industrial capitalists enter politics they apply the same standard and adopt as their own the party and outlook which prevails. In England and the United States the struggle between liberalism and arbitrary power had long been fought out. The execution of Charles I, the overthrow of the army, and the glorious Revolution in England, the defeat of the red-coats and royal government in America, established the great principles of constitutional freedom and the rule of law. The English and American capitalists found the civilian politicians and lawyers in control. Therefore they too became liberals, advocates of individual freedom and upholders of constitutional government. In France, despite the great revolution, the verdict of success was less clear: therefore the industrial capitalists were confused – some became republicans, some Bonapartists, some corrupt and unprincipled. But in Germany there could be no doubt where success lay. The German capitalists became dependants of Prussian militarism and advocates of arbitrary power as naturally and as inevitably as English or American capitalists became liberals and advocates of constitutional authority. Where Anglo-Saxon capitalists demanded *laissez-faire*, German capitalists sought for state leadership; where Anglo-Saxon capitalists accepted democracy, however grudgingly, German capitalists grudgingly accepted dictatorship. This was the fateful legacy of 1848.

5

THE ASCENDANCY OF AUSTRIA, 1849–60

The German liberal movement had failed; but the old stability of the Vienna system was not to be restored. The temptation to reorder Germany was too much for both the German powers, and 1849 began not a new period of co-operation, but a long conflict. In the early part of 1849 all the advantages seemed on the side of Prussia, but she could make nothing of her opportunity, and, within a little more than a year, the advantage passed to the side of Austria, only to be lost in its turn. The military power of both Austria and Prussia had been restored by the end of 1848, but not each was equally free. In Austria the air of military success which had accompanied the new Emperor and the new ministry proved premature. In the spring of 1849 the Austrian army in Italy was engaged in renewed war with Piedmont; and, a more serious setback, the attempted reconquest of Hungary ended in failure. Piedmont was decisively defeated, but peace was not made until July 1849; and Hungary was not conquered, with Russian help, until the end of August. Even then large armies of occupation were needed both in Hungary and in northern Italy; and the programme of reorganizing the entire Austrian Empire as a centralized unit absorbed as well all the administrative energies of the Schwarzenberg-Bach government.

Thus, Austria had neither force nor policy to spare for the affairs of Germany. She stood aside, asserting her rights, but not defending them, intending to reconquer her position in Germany when her internal strength had been consolidated.

Prussia's opportunity was thus thrust upon her. She became, not through her own efforts, but as the result of events in Hungary and Italy, the sole power in Germany. The Prussian army had no distractions. It did not need to divert forces to Posen; and its bloodless November victory in Berlin had been so complete that it did not need even to leave a large garrison in the capital. It was free to send forces to the assistance of any German prince menaced by disorder – to Dresden, to Cassel, to Frankfurt, to Baden. In fact, by the summer of 1849, the Prussian army dominated Germany as completely as the French army had dominated Germany in the great days of Napoleon. The German princes owed their continued existence to its support. What should Prussia do with the position she had so easily won? The generals and the conservative ministers wished merely to defeat the nationalist movement and to defend the social order, to restore the princes and to maintain the traditional disunion of Germany, at most to improve Prussia's military position by alliance with the princes and the acquisition of military rights of way. But Frederick William IV was not a Junker king. Indifferent to Prussia's military position, he held to his romantic vision of Germany and still hankered after the Imperial Crown which in April 1849 he had grudgingly refused. His advisers had objected to the Crown as German; he had objected to it only as democratic, and his aim now was to extract from the princes the offer which he had postulated as essential. He was totally at odds with his Prussian ministers and took a private adviser, Radowitz, not a true Prussian, but a Roman Catholic nobleman from western Germany. The policy of Radowitz was not Prussian, but German; conservative, indeed, or rather anti-liberal, but pursuing the aim of German union. Frederick William IV harked back to his saying of March 1848: 'Prussia merges in Germany.' He had objected to the liberalism, not the nationalism, of Frankfurt, and hoped now to square the circle – to unite Germany and yet preserve the conservative order.

Outcome of Radowitz's policy was the Erfurt Union, a defensive association of the princes under Prussia's protection. The old

Confederation, it was argued, had been dissolved by the events of 1848; the Federal Act had lapsed, and new and more limited unions could be established. The German princes had no choice. They owed their independence to the balance between Austria and Prussia, and with Austria engaged in Hungary and Italy this balance no longer existed. Therefore the German princes had to acquiesce in Radowitz's schemes, to accept the idea of a close political union, and to agree to the pooling of their military resources. Frederick William IV imagined that he had accomplished a great German work, but in fact he had made the same mistake as the liberals of Frankfurt: he thought the princes converted, when they were merely frightened, frightened of their own radicals, still more frightened of the Prussian army. The only real basis of the Erfurt Union was the withdrawal of Austria from German affairs; and it could only endure if this withdrawal was permanent.

Quite the reverse happened. The achievements of the Austrian army in Italy and in Hungary gave to Austrian policy a confidence and assertiveness even more exaggerated than Metternich's hopeless gloom before 1848. In fact Austrian policy had not been so confident since the days of Prince Eugene. Schwarzenberg was a relentless enemy of liberalism, but just as violent against Metternich's conservatism or the romanticism of Frederick William IV. He held, quite simply, to the rule of the sword and believed that the Austrian sword could rule Germany. The Schwarzenberg ministry made the Austrian Empire a united state for the first time in history. The traditional differences between Hungary and the rest of the Empire were obliterated; the customs barrier between Hungary and the rest of the Empire abolished; the entire Empire subjected to a single code of law, to a single fiscal system, and to the rule of an Imperial bureaucracy. Schwarzenberg had no ideas of his own, but he was quick to pick them up from others; and having picked up the idea of a unified Empire from one renegade German liberal, Bach, he went on to pick up from another, Bruck, the even more grandiose project of a unified central Europe – Mittel-europa, to give it its later name. Bruck, the Minister of Commerce, was a German merchant on a grand scale. Himself the founder of the commercial greatness of Trieste, he believed that Germany's destiny lay not westwards across the oceans, but south-eastwards to the Balkans and beyond into

Asia Minor. Bruck wished to save the German communities of eastern and south-eastern Europe for national Germany, but he had no illusions about national Germany's strength. Only the Habsburg monarchy, he held, could protect the German cause; and in return for this protection he was prepared to subordinate national Germany to the Habsburg monarchy. The essence of Bruck's plan, which Schwarzenberg adopted, was that the German Confederation should be first revived and then that the entire Austrian Empire should be incorporated in it. No more conservative Austro-Prussian partnership, but instead Germany dominated by the Austrian Empire and the Austrian Empire run by Germans.

The first stage was the defeat of Prussia and the dissolution of the Erfurt Union. In this stage Austria had every advantage. The German princes hated subordination to Prussia and began to break away from the Union, as soon as they saw a chance of Austrian protection. The Prussian ministers were jealous of Radowitz and were delighted to see his plans go awry. The Prussian generals were resolved not to risk their army in a German cause and, in any case, believed both Austrian army and Austrian leadership superior to their own. The reactionary Junkers demanded a breach with Germany and a return of Austro-Prussian partnership. In addition Schwarzenberg enlisted Russian support against Prussia in 1850 as he had against Hungary in 1849. Tsar Nicholas did not much care whether schemes for German unification were liberal or monarchist. He was opposed to German unification of any kind. Therefore he threw his weight on the Austrian side. In the autumn of 1850 the dispute turned into open conflict. The Elector of Hesse-Cassel, a member of the Erfurt Union, was at odds with his subjects. Prussia prepared to intervene. But Schwarzenberg declared the Confederation revived and induced the Federal Diet – a packed rump – to entrust intervention to Bavaria. Prussian and Bavarian troops met in Hesse. The Austrian forces were moved into Bohemia, and the great Radetzky, victor of two Italian wars, came north to take command. Schwarzenberg would probably have preferred war: he would have liked to settle with Prussia once and for all. He failed to get his way. Francis Joseph was reluctant to fight a fellow monarch; the Prussian ministers were eager to give way; above all, the Tsar forbade war – he no more favoured an Austrian than a Prussian domination of Germany.

The result was the agreement of Olmütz (November 29th, 1850), by which Prussia renounced the Erfurt Union and accepted the revival of the German Confederation.

Olmütz was a total defeat for the plans of Radowitz and Frederick William, and to a lesser degree a defeat for Prussian power. But it was not a complete victory for Austria, certainly not a victory for Bruck and Schwarzenberg. Early in 1851 Schwarzenberg called a conference of the German princes at Dresden and proposed the incorporation of the entire Austrian Empire in the German Confederation and in the Zollverein. His proposals were defeated. The German princes saw in them another version of the Erfurt Union and supported the negative of Prussia as enthusiastically as they had supported Austria's negative in 1850. Nicholas I backed up the German princes. In fact, after Olmütz Germany was kept disunited by Russian decree. Besides, the constructive energy of the Schwarzenberg ministry was waning. The Austrian Empire had not really been regenerated by the events of 1848. There had been a sort of electric shock which had burnt up some of the old wood, but there was no new growth. Francis Joseph, despite his youth and energy, was at heart obscurantist, without a flicker of sympathy with constructive ideas. The constitution devised by the Constituent Assembly had been torn up in March 1849, and replaced by a dictated constitution, liberal but unitary; but this constitution was never put into operation and was in turn torn up in December 1851. Austria then formally reverted to the irresponsible erratic absolutism which in practice she had never left. The landed aristocracy, frivolous and discredited, began once more to predominate in Imperial counsels; and the middle-class German ministers who had promised to bring to the Empire a new life and vigour withdrew in disgust. Bruck, the Minister of Commerce, and Schmerling, who had defended the Austrian cause in the Frankfurt Assembly and then become Minister of Justice, retired to private life. Schwarzenberg himself died early in 1852 and was succeeded as Foreign Minister by an ignorant, arrogant fool, Buol. No new Prime Minister took his place; Francis Joseph himself took over the supreme direction of affairs. Of the great reforming ministers Bach remained alone and isolated, still giving to internal administration a certain grandeur, but quite unable to change the spirit of the system; and in 1855 Bach, to retain his position, had to swallow the Concordat with the Papacy, which gave to the Roman Church in Austria privileges and power unparalleled since the worst days of the Counter-Reformation. The Concordat did not merely make reform impossible in Austria; its obscurantism alienated from Austria all German Protestants and even the German Roman Catholics of the liberal western states.

Thus Austria, despite her apparent triumph of 1850, achieved nothing in Germany and had nothing to offer Germany. The finances were in disorder, the debt mounting every year. The army, despite its victories of 1848 and 1849, was inadequate to its tasks. Its equipment was neglected and outmoded, the generals chosen for their family connections and their standing at court. Both northern Italy and Hungary needed large armies of occupation and threatened to explode into insurrection if ever these were reduced. Metternich's Austria had had every defect of administration, but had been redeemed by a skilful and vigilant diplomacy. The diplomacy of the new Austria was the most inept part of its government. The Habsburg monarchy owed its preservation to Russian support; yet when the Eastern Question reached a new crisis in the early 'fifties Austria committed every conceivable blunder. Greedy for territory at the mouth of the Danube, Austria estranged Russia and yet failed to get on good terms with England and France, the allies of the Crimean War. Every opportunity was lost; and Austria emerged from the Crimean War isolated, and disliked by all the Great Powers. In such circumstances the only wise course would have been at least co-operation with Prussia; but here too, Austrian policy seemed deliberately to aim at estrangement. The Austrian diplomats had failed to carry through their German plans; but instead of making the best of things they harboured an impotent resentment and took a futile revenge in humiliating Prussia at the Federal Diet. Instead of the former Austro-Prussian co-operation, by which the two Great Powers agreed on a common Federal policy and together made proposals at the Diet, Austria now combined with the lesser states to put Prussia in a ceaseless minority. The lesser states would not have followed a constructive Austrian lead, but they enjoyed baiting Prussia and flattered themselves that they at last counted for something in German affairs. Austria accomplished nothing at the Diet except to implant in the mind of the greatest of all

Prussians a ruthless determination to reassert Prussia's greatness and independence.

In 1850 Prussian policy had seemed to end in complete failure. Within a decade Prussia was on the threshold of complete success. The humiliation of Olmütz had been evidence of diplomatic error and of confusion of counsels between Frederick William IV and his ministers; it had not been evidence of deep-seated weakness. The Prussian monarchy had not succumbed completely to the revolution in 1848; for that very reason the counter-revolution was less complete in the following years. The revolutionary parliament had been dissolved in November 1848, but its place had been taken by a more moderate body, and in 1850 the King issued a definitive constitution, which was to remain unchanged until 1918. This constitution was by no means radical. The King retained most of his power and it was not even clear that the ministers must conform to the will of the majority of the Lower House. The restricted electorate was divided into three classes – high taxpayers, medium taxpayers, and small taxpayers – and each of these classes exercised an equal franchise. Still, in comparison to conditions in Austria, Prussia appeared liberal. Her administration remained first-rate, and many of the reformers of 1848 found an outlet in administrative reform. Her finances were well conducted. The army leaders drew a lesson from the failure of 1850 and began a long period of army reorganization. Above all, Germany after 1850 began to imitate in earnest the British industrial system; and this strengthened Prussia in more than one direction. The greatest coalfields on the Continent were in Rhenish Prussia in the Ruhr valley; and these now came seriously into production. On them was founded an iron and steel industry which soon rivalled and at length surpassed the old-established industry of Bohemia. Prussia became, for the first time in her history, an industrial power. Not yet a great industrial power, towering above all the Continent and ultimately challenging even Great Britain; but still no longer an exclusively rural state. By 1871 the town-dwellers of Prussia had risen from one-quarter to a third of her population; not as great as the proportion in England, but already slightly greater than the population in France, 33 per cent against 31 per cent, and considerably greater than the proportion in Austria.

The industrial development made railway building faster and easier than it had been before 1848. New railways, even the *Ostbahn*, were built by private capital. But they did not escape the control of the army leaders. The Prussian generals had never been inventive, never pioneers in the art of war, but they had always been quick to adapt inventions to their own purpose. The Austrian general staff opposed the building of railways as an interference with their strategic plans and allowed the railways of northern Italy to be sold to a French company, at the very moment when they were preparing for a war in Italy against France. The French general staff did not bring railways into their calculation even at the time of the war of 1870. The Prussian general staff designed a plan for strategic railways, and the Prussian state gave its consent only to the railways which conformed to this plan. These railways were first used for the mobilization of 1859, and the lessons of 1859 were the essential prelude to the achievements of 1866 and 1870 which left contemporaries breathless. Nature and history had made Prussia geographically formless, rambling, and disconnected; the railways gave her unity and backbone. In this too, Prussia was a 'made' state, a triumph of art over nature.

Prussia's German policy seemed to stagnate during the eighteen-fifties. The Prussian governing class had disliked Frederick William's romantic policy and had desired a reconciliation with Austria. Still, they resented their apparent humiliation in 1850; and after Olmütz only a very few advocated a frank return to a conservative cooperation with Austria. One of these few was the 'wild Junker' Bismarck, and it was as the friend of Austria that Bismarck became Prussian representative to the Federal Diet, a strange beginning to his public career. Bismarck's mission to Frankfurt opened an epoch in German and in European history, the epoch in which we still live. For no man has had so profound an effect on Germany and none a more profound effect on Europe. Bismarck was the greatest of all political Germans and assembled in his own person all the contradictions of German Dualism. Outwardly harsh, resolute, and fearless, he was in reality highly strung and hysterical. He bullied his way over obstacles, yet serious opposition reduced him to impotent frenzy and high-pitched abusive rage, and the criticism which any British minister takes in his stride in the House of Commons would have sent him sheer out of his mind. Himself always plotting combinations against others, he was convinced that all the world was plotting combinations against him and lived in a half-mad imaginary world in which every statesman was as subtle and calculating, as ruthless and assiduous as he was himself.

Bismarck always talked of himself as a Junker and gave himself Junker airs – dressed like a Junker, affected a Junker brutality of speech, became absorbed in agricultural pursuits. In fact he was only half-Junker by birth and hardly at all by upbringing. His mother came of a middle-class bureaucratic family in Berlin, and he received a middle-class urban education, knowing nothing of farming until, as a grown man, he took over and rescued the derelict family estates. He was the highly educated sophisticated son of a highly educated sophisticated mother, masquerading as his slow-witted rural father and living down his middle-class origin by an exaggerated emphasis on the privileges of his class. He said to one of the liberals of 1848: 'I am a Junker and mean to benefit by it.' Junkerdom was an anachronism in the nineteenth century, politically barren, economically bankrupt. Without Bismarck the Junkers would not long have kept up the fight against liberalism and could have resisted industrial capitalism not at all. Bismarck saved them. A convert to Junkerdom, he outdid the Junkers in determination to defend their social and political position; but his superb intelligence told him that this position could no longer be defended by a policy of resistance. The prevailing forces of the day must be dominated and perverted, as Stein had planned to pervert the ideas of the French revolution. So, at one time or another, Bismarck made or planned alliances with every power in Europe – with England, France, Russia, Austria, and most of the smaller fry. So, at one time or another Bismarck worked or planned to work with every social and political force within Germany – with the great industrialists, with the Roman Catholics, with the anti-Catholics, even with the Socialists. He despised the Germans and loathed democracy. Yet he brought national Germany into existence and gave the Germans universal suffrage.

Completely flexible in his means, Bismarck had one permanent aim, the preservation of his class, and one permanent enemy, all those who sought to substitute ideas and reason for force as the decisive factors in politics. The advocates of a liberal Germany, the exponents of a Concert of Europe, threatened the basis of Bismarck's political philosophy. The Junkers were predatory militaristic landowners, conquering their lands by force and holding them by force; and force was all that Prussia had to offer Germany or the world. Bismarck was right to despise the academic scheming liberals of 1848. He was wrong to suppose that they were the best which liberalism could offer or that liberal ideas necessarily went with impotence. Bismarck once shook off the warnings of a British diplomat about European disapproval with the words: 'What is Europe?' The Englishman replied: 'Many great nations.' In the long run the men of liberal ideas and the many great nations were to have more force than the successors of Bismarck; but it was too long a run to be pleasant. Still, it would be unfair to blame Bismarck for all the events of the last seventy years. He had to deal with Germans, to deal, that is, with a nation which had learnt from long centuries of bitterness and disappointment to admire only force and to follow only authority. Bismarck was a representative German, except that he had political sense and perhaps even political wisdom. He had the typical German religion: rather exaggeratedly emotional, probably genuine, but unrelated to his secular life. He was perhaps genuinely loyal to the Hohenzollerns, though only so long as they were the obedient instruments of Junker power. At bottom he was a barbarian of genius, mastering in the highest degree the mechanical and intellectual side of civilization, altogether untouched by its spirit. But his genius gave him a sense of moderation, and this acted often as a substitute for idealism. As a result, though his ultimate legacy to Germany was boundless tyranny and to Europe boundless war, his immediate achievement was to give Germany a long period of prosperity and legal government and Europe a long period of peace.

In 1851, after Olmütz, Bismarck still held to the simple recipe of preserving Junker Prussia by co-operation with Austria. His aim was to return to the Holy Alliance. A few weeks in Frankfurt convinced him that the friendship between Austria and Prussia was dead, and a visit to Vienna convinced him that the friendship between Austria and Russia was dead also. Feebly arrogant, Austria humiliated Prussia at the Diet and challenged Russia in the Near East. The Holy Alliance was beyond revival. Bismarck gave the first sign of his political genius when he abandoned his accepted beliefs overnight and began to search round for alternatives. If the partnership of the three absolute monarchies was dissolved, then Prussia could not hope to hold her own alone either against France or against the national movement in Germany; she must seek for new allies. Bismarck was fertile in expedients. He insisted that Prussia must not be dragged in the wake of Austria's anti-Russian policy, but must hold aloof in the Near East. He responded insolently to the Austrian assumption of leadership at the Diet, and urged the Prussian ministers to form an anti-Austrian alliance with the revolutionary Emperor of the French, Napoleon III. These wild proposals shocked the reactionary ministers of Frederick William IV. Against Bismarck's realism they still opposed an outworn legitimism and hoped that somehow the Holy Alliance would be restored. They drifted into a defensive alliance with Austria, but escaped from it when, at the beginning of the Crimean War, it threatened to draw Prussia into war with Russia.

The Crimean War gave the death-blow to the European order which had been created by the Congress of Vienna, and so in particular to the balance of the German Confederation. Both German powers were discredited and threatened. Austria who had tried to profit from the war earned the hatred of the Tsar and, though she became formally a member of the 'Crimean coalition', of England and France as well. Prussia had evaded all commitments and was merely despised by all parties, so much so that the Great Powers almost forgot to invite her to the Congress of Paris at all. Both France and Russia had made the maintenance of German disunity the cardinal principle of their policy, France since the time of Richelieu, Russia since the Peace of Teschen in 1778 and as recently as the agreement of Olmütz. Now both abandoned this principle and followed a policy of adventure. In France Napoleon III was bewitched by the idea that his uncle had been ruined by opposing German and Italian nationalism; and he wished to dazzle French opinion by a drastic overthrow of the system of the Congress of Vienna. The Tsar was obsessed by the humiliating peace terms which forbade Russian armament on the Black Sea; and for fifteen years Russian policy, blind to all else, pursued the single object of tearing up these clauses of the Treaty of Paris. With every extension of education German national sentiment was growing deeper and stronger; with the development of industry Germany was growing more powerful. Yet this was the moment chosen by both France and Russia to abandon the precautions against a great Germany which they had applied for centuries.

Such is the force of even the most outworn institutions that the

Austro-Prussian balance lasted, to outward appearance, until the end of the 'fifties. The first obvious blow to it was the disappearance of Frederick William IV, mad in 1858, dead in 1861. His brother William, who succeeded him, was by no means a liberal. Indeed he had had to be smuggled out of Prussia to England during the revolution of 1848. But he was hard-headed, immune from romantic ideas, and therefore influenced by day-to-day events. In theory he believed, as Frederick William had done, in the wickedness of liberalism and in the traditional superiority of the house of Habsburg. In practice he resented being under Habsburg orders and was ready to play for liberal support in Germany. His coming to power began in Prussia the brief 'new era', when liberal ministers were appointed and Prussian policy took on an avowedly German tone. The Prussian governing classes were not converted to liberalism. But they could no longer live in a dream-world of the Congress of Vienna. They were conscious of the threat from Austria and, appreciating the anarchy which had overtaken the relations of the Powers, they could think of no other ally than German liberalism. The moderate liberals, still disheartened by the events of 1849, responded eagerly to this approach and revived, in the National Union, the programme of Prussian leadership in Germany. Only Bismarck protested against this alliance with liberalism, and early in 1859 he was sent out of the way – 'put on ice', as he said – as Prussian Minister at St Petersburg.

In 1859 Napoleon III put into operation the first part of his programme by engaging in war with Austria for the liberation of Italy. The Franco-Austrian war brought the dilemma of Prussian policy to a head. A few daring radicals, and Bismarck as well, wanted Prussia to exploit Austria's danger or even to go to war on the Italian side. The liberals wanted to defend the national cause, and the conservatives the cause of monarchy, by an alliance with Austria. Prussia made half-hearted promises to Austria, mobilized, talked of defending the Rhine, and in the end did nothing. She was once more discredited in the eyes of liberal Germany. Austria lost Lombardy and, what was more important, her absolutist system was shaken beyond survival. The defeat of 1859 began in Austria the long search for a more stable basis of government which lasted until 1867. The first experiment was reaction: back from the levelling absolutism of Bach to the traditional muddle of the days of

Metternich; back from bureaucratic centralization to provincial autonomy. This aristocratic revival was hostile to German nationalism and, in a fraudulent way, sympathetic to the nationalism of the subject peoples. It offended in Germany both liberals and nationalists, strengthened the arguments of the Little Germans, and thus, in a negative way, improved Prussia's standing. But the aristocratic programme was tried in Austria only to be abandoned. In February 1861 the course of Austrian policy was once more reversed. Schmerling, the leader of the Austrian party at Frankfurt in 1848, became the chief minister; a parliament for the entire empire was set up at Vienna, with the constituencies and the franchise so arranged as to give the Germans a sure majority; and the Schmerling ministry began to press for a reform of the German Confederation. Austria had recovered her primacy in the eyes of Germany, and it seemed impossible for Prussia to hold her own against her without a surrender to middle-class liberalism which would cut the roots of Junker power. Such were the circumstances which led the Junkers and the King to play Bismarck, their last, despairing card. They were engaged in a mad act – to preserve Junker Prussia into the twentieth century – and it needed a mad Junker to succeed. But Bismarck was mad in ways that his fellows never appreciated and he was to lead them into paths beyond their imagining.

6

THE CONQUEST OF GERMANY BY PRUSSIA, 1862–71

The issue which brought Bismarck to power was not the survival of Prussia in Germany, but the survival in Prussia of the military monarchy and the military caste. William I was by upbringing and taste a soldier, anxious to redeem the army from the failure of 1850 and to repair the defects shown by the mobilization of 1859. In particular, he wished to provide for the increase in the size of the annual classes of conscripts. Since 1815 the population of Prussia had increased from ten and a half to eighteen million, the yearly intake of the army not at all, so that one out of every three Prussians escaped military service. Roon, the Minister of War, therefore planned to increase the military establishment by creating new regiments and providing new barracks. But he had a further object. The only conservative in the liberal ministry, he was determined to make the army at least a stronghold of conservatism. Therefore he planned also to remove from the army the few scraps of liberalism remaining from the days of Stein and Scharnhorst and the war of Liberation. The serving army was not only to be increased; it was to become the only army. The reserve, with its middle-class officers and its connections with civilian life, was to be reduced and later eliminated. Roon had the typical barrack-room

mentality. Far from valuing the 'citizen soldier', he envied the professional armies of France and Austria and, if he had had longer to operate
his plans, he would have made impossible the great mobilizations of
reservists which secured the victories of 1866 and 1870. Surrounded
by liberal ministers, Roon actually feared the liberalism of the reservists
– a compliment, though an undeserved one, to the Prussian people.

The Prussian parliament was by no means the revolutionary parliament of 1848. Elected on the three-class franchise, it was composed
not of radicals, but like the Frankfurt Assembly, of 'notables', lawyers
and civil servants, anxious to establish constitutional principles and to
prevent a military monopoly of the Junkers, but in a strictly legal
manner. They carried on their conflict with the King by means of
resolutions and protests without attempting to appeal to the Prussian
masses, and unanimously rejected a radical suggestion that they should
refuse to meet in order to expose the fraud of Prussian constitutionalism. They put their faith still, as they had done at Frankfurt, in principles without power, and would have been ashamed of a liberty that
had been fought for. The liberal majority did not oppose the increase in
the size of the army. This was a myth subsequently invented by
Bismarck's following of sycophantic historians. On the contrary,
inspired by the legend of 1813, they believed universal military service
to be a liberal institution. Their aim was to preserve in the army some
liberal middle-class element. They agreed to the increase in the annual
intake of conscripts, but proposed to balance it by reducing the period
of service from three to two years, so that the size of the standing army
would remain the same and the reserve, therefore, would still be an
essential part of the military organization. Most of the military experts
would have accepted this proposal. In fact those of them who kept alive
the traditions of Scharnhorst thought the parliamentary scheme an
improvement. Roon resisted the proposal not on military, but on class
grounds: he was more concerned to abolish the middle-class reservist
officers than to increase the fighting strength of the army.

In 1861 the Prussian parliament agreed to the increased army
expenditure for a single year, on the assumption that Roon's far-
reaching changes would be postponed. Roon, however, set on foot his
reactionary reforms; and in 1862 therefore the parliament refused to
make the increased grant. William I believed that he was faced not

merely with a constitutional, but with a real political crisis, and could see no way out but abdication. Roon persuaded him to try Bismarck as a last expedient. On September 22nd, 1862, Bismarck became Prime Minister of Prussia and the Junkers' saviour. He formulated his policy in the famous phrase: 'The great questions of the day will not be settled by speeches and the resolutions of majorities – that was the great mistake from 1848 to 1849 – but by blood and iron.' The parliament was allowed to remain in being, but Bismarck ignored its resolves. The army reforms were carried through and the increased taxes, which had not been voted, collected. Bismarck even invented a theory that there was a 'hole' in the constitution, which laid down that the agreement of King and parliament was necessary for legislation, but did not say what was to happen when they disagreed. Therefore the King must fill this 'hole', until a constitutional agreement was reached. Bismarck did not believe in his own theory and admitted in the sequel that he had been acting illegally; but at the same time it was a good talking point, which kept the parliamentary lawyers occupied. The liberal majority were helpless. Short of appealing to the people, they had no weapon and were eager, long before 1866, to compromise with the King. Most of the Junkers, on their side, disliked the openly illegal position into which they had drifted, and even Roon offered a compromise acceptable to the parliament. Bismarck for his own purposes kept the conflict going and whipped the parliament up to new outbursts whenever it showed signs of conciliation. William I feared his daring, and his fellow Junkers resented his frank contempt for them. King and Junkers alike clung to Bismarck only so long as they felt threatened by a political revolution, and Bismarck therefore had to keep this imaginary threat in being. The opposition of the Prussian liberals was invaluable to him. Without it he would have achieved nothing at all.

Bismarck cared nothing for the constitutional struggle in Prussia, except as a means of staying in office. He knew perfectly well that it was without real significance. His real anxiety was to preserve Prussia as a great power and therefore above all to reorder Prussia's relations with Austria and with Germany. Bismarck always liked to show that he had intended to do whatever he actually did; in fact that he made events. In later life he gave out that he had always intended to fight Austria and to unify Germany; and this version was generally accepted by his admirers and by most historians. In reality, Bismarck's greatness lay not in mastering events, but in going with events so as to seem to master them. He had no rigidly defined programme when he became Prime Minister in 1862, beyond preserving the Junker social order. Sentimentally, as a matter of private taste, he would have preferred a return to the conservative order of the days of Metternich: Austria and Prussia co-operating to resist liberalism within Germany; Austria, Prussia, and Russia co-operating to resist liberalism in Europe. But this Holy Alliance had broken down. Austria and Russia were hopelessly estranged in the Near East; and if Austria persisted in Schwarzenberg's policy of degrading Prussia to the level of the lesser states, still more if Austria pursued wholeheartedly Schmerling's aim of winning the leadership of liberal Germany, then conflict with Austria was inevitable. Bismarck did not follow a single aim, but rather two contradictory aims: the policy which he liked but did not expect to succeed, of winning Austria back to the conservative alliance with its centre moved, of course, from Vienna to Berlin – and simultaneously the policy which he disliked but strove to make as harmless as possible of seizing the leadership of Germany and bringing Austria to her senses by defeat.

One aim Bismarck never pursued: that of uniting all Germans in a single national state. Greater Germany would mean the end of Junker Prussia. The Junkers had neither the numbers nor the capacity to run all central Europe; instead German radicalism would run Prussia. A Prussian diplomat once said to Bismarck: 'Our power must find its limits when the supply of Junker officers gives out.' Bismarck replied: 'I cannot say that in public, but it is the basis of my plans.' Greater Germany, too, would be predominantly Roman Catholic: in 1855 52 per cent of the population of the German Confederation was Roman Catholic, as against 35 per cent if the Austrian lands were excluded. Above all, Greater Germany would mean a Greater German foreign policy, protection, that is, of the German communities in eastern and south-eastern Europe, conflict therefore with Russia to the ruin of the Junkers. For co-operation between Russia and Prussia was vital for the subjugation of Poland and so for the security of the Junker estates. Ultimately Greater Germany, with its programme of central Europe united under German authority, implied conflict not only with Russia, but with all the world; a conflict which Bismarck knew the Junkers were not powerful enough to sustain. Bismarck was ceaselessly active and his mind endlessly fertile in expedients, but in the last resort his policy was, like Metternich's, negative: to bar the way to Greater Germany. Metternich and Bismarck both despaired of the old order for which alone they cared. Metternich defended the old order without hoping for success. Bismarck went with the new forces in order to draw their sting. He conjured up the phantom of unification in order to avoid the reality.

Bismarck's first achievement in foreign policy was the consolidation of Russo-Prussian friendship over the body of Poland. Prussia's aloofness during the Crimean War had already won the Tsar's favour, but it needed the Polish revolt of 1863 to make things certain. In 1846 and 1848 Prussia had sympathized with Poland, and Austria had been the pacemaker in oppression. In 1863, Austria, estranged from Russia and aspiring to liberalism, supported the Poles, though ineffectively; Bismarck, breaking finally with the programme of Prussian radicalism, supported Tsarist conquest. The anti-Polish agreement between Prussia and Russia (the Alvensleben convention) was a symbol, not an expression of practical need. There were no Polish disturbances in Prussian territory, and the risings in Russian Poland were far from the Prussian frontier. Indeed, Gorchakov, the Russian Chancellor, opposed the convention as humiliating and unnecessary; and it was pressed on by the Tsar in the name of monarchical solidarity. The Alvensleben convention determined the character of future Germany. Bismarck and the radicals both held that Germany could be united only by means of foreign war; and the experience of the great French revolution showed that they were right. But the radicals hoped for a revolutionary war against Russia which by liberating Poland and overthrowing Tsardom would also destroy Junker Prussia. The Alvensleben convention determined that the coming war would be a war against France, against the liberal west, a war therefore which would actually strengthen Junker Prussia and cut off liberal Germany at the roots.

Secure in Russia's favour, Bismarck turned next to the conflict with Austria, the conflict which within three years was to change the face of Europe. In 1863 Austria still seemed in the ascendant and could still take the initiative. Bismarck's rupture with parliament discredited Prussia in the eyes of all liberal Germans. Even the cautious Protestants of

Northern Germany who had made the National Union despaired of Prussian leadership. In Austria, on the other hand, the liberal parliament with its German majority set up in 1861 enjoyed a growing prestige; and all the forces which had supported Habsburg leadership in Germany in 1848 revived after long years of discouragement. Radicals who desired a Greater Germany; traditionalists who wished to see again the mythical glories of the Holy Roman Empire; the princes who feared the tyranny of the King of Prussia but who would accept the primacy of the Habsburg Emperor; the Roman Catholics of western Germany; all those who hoped for a Germany somehow united by peaceful agreement; in fact almost every body of opinion in Germany except the Prussian officer corps looked to Vienna for leadership. Highwater mark of this leadership was the meeting of the princes which Francis Joseph summoned to Frankfurt on August 16th, 1863, the last and most grandiose attempt to unite Germany by consent. Austria proposed a strengthening of the federal authority, the establishment of a federal assembly composed of delegates from the parliaments of the separate states, and the voluntary surrender by the princes of part of their sovereignty. This sovereignty was fictitious, and the princes would have given in to Austria, as they gave in to Prussia at the Erfurt Union in 1849, if Austria had been alone in Germany. But Austria was not alone. Prussia existed, and the princes made their agreement conditional on the agreement of Prussia.

The invitation of William I to the meeting at Frankfurt provoked the decisive and most serious crisis of Bismarck's career. William I was King of Prussia, but he was a prince and a German, and he was reluctant to stand aloof when the princes were proposing to unite Germany by consent. This seemed like a squaring of the circle: German national sentiment would be satisfied, yet the rights of the princes would be preserved. Bismarck forbade William to accept the invitation and after a struggle got his way. For Bismarck held the trump card. If he resigned, William would have to give way to the demands of his parliament. Constitutional monarchy in Prussia was too high a price to pay even for the friendship of the German princes. As with the Prussian parliament so with the meeting of the princes Bismarck refused to accept the conventional rules, and appealed to the Prussian army as the true basis of Prussian existence. He would not be bound by the clauses of a constitution which was a legal fiction, not the outcome of a conquest of power by the middle class; and he would not acknowledge obligations to German princes, who were also unreal. Bismarck's challenge could not be met by argument; it could only be answered by force. The liberals of the Prussian parliament would not contemplate a revolution; the princes of Frankfurt would not contemplate war. The only real force at the Frankfurt meeting was the Habsburg Emperor, but his presence there did not make sense and nothing came of it. Francis Joseph was a narrow-minded autocrat, head of the most obscurantist dynasty in all Europe. His alliance with the liberals of German Austria, even more his appeal to German liberalism, was fraudulent, the mere accident of policy without meaning or significance. Francis Joseph was certainly jealous of Prussia and willing to wage against Prussia an old-fashioned dynastic war; but the traditions of his house, centuries old, prevented his fighting this war as the leader of revolutionary German nationalism. The judgement passed by Francis I in 1815 remained true: 'Only a Jacobin could accept this crown.'

The failure of the Frankfurt meeting ended all chance of a Germany achieved by negotiation and so broke the last frail link of historic continuity. The ghost of the Holy Roman Empire, the ghost of a civilized stable Germany, the ghost of the Free Cites and of German liberalism, all these were laid at Frankfurt in August 1863. Defeated too was the Schmerling policy of a liberal Austria under German leadership. If the conduct of Austrian affairs had followed rational lines, if Francis Joseph had ever been able to adopt a single policy without reservations, Austria in 1863 would have reverted to Metternich's conservatism and would have revived the reactionary partnership with Prussia. But the supreme government of Austria was in chaos, Francis Joseph inclining first to one side, then to the other, too autocratic to go with the liberals, too ambitious to be satisfied with a negative conservatism. Bismarck tried, perhaps without conviction but certainly with persistence, to restore the co-operation of the Holy Alliance; but Francis Joseph and his ministers would not return openly to the days of Metternich. It would be a distraction, relevant only to the personal history of Bismarck, to attempt to decide when he gave up the hope of winning the alliance of Austria without war or to estimate how the genuine offers of friendship gradually merged into subterfuges designed to provoke a conflict. Bismarck certainly sought Austrian friendship for longer than he later made out or than appears in the versions of Bismarckian historians; but he was not so long-suffering or so sincere as some conservative German historians have recently argued. Yet however hostile in method his essential object was the restoration of the Austro-Prussian alliance, a monarchical union against liberalism, and still more an insuperable barrier (as it had been in Metternich's time) against a complete German unification and Greater Germany.

The means by which Bismarck asserted his ascendancy in Europe and set the stage for adjusting relations with Austria was the question of Sleswig and Holstein, the great romantic issue of 1848 now revived in a new form. The conflict of 1848 had been postponed, not settled, by a treaty of peace, signed in London in 1852: the two Duchies had remained under the sovereignty of the King of Denmark, the national claims of both Denmark and Germany ignored. Late in 1863 the last King of Denmark of the male line died, and the problem of the Duchies was opened once more. But the circumstances were very different. In 1848 a humiliated Prussia obeyed the summons of a self-confident National Assembly and sought to liberate the Duchies for national Germany. In 1864 German nationalism, still discouraged, trailed after the Prussian army and cheered on the conquest of the Duchies by the Prussian monarchy – strange victory of liberalism which substituted autocratic Prussian rule for the wide autonomy which the Duchies had formerly possessed. Denmark controlled the entrance to the Baltic, and the two Duchies were as much the key to the security of the Sound as was, say, Gallipoli to the security of the Straits. But England and Russia did not repeat their negative of 1848. Russia was blinded by the defeats of the Crimean War and bewitched by the monarchical solidarity of the Alvensleben convention. England relied only on the prestige of her sea-power, this time without effect. She had no Continental ally, for Napoleon III was determined not to oppose German national feeling and so set his foot on the path which led to the destruction of French power in Europe. Austria acted most foolishly of all. She was too conservative to follow the liberal course of liberating the Duchies for Germany; but she would not altogether estrange national sentiment in Germany by following the conservative course of upholding the treaty settlement of 1852. Therefore she followed the worst course of all: she helped to

conquer the Duchies for Prussia, and so offended both German nationalism and foreign powers. In August 1864 Denmark, isolated and
defeated, made peace and surrendered the Duchies into the joint hands
of Austria and Prussia.

There followed eighteen months in which Bismarck offered alliance
to Austria with one hand and prepared for war against Austria with the
other. His offer of August 1864, in which he proposed that Austria
should surrender her rights in the Duchies in exchange for Prussian
assistance in the reconquest of Lombardy (the abortive treaty of
Schönbrunn), was probably sincere. And there was genuine regret in
the final refusal of October 1864 to admit Austria to the Zollverein.
Highly characteristic of Bismarck was his slipping off on holiday to
Biarritz so as to saddle his colleagues with this decisive irreparable step,
against which he could safely, but impotently, advise. Probably fraudulent was the treaty of Gastein (August 1865) by which Bismarck divided the Duchies – Sleswig to Prussia, Holstein to Austria. Certainly
fraudulent was his last proposal of May 1866, for a partition of Germany between Prussia and Austria; fraudulent not in the sense that it
did not represent Bismarck's aim, but in that he had learnt from long
experience Austria's unwillingness to conform to his plans. All these
projects ran up against the indelible effects of the events of 1848.
Junker Prussia, despite its concessions to liberalism, emerged fundamentally unshaken by the revolution. Aristocratic Austria, despite the
military victories of 1849, could never be restored. In the days of
Metternich the Austrian Emperor was really a free agent; he balanced
not between, but above, his peoples. In the 'sixties the Habsburg monarchy could keep going only by taking one group or other of its subjects into partnership. Co-operation with the middle-class Germans,
Schmerling's line of policy, committed Austria to seeking the approval
of national feeling in Germany and debarred her from a conservative
alliance with Prussia. Return to aristocratic conservatism, the policy
followed in 1860 and revived in 1865, certainly relieved Austria from
any obligations to the German liberals, but these aristocrats would
never accept the uncouth Prussian Junkers as equals and moreover,
conscious of their weakness, they sought the support of the backward
Slav peoples within the Austrian Empire. 'Austroslavism', the strange
federal mixture of feudalism and Slav nationalisms, made agreement

with Prussia impossible. For how could the Junker oppressors of the Poles go hand in hand with an Empire in which the Slav peoples were allowed even a moderate existence to the detriment of the 'master nations', Magyar and German?

Thus Bismarck's real task, whatever his inclination, was the isolation of Austria and the search for alliances. To break down the German balance established by the Congress of Vienna, while the members of the Congress looked impotently, or even encouragingly, on – this was his master work. For more than three hundred years the powers of the circumference – France on the one side, Sweden and later Russia on the other – had laid down the law to central Europe. In the two years 1864 to 1866 the situation was reversed, and soon central Europe claimed to lay down the law first to France, then to Russia and finally to all the world. Tsarist policy was monotonously fixed on the undoing of the Black Sea clauses of the Treaty of Paris, and Russia would pay any price to see Austria made of no account in the Near East. The attitude of France was not so simple. Every French interest demanded a balance of power in Germany and a strong Austria in the Balkans, but the interests of Napoleon III did not coincide with the interests of France. To shore up his regime in France, he needed foreign successes, a policy therefore of disturbance not of conservatism; and so urged Bismarck on against Austria. French policy was pulled this way and that until the last moment, but when it came to the point Napoleon III came down on the side of a general upheaval in Europe, an upheaval of which he was the immediate victim.

Bismarck secured the neutrality of France and Russia, but he needed more. Moltke, the chief of the Prussian General Staff, was confident of victory only in a short war. For, while Prussia's front-line strength was greater than that of Austria, the population of Prussia was only half that of Austria; and besides, Bismarck's diplomatic precautions might not withstand a long strain. To finish Austria off quickly, Bismarck made alliances with the three revolutionary 'master' nations of 1848 – with Italy, with the Magyars, and with German radicalism. With Italy, the alliance (made April 8th, 1866) was formal, an offensive alliance of two states. With Hungary, the alliance was implicit, but none the less real: the Magyars, still subjected to Vienna, hampered the Austrian defence, and Bismarck's victory gave them virtual independence. With the German radicals, the alliance was political, expressed in Bismarck's proposal of April 9th, 1866, for a German parliament elected by direct universal suffrage. This proposal marked the decisive breach with conservative Austria and the idea of the Holy Alliance; it marked equally the final breach with the Prussian liberals and with all those who hoped for reform in Germany by consent. Universal suffrage was not liberal, but revolutionary; and it had been persistently urged on Bismarck by the revolutionary Socialist, Lassalle, as a means of swamping the liberal lawyers of the Prussian parliament, with their middle-class constitutional principles. Bismarck stood Lassalle's idea on its head. Lassalle intended to enfranchise the industrial workers, trained by economic disputes to be the enemies of the liberal capitalists. Bismarck was concerned, in a Germany where two-thirds of the population lived on the land, to enfranchise the conservative peasantry. When later Germany became predominantly urban Bismarck's calculation seemed to have failed; and in his long struggle against the Social Democrats he himself confessed as much. Yet in an even longer run his calculation proved right. The masses, whether rural or urban, cared for material benefits, not for legal principles; and the revolutionary idea of the sovereignty of the people killed the liberal doctrines of respect for law and for established rights. Lassalle had already offered Bismarck his alliance to smash the Prussian constitution, if Bismarck in return would curb the economic absolutism of the capitalists and give the workers social security. Lassalle was a visionary, a general without an army – as Bismarck said: 'What could the poor devil offer me?' He was repudiated by his fellow Socialists, Marx and Engels. But they too wrote triumphantly of Bismarck doing their work for them: the more centralized and powerful the German state, the easier it would be for them to take it over. Despite their theoretical enthusiasm for the great ideas of the French revolution, they saw in the Junker conquest of Germany and the Junker defeat of the German middle class nothing but gain. Thus the offer of universal suffrage completed the squaring of the circle by which Bismarck made the Junkers, the weakest and most reactionary social force in Germany, the welcome allies of all that was most progressive and powerful. The capitalists accepted Junker rule because it gave them prosperity and unification; the working classes accepted Junker rule because it gave them social security and the vote. The only loss was Freedom, and that is not an item which appears in a balance sheet or in a list of trade union benefits.

The proposal of universal suffrage shaped the future character of Germany. It miscarried in April 1866 as a practical manoeuvre. The masses did not yet count as a political force; they could not be conjured into existence overnight by a Prussian manifesto. The few middle-class radicals, whether in Prussia or outside it, were not won over. For, despite their radicalism, they still attached importance to constitutional procedure, and could not so easily forget Bismarck's unconstitutional rule in Prussia. Moreover, universal suffrage estranged the moderate realist liberals of the National Union, who had hitherto favoured Prussian leadership in Germany, as the easier, more moderate way. As a result when, in June 1866, the dispute between Prussia and Austria broke out into war, all German opinion, except that of a few anti-Austrian irreconcilables, was on the Austrian side. Nothing could be more false than to suppose that the war of 1866 was, on the Prussian side, a people's war. In those parts of Prussia which were more German than Prussian, in the Rhineland in particular, there was considerable resistance to the call-up of reservists, and demonstrations against the war took place even in Berlin. At the Federal Diet, all the states not absolutely under Prussia's guns voted in condemnation of Prussia; and though this vote expressed primarily the opinion of the princes, it represented also the feeling of their liberal middle-class parliaments. The armies of the German states fought against Prussia willingly if not enthusiastically. None of the states except Saxony would agree, even at this crisis, to a common plan of defence or to make sacrifices for the common cause; this did not prove that they desired a Prussian victory, but merely demonstrated that a league of sovereign states is incapable even of self-preservation. In short, Germany was conquered not united.

The war between Austria and Prussia lasted three weeks (seven to the formal conclusion of hostilities), only long enough in fact to get into position and fight a decisive battle. On July 3rd the Austrian army was defeated and broken at the battle of Sadova (Königgrätz). At once Bismarck renewed the offers of a moderate settlement which he had made before the war. Although during the war he had encouraged attempts at revolt in Hungary and although he even made offers of independence to the Czechs in Bohemia, the last thing he desired was the destruction of the Habsburg monarchy. The Habsburgs were his essential allies against Greater Germany. Austria, therefore, lost no territory to Prussia, except her theoretical share of Sleswig and Holstein. But she withdrew from German affairs, and the German Confederation was dissolved. Of the German states north of the Main, Prussia annexed all those which had fought against her, except Saxony, who was rewarded for her cooperation with Austria by the successful Austrian defence of her existence; and all the states north of the Main, whether they had fought against Prussia or not, were forced into a new North German Federation under Prussian control. The establishment of this Federation made annexation pointless and indeed undesirable. Whether annexed or not, North Germany would be subordinated to Prussia in war, and in peace-time the princes were useful allies for Bismarck against liberalism. But William I could not free himself from the idea that the princes who had fought against him deserved punishment, and Bismarck had to tolerate this moral interference with his plans.

The Prussian parliament had been dissolved at the beginning of the war, and new elections were held on the day of the battle of Sadova. The liberals, though reduced, were returned with a majority; but they realized that a new dissolution, after the news of victory, would ruin them. The moderates broke away from the Progressive party to form the National Liberal party, and on September 3rd, 1866, the Prussian parliament gave Bismarck by 230 votes to 7 an indemnity for the unconstitutional collection of taxes. The vote of September 3rd was as decisive a landmark in the history of Germany as was the Bill of Rights in the history of England or the oath of the tennis court in the history of France. In each case the struggle between crown and parliament reached its term; but in Prussia it was the crown which won. German liberalism, as expressed in the Frankfurt assembly of 1848, had never fought a real enemy and therefore had no prospect of real success. Prussian liberalism had been fighting a real battle, however feebly, and would have won a real victory, if Bismarck had once lost his grasp on affairs. After September 3rd liberalism was dead in Prussia. The Prussian crown was a military monarchy and needed a parliament only to consent to its expenditure for military purposes; yet the liberals agreed that the King had done right to raise money for the army without the agreement of parliament. The liberals did not sacrifice their principles from fear or for material gain; they were bewitched by success, and success was the condition on which the Hohenzollern monarchy retained its power. The capitalist middle classes ceased on September 3rd to demand control of the state; they accepted Junker rule and confined their liberalism to hoping that this rule would be exercised in a liberal spirit – 'liberal administration', not liberal government became their aim.

The abdication of the Prussian liberals and the defeat of parliamentary government had a profound social result. Parliament did not control the state; therefore it could never be for the individual the path to power. Henceforth only men of the second rank went from the middle classes into politics. The intellectual ability of the politicians steadily, relentlessly, declined; all that survived was the gift of sterile negative criticism. Political parties became inevitably interest groups, solely concerned to win concessions from the state, but never supposing that they might have to accept responsibility themselves. The really able and ambitious members of the middle class shunned politics and turned exclusively to industry and finance. As Sombart, the great economic historian, wrote in 1903: 'With us there is no diversion of talent into the field of politics, as in other countries. Neither the rich, nor what is more important, the gifted members of the middle class are withdrawn from economic life to devote themselves to politics.' As a result the direction of German economic development was far more skilful, far more systematic than it was in other countries. German industry was directed by men of education and vision; no wonder it soon surpassed all the rest of the world. But there was something more. The leaders of industry were not primarily concerned with wealth nor with mere technical achievement. They were driven on by the same longing for power and the same desire to make their country great as in England and France led men to take up a political career. German industry therefore was a fighting, conquering industry, concentrating on the goods which make a state powerful, not on the goods which make a people prosperous. Germany predominated in heavy industry and in chemistry, in the weapons of war and in the scientific substitutes which lessened her dependence on supplies from overseas – again a preparation for war. All the talent of Germany sought a substitute in industry for the political power which they had renounced on

September 3rd, 1866. They strengthened the military monarchy and urged it on to conquer others in order to console themselves for the fact that they had been themselves conquered.

The defeat of Austria broke down the balance which had existed in Germany ever since the failure of Charles V in the sixteenth century. Prussia was now the only power in Germany. Sole barrier to her domination was France, who soon reaped the reward of having allowed the destruction of the work of Richelieu. In 1866 Bismarck was not ready for war against France, and he agreed to give the German states south of the Main 'an internationally independent existence'. These states had no power or reality. They had been as much conquered as the states north of the Main. But they survived for four more years under the shadowy protection of Napoleon's palsied hand. Bismarck was in no hurry. He had to create, almost single-handed the North German Federation; and the outburst of national enthusiasm which followed the events of 1866 stirred up his Junker fear of German radicalism. In 1867 he said: 'We have done enough for our generation'; and he would have been prepared to leave south Germany for the future, if Napoleon III on his side had acquiesced in failure. But Napoleon needed success more desperately than ever; and the moment the war was over he began to intrigue for the alliance with Austria which he ought to have made before the war started.

He was too late. After 1866 the Habsburg monarchy finally lost its freedom of manoeuvre. Early in 1867 Francis Joseph made with the Magyars the political bargain known as the 'Compromise', by which the Magyars accepted a common Habsburg army and a common foreign policy in return for a Hungary internally independent and under Magyar domination. The Magyars became the most powerful political force in Austria-Hungary. Magyar domination of Hungary and Hungarian domination of Austria-Hungary was as much a product of Bismarck as Junker domination of Prussia and Prussian domination of Germany. The Magyars recognized this and resolutely barred the way against any attempt to undo Bismarck's work. Nor were they alone. The Germans of the Habsburg monarchy had supported Schmerling's attempt to establish Habsburg authority over Germany; and they were the defeated party of 1866, excluded from the Reich for the first time in a thousand years. Yet they now opposed any attempt to undo the verdict of Sadova. Francis Joseph gave Austria a constitution and the Austrian German liberals predominance in that constitution as a necessary part of his compact with the Magyars. A Habsburg victory over Prussia would not merely undo Hungarian independence; it would also end liberalism in Austria and would put the Habsburg monarchy in the hands of the Slav peoples. Rather than accept equality with the Slavs and run the risk of counting as a minority in Austria – which they were – the German Austrians, too, became guarantors of Bismarck's work. The few Habsburg politicians who still hoped for revenge were hamstrung. They could renew the struggle with Prussia only if they were prepared to struggle against the Magyars and German Austrians as well and to seek the alliance of the Slav peoples. But the anti-Prussians in Austria were aristocrats, great landowners of clerical conservative views. It was inconceivable that they could become the radical leaders of land-hungry peasants. Therefore, despite dynastic distaste, the Habsburg monarchy was doomed to remain the satellite of Prussia-Germany. The alternative was agrarian and social revolution.

Thus France was isolated in 1870 as Austria had been in 1866. Russia was offered a last chance to prevent the rise of a great power in central Europe, but the Tsar held doggedly to his purpose of ending the disarmament of the Black Sea. He received his reward: early in 1871 the offending clauses of the Treaty of Paris were torn up. But at a terrible price. In July 1870 Bismarck went to war with France over a trumpery issue; all the states south of the Main joined in the war; the French armies were defeated and destroyed on the frontier, at Sedan, and in Metz; and early in 1871 Paris surrendered to the Germans. The French republic, crippled and friendless, had to surrender Alsace and Lorraine, which had been French for two hundred years, and to pay a great indemnity. Still more, the German princes were induced by Bismarck to offer the German crown to William I, and on January 18th, 1871, the German Empire was proclaimed in the palace of Versailles. Within nine years, between 1862 and 1871, Prussia had risen from being the weakest and least regarded of the Great Powers to become the dominant state of the European continent.

The success of Bismarck was so rapid and so perfect that many observers, both then and later, accepted it as inevitable. The development of German nationalism, and perhaps even the growth of German economic power, were inevitable; but there was nothing inevitable in the particular form they took. Without Bismarck the unification of Germany might have been accomplished against both the Prussian monarchy and the Prussian landowners; and without Bismarck's success German industrial development would certainly have taken other, less brutal, forms. To unite Germany under Prussia was to fly in the face of all the rules, a gigantic *tour de force*, and one which had later to be paid for by Germany, and still more by Europe, in many years of suffering. Still less inevitable was Bismarck's victory over the European Powers who had for so long maintained German disunity. Bismarck owed his success to the disunion and lack of will of his opponents. A coalition, or even a prolonged war, would have ruined him. But all sense of European solidarity had vanished. Each Power pursued its own ends recklessly: Russia thinking only of the Black Sea, Napoleon III scheming for a stroke of prestige, and Austria conducting a series of contradictory policies, all of them selfish. The old community of aristocratic interests had broken down; a new community of interests between the peoples had not grown up. Bismarckian Germany was Europe's reward. The isolated combatants lacked all persistence. Neither Austria in 1866 nor France in 1870 would bid *va banque*, and that was the only call to make against a state and a class which had always lived on the margin of existence. After Sadova the Habsburg monarchy thought only of preserving its dynastic position; after the fall of Paris the French peasantry and bourgeoisie thought only of preserving their comfortable economic position. The price of resistance which they then refused to pay was later charged a hundredfold against their descendants.

But it seems inadequate to explain Bismarck's success solely by the mistakes of his opponents. At the time, and for many years after, the Prussian victories were regarded as a proof of the strength of nationalism, and by a strange chain of reasoning Bismarck, thus supposed to owe his victory to nationalism, was himself decked out as a national enthusiast. In fact German nationalism had little more to do with the victories of 1866 and 1870 than with the victories of 1813. In 1866 German national feeling, so far as it existed, was almost united against Prussia; in 1870 nationalist professors killed Frenchmen from their university chairs, but the real war was fought by a Prussian officer class to whom national enthusiasm was altogether repugnant. William I represented the sentiments of his fellow officers when he tried to evade the Imperial Crown and when he refused to speak to Bismarck on the day that the Crown was forced upon him.

A later, more materialist generation found the explanation of Prussia's victory in her superiority in men and in material equipment. But this was to date back to 1866 and to 1870 the circumstances of 1914 or of 1940. In 1866 Prussia had a population of 18 million against Austria's population of 33 million. She added 3 million by the annexations of 1866 (a majority of them, however, unwilling and discontented subjects) and controlled a further 3 million through the North German Federation. Alliance with the south German states brought the total in 1870 to just under 40 million (annexation of Alsace and Lorraine carried the total to 41 million in 1871), but only the Prussian element in these was effectively organized for war. The French population was 37 million, and, as the birth-rate was lower, the proportion of men in the fighting years was higher than in Prussia. Equally mythical was Prussia's economic advantage. Her production of coal passed the French figure by about 1860, and by 1870 was about double; her production of iron and steel did not surpass that of France until after 1871. Moreover Prussia was actually inferior in the application of industry to war. In 1866 she possessed a rifle much superior to the Austrian musket; but Prussian artillery was inferior in number, calibre, and conduct to the Austrian. In 1870 not only was French artillery superior to Prussian, but the *chassepot*, the French rifle, was superior to the Prussian needle gun. In fact Prussia won despite the fact that Krupps were inferior to Skoda in 1866 and to Schneider-Creusot in 1870. Prussia had not even more railways than France: the difference was that she knew how to use them.

That was the core of the matter. Prussia's triumph was a triumph of will, not of material superiority, a triumph of planning, of forethought, of conscious direction. The Prussian generals were commonplace enough. Not only Bismarck, but Prince Frederick Charles, himself a distinguished general, spoke contemptuously of them. What was not commonplace was the Prussian General Staff, applying business methods to the conduct of an army. As always, 'war was the national industry of Prussia', and the Prussian staff officers brought to war accuracy, precision, system. The basis of their success was the railway time-table. And behind that lay the sandy wastes of eastern Germany which had compelled their owners for long centuries to a ruthless relentless efficiency. But there was something more. Not all the planning of the general staff could have brought victory without the endurance of the Prussian soldier. He could march further, live on harder rations, stand heavier casualties than the soldiers of Austria or of France. Yet he was not, like the Austrian or French soldier, a long-term conscript, hardened by long years of military discipline. He was a citizen, recalled from civil life or soon to enter it. Therefore, added to his hardness, he possessed initiative, a civilian readiness to act for himself but in conformity to a military purpose. Against the well-drilled obedience of regular armies or even the patriotic enthusiasm of national levies, the Prussians brought the irresistible spirit of Crusaders. They were Ironsides like the men of Cromwell, inspired by belief in a cause. But in what cause? In nothing higher than the cause of conquest. German nationalists had long regarded the weakness of Germany as evidence of their lack of freedom; therefore, if Germany was powerful, Germans would automatically be free. Tamed by the Lutheran tradition, itself the product of the failures of the sixteenth century, and dispirited by the political failures of the nineteenth century, the Germans sought freedom in the conquest of others.

Convinced that they were fighting in a sacred cause, the Germans felt morally superior to their opponents as, centuries before, the Teutonic Knights had felt superior to the heathen of the Baltic, and introduced into the warfare of civilized nations the ruthless barbarity which they had inherited from their eastern borders. For long enough, and particularly since the time of the Enlightenment, the western world had seen only the western face of Germany – the Germany of literature and music, the Germany of liberalism and scholarship, the Germany of peaceful industry. In 1870 Germany first turned to the west her eastern face, the face which she wore towards the Slavs, the face of the intolerant exterminator and overlord. In England, and even in France, men of liberal mind refused to believe the record of German brutality or, at the most, expected the Germans to improve when they had had more experience of the ways of conquest. The Germans, it was argued, were merely conquering France, as seventy years before Napoleon had conquered Germany. But Napoleon's armies marched under the banner of an idea, the German army under none. Prussia for the sake of Prussia; Germany for the sake of Germany; ultimately, world power for the sake of world power: such was the creed of the new Crusaders, a creed which could never win converts. The war of 1870 made Germany the strongest power in Europe, dominant as Spain had been in the sixteenth century and as France had been first under Louis XIV and then under Napoleon. Each of her predecessors had stood for something: Spain for the Counter-Reformation, Monarchist France for aristocratic civilization, Napoleonic France for equality and civil liberty. Germany stood for nothing, except German power. The organizing capacity, the selfless devotion, the critical intelligence, the scientific curiosity, which in western Europe were liberating men from the tyranny of others and, still more, from the tyranny of nature, were in Germany employed to liberate the German state from the control either of its neighbours or of its subjects. The highest faculties of the mind, and these the Germans possessed, were put to the service of a mindless cause.

7

BISMARCKIAN GERMANY: THE ASCENDANCY OF PRUSSIA, 1871–90

The Reich which Bismarck established in 1871 is often spoken of as a compromise. But this is the wrong term. Compromise implies a mutual acceptance of the claims of opponents, an agreement to give way in the last resort. British history has been made by a series of true compromises. The landed classes compromised with the merchants at the beginning of the eighteenth century; this coalition compromised with the industrial capitalists in the time of Peel; and Peel's coalition has compromised with the industrial workers in our own day. Since the days of Cromwell there has never been in England a class or a party determined to force through its extreme claims, whatever the cost; the terrible exception was in the early months of 1914. No such compromise took place in Germany. The Bismarckian Reich was a dictatorship imposed on the conflicting forces, not an agreement between them. The parties did not compromise; they were manipulated by Bismarck – pushed down when they threatened to become strong, helped up when they appeared weak. Bismarck stood at the centre of a multiple seesaw, tilting it now this way, now that in order to keep his artificial creation in some sort of equilibrium; but the inevitable result was to give Germany ever more violent and uncontrollable oscillations. Bismarck's only asset was success. He had defeated liberalism; therefore the Junkers accepted him despite the national Germany he had forced on them. He had united Germany; therefore the middle classes accepted him despite the defeat of liberalism. But success is a wasting asset. It was effective in 1866 and in 1871; the memory of it was effective for the last time in 1887. In the long run Bismarck's system could not run on the reputation of the successes he had achieved twenty years before. A new justification had to be found – or else new successes had to be won against foreign powers. Bismarck's Reich was designed to give Germany stability and peace; but ultimately it doomed Germany to upheaval and war. Bismarck possessed political genius of the highest order; and he used that genius to prevent in Germany the liberal revolution which had transformed England in the seventeenth century and France in 1789. As a result nothing was solved. The disease was forced inward until it poisoned the body of Germany incurably, and the body of all Europe as well.

The Imperial constitution of 1871 was a hotch-potch, hastily put together by Bismarck to serve his own ends. Except for the change of name it was little more than an enlargement of the constitution of the North German Federation of 1867. Show-piece of the constitution was the Reichstag, elected by universal suffrage, the incorporation of German radical demands. The Reichstag could hold debates and could pass (though not initiate) laws; its consent was necessary to the expenditure of money. But it possessed no powers. The constitution laid down that the Imperial Chancellor was 'responsible', but it did not say to whom – certainly not to the Reichstag. A majority in the Reichstag could do nothing against the Chancellor: if they voted against him, he did not resign, but dissolved the Reichstag. The Reichstag could certainly reject laws proposed by the Chancellor, but these laws contained reforms which the majority desired: their complaint was not against laws, but against a failure to legislate. The financial control was illusory. The revenue of the Reich was entirely derived from customs and excise, dues permanently fixed; and whenever these were changed the discussion usually turned on the economic policy involved, not on the way in which these dues would be spent. If the balance sheet of the Reich

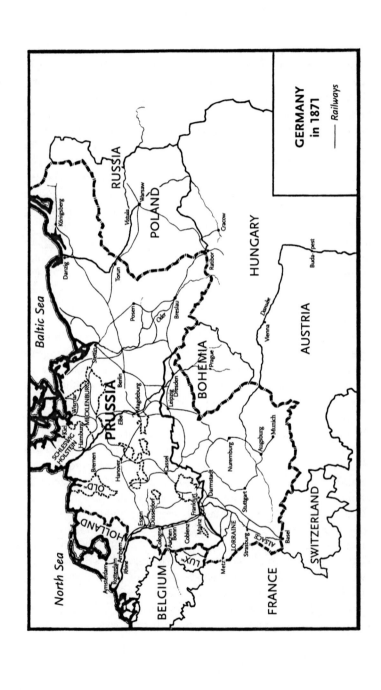

GERMANY
in 1871

——— Railways

showed a deficit, the Reichstag was not asked to vote taxes to make up the balance: the states had to provide 'matricular contributions' from their internal revenue, deficiency grants levied in proportion to the population of each state. When later the expenditure of the Reich increased, these matricular contributions became a regular annual item. The Reichstag which approved the expenditure did not have to provide the money; and the states which provided the money had no control over its expenditure. In any case much of the expenditure of the Reich – the Civil List, the administration, the diplomatic service – was included in the constitution and did not come up for annual review. Bismarck attempted to make the army grant permanent also, but in this he failed and had to be content with a grant for seven years at a time. Hence the crises which occurred at septennial intervals – in 1879, 1886, and 1893, when it was necessary to whip up enough enthusiasm to carry the army grant for a further seven years. Bismarck did not provide for a navy. Hence, in the twentieth century, another series of crises had to be manufactured, first to establish a permanent naval grant, and then to increase it.

Bismarck's constitution was supposed to be federal, but its federalism was fraudulent, window dressing to make the dictatorship of Prussia more respectable. The few states which had been allowed to survive in 1866 were humble Prussian dependencies. The States south of the Main, Bavaria in particular, put on a brave appearance of independence and bargained obstinately before they accepted the Reich in 1871. But they too were unreal: they had owed their existence solely to the protection of Austria and of France, and this protection had ceased. Their military effort of 1866 had been contemptible, and Bismarck, if he wished, could have ordered them out of existence. Their survival suited Bismarck's purpose. Their abolition would have put Bismarck too much in the hands of the radical nationalists and would have left the King of Prussia in undesired isolation. The sham existence of these kings and princes helped to cloak the very real existence of the Prussian monarchy and of Prussian military power. Bismarck played off the states against the Reichstag, as in his system of taxation; and the kings and princes kept their titles in return for acting as Prussia's agents in the government of Germany, much as they had acted as the agents of Napoleon at the beginning of the century. It made things much easier for Bismarck, for example, that in Bavaria, the most Roman Catholic state, the struggle against the Roman Catholic Church was carried on at his request by the Bavarian government; it would have been a nuisance to have to import Prussian officials for the purpose. In return the Bavarian government got certain empty rights, interesting to constitutional lawyers, such as a separate Bavarian army in peace-time; but the states were no more consulted or even informed by the Imperial German government than they had been by the Imperial French government in the time of Napoleon. The Federal Council, or Bundesrat, composed of representatives of the states, was supposed to act both as the German government and as the upper house of the legislature; and a great parade was made of the fact that Prussia only possessed a minority of members. But Prussia had seventeen and fourteen were enough to bar any constitutional change – which was all that mattered. The Federal Council, in fact, counted for even less than the old Federal Diet which had dragged out fifty years of existence at Frankfurt. Few Germans ever knew of its existence, and it was never consulted on any important question. Thus, during the crisis of July 1914, which preceded the First World War, the Federal Council, which was supposed to decide the policy of Germany, met only to pass routine orders forbidding the export of foodstuffs, and the state governments were left to learn the course of events from the gossip which their representatives could pick up in Berlin. It would be wrong to conclude from this that Germany was a completely unified state. What existed was not state patriotism but particularism, a feeling of local pride and loyalty which was especially strong in the former Free Cities. The citizen of Nuremberg still thought of himself as a citizen of Nuremberg, not as a Bavarian; and for that matter many Rhinelanders still thought of themselves as Rhinelanders, not as Prussians. As a result, the political energies of the best Germans went into local government and made of it a model to all the world. But this admirable development had no relevance to imperial affairs, or to the story of Germany as a great power.

The government of Germany, in fact, was a dictatorship in the hands of the King of Prussia. He delegated his powers to two agencies: military matters to the general staff, civil matters to the Imperial Chancellor, and the two dealt with each other as independent, often hostile, authorities. The chief of the general staff was, in his sphere, absolute.

He made his military plans and conducted his own foreign policy without consulting the Chancellor; and on each septennial interval issued orders to the Chancellor and the Reichstag as to his military needs. In Bismarck's time, the soldiers were kept in their place not by any constitutional provision, but through Bismarck's personal influence with William I; after Bismarck's time the situation was reversed and the Chancellor was kept in his place by the influence of the soldiers. On the Chancellor rested the conduct of all German affairs other than the army. Bismarck had at first assumed that these affairs would mean only foreign policy; and he designed the Chancellorship as a branch of the Prussian Foreign Office, throwing in the assistance of a few officials to manage the Zollverein and the Post Office. But Imperial Germany soon transcended this conception of a league of princes. The creation of a common German law made necessary something like a Minister of Justice; financial problems made necessary a Minister of Finance, and economic problems a Minister of Commerce; soon Bismarck himself embarked on a German social policy; later the growth of a navy demanded a Secretary for the Navy, and later still there was needed a Secretary for the Colonies. As a result, Bismarck in 1879 promoted a law of Substitutes, allowing the Chancellor to appoint secretaries to do his work for him. These secretaries were not a government, but like everything else in the system, substitutes, *ersatz*: they were individual agents of the Chancellor, not consulting each other, often indeed pursuing different policies and openly hostile to each other. Some of them attended the Prussian cabinet as ministers without portfolio: but they were there rather to receive the orders of the Prussian government than to discuss German policy. So clear was this subordination that the Secretaries of State usually acted as Prussia's representatives at the Federal Council. Later, after Bismarck's time, some of the secretaries were men of ability or of strong personality and imposed themselves on a weak or ignorant Chancellor; so Marschall (Secretary of State, i.e. the substitute for foreign affairs, from 1890 to 1897) and Kiderlen (Secretary of State from 1909 to 1912) each counted as individuals. The most famous of all, Tirpitz, Secretary of the Navy from 1897 to 1916, was forced on the Chancellor by William II and went on his way as independently as the chief of the general staff. But these personal variants had no constitutional significance; they were merely the outcome of intrigues in a Byzantine court. In theory, and usually in fact, the civil government of Germany remained in the hands of the Chancellor alone.

Technically, and in practice, the Chancellor was the agent of the King of Prussia, now by hereditary right also German Emperor. The Reichstag could do nothing to turn the Chancellor out of office if the Emperor wished to keep him in; it could do nothing to keep him in (though such a constructive wish never occurred to it) if the Emperor wished to turn him out. The legislative system of Germany was outwardly democratic; the government of Germany was as autocratic as the government of Tsarist Russia, in flagrant contrast not only to the government of the countries of western Europe and of Hungary, but even of Austria, where, until the beginning of the twentieth century, the Prime Minister was supported or overthrown by a parliamentary majority. The fate of Germany was determined by the King-Emperor's absolute will, influenced in Bismarck's time by good advice, influenced after his time by bad advice or by none at all. The King-Emperor straddled between Prussia and Germany: kept Germany under Prussian control and, at the same time, tried to persuade the Junkers not to be too openly contemptuous of the German middle classes. This straddling was made easier by the fact that the Imperial Chancellor was usually Prime Minister of Prussia (as well as being always Prussian Foreign Minister), a union useful though not essential. As the King-Emperor combined two functions, the system could have worked with a separate adviser for each; and in fact Bismarck gave up the Premiership of Prussia to Roon for a few years, and Caprivi also gave it up in 1892. This arrangement was harmless when the two men were in close sympathy as were Roon and Bismarck; but the King-Emperor could not afford a quarrel between the two sides of his own personality, and after the disputes of Caprivi's time, the experiment was never repeated. The Prussian parliament, with its defined constitutional position, had rather more control over the Prussian Prime Minister than the Reichstag had over the Chancellor – of course only in internal affairs; but this control had very strict limits. As Bismarck's early days in power had shown, the Prussian parliament could not force a Prime Minister out of office or even limit expenditure on any essential matter. It could criticize; and its criticism carried more weight, being the criticism of loyal Junkers, not of liberal lawyers. But the King-Emperor, and therefore the Chancellor, was not the mere agent of the Junkers' will. The essence of Bismarck's system was that he was saving the Junkers despite themselves. Bismarck recognized that the Junkers could survive only by putting themselves at the head of national Germany; and he put them there despite the Junker distaste, to call it no more, for nationalist enthusiasm. Most of the Junkers hated the German idea and hankered for the gentlemanly days of the Holy Alliance. They were jealous of Bismarck – a landowner like themselves who had become a European statesman and a prince – and they resisted many of his administrative concessions to the liberal classes. Hence the period of Bismarck saw a paradoxical system of government in which the long-term interests of the Junkers were served against the wishes of the Junkers themselves. In fact, just as Bismarck gave national Germany the unity which it lacked the confidence to achieve for itself, so he tried to give the Junkers the vision and commonsense which they could not find in their own brains.

The most obvious side of the Bismarckian system was thus a balance between the landowners of eastern Germany and the liberal middle classes: military power in the hands of the Junkers, economic power in the hands of the capitalists, the power of the state in the hands of Bismarck. For each the bargain implied certain conditions. The Prussian nobles retained their social superiority and the monopoly of the army commissions, on the condition of acquiescing in liberal reforms and nationalist clap-trap. The liberals obtained all the classical liberal demands – modern administration, freedom of enterprise, secular education – on condition that they did not insist on office, still less power, in the state. Bismarck rode above both sides on the condition of success: his unrivalled ability foresaw and anticipated every danger. But these two classes were a minority in Germany, a minority not only in numbers, but – what was more important – in opinion. They were the classes of the establishment, but that establishment was rejected by much of Germany. Both classes were 'Little German', hence their readiness to accept Bismarck's bargain. The Junkers disliked any German nationalism and put up with Little Germany as its least offensive form: it reduced to a minimum the sacrifice of Prussian resources for a non-Prussian cause. The middle-class National Liberals were the same sensible moderate nationalists who had founded the Little German movement in 1848, quite content with less than the whole, if they could have a flourishing industrial system and security for their property. Over against them stood all the classes and opinions which had been Greater German from the beginning and which still rejected both the incompleteness and the Prussian inspiration of Bismarck's work. These classes were themselves disunited and indeed hostile; this alone enabled Bismarck to succeed.

The forces which opposed Bismarck had first shown themselves in the Greater German coalition at Frankfurt in 1848, the coalition of romantic conservatives who looked back to the Holy Roman Empire and of extreme radicals who would accept no less a Germany than the whole. In 1848 the two extremes united on a Greater German programme of a Habsburg Emperor and universal suffrage; and they were not won over by Bismarck's programme of a substitute Reich, a Hohenzollern Emperor, and an impotent Reichstag. In Bismarck's time both took on new forms. The conservatives, severed from the Habsburgs, rallied openly round their religion and became the Centre, the party of Roman Catholics; the radicals, seeking mass support, became Social Democrats, followers of Karl Marx. The Centre objected to the rule of Protestant Junkers and secularist liberals, the Social Democrats to the rule of landowners and industrialists. The Centre objected to the Junker treatment of Catholic Poles, the Social Democrats to the Junker exploitation of Polish peasants. The Centre repudiated the materialist values, the Social Democrats resisted the exploitation, of the factory owners. Both rejected Bismarck's partition, the frontier erected between Germany and Austria in 1866: the Centre would not be severed from their fellow Roman Catholics, the Social Democrats from their fellow workers. Neither party was opposed in principle to the strong authority of a central state: the Social Democrats believed theoretically in dictatorship for themselves, and Roman Catholics have never opposed absolute power, so long as it is safely in Roman Catholic hands. But Greater Germans, Roman Catholics and Radicals alike, had been the defeated party in the struggle of the 'sixties. In the struggle for power they had lost. Therefore both came out as opponents of the central power, the Centre as the defenders of federalism, the Social Democrats as defenders of individual liberty. They could not hope to capture the German Reich; but they might hope to control municipalities or even separate states. Thus, their rejection on Greater German grounds of Bismarck's Reich, when translated into practice, became particularism; and Bismarck's struggle against the Greater German policy of limitless expansion was expressed in the attempt to enforce the authority of the Reich on recalcitrant classes and creeds. This seems an absurd conclusion, but it was an inevitable consequence of Bismarck's initial paradox of carrying through a partial unification of Germany in order to make a complete unification of Germany impossible. The groups of the Bismarckian coalition arrogated to themselves the national label, yet each was in fact a sectional party: the National Conservatives served the interests of the Prussian landowners, the National Liberals the interests of the great industrialists. The Centre, on the other hand, united German Roman Catholics without consideration of class, the Social Democrats united German workers without consideration of state or province. The parties against whom Bismarck evoked national feeling were in reality more national than the parties which supported Bismarck. This contradiction conditioned not only the politics of Bismarck, but determined the development of the Reich until the present day. Bismarck's line of policy was not, of course, clear cut from the beginning. In fact many of his projects were abandoned or modified within the first decade. He had formed his ideas in the age of Metternich and the Holy Alliance; and he achieved his greatest successes in a Germany that was still two-thirds agricultural and rural. He imagined in 1871 that the period of upheaval in Germany was over and that, after the adjustments he had made, Germany would enter a new period of social and economic stability. Only at the end of the 'seventies did he appreciate that his political changes, far from ending the German revolution, had released forces almost unmanageable; and in 1879 he was driven to begin a new, and ultimately unsuccessful, process of balance and manoeuvre. Thus, the classical Bismarckian system only lasted eight years, from 1871 to 1879; after that came a series of ever more daring and impossible expedients until the system crashed in 1890.

The Bismarckian order of 1871 had a simple pattern: Junker Prussia and middle-class Germany, the coalition which sprang from the victories of 1866. Bismarck did not make much effort to reconcile the Junkers to National Germany: like most aristocratic statesmen of ability, he despised his fellow nobles, and he did not put himself out to make them realize that everything he had done was for their good. All his effort, in these first years, went into reconciling the liberals to the continuance of Junker rule. Between 1867 and 1879 the German liberals achieved every liberal demand except power; and in Germany the demand for power had never bulked large in the liberal programme. Never have liberal reforms been crowded into so short a period: the English 'age of reform' (say, from 1820 to 1870) was in comparison hesitant and lethargic. The speed was even more breakneck, in that most of the greatest reforms were carried through at once – in 1867 for northern Germany, in 1871 south of the Main, a more rapid change than even France experienced during the great revolution. Germany was given at a stroke uniform legal procedure, uniform coinage, uniformity of administration; all restrictions on freedom of enterprise and freedom of movement were removed, limited companies and trade combinations allowed. It is not surprising that in face of such a revolution the liberals did not challenge Bismarck's possession of power: he was carrying out their programme far more rapidly than they could ever execute it themselves.

The policy of appeasing the liberals brought Bismarck into conflict with the Roman Catholics, the conflict so ambitiously named 'the conflict of civilizations' (*Kulturkampf*). The conflict began with the attempt to break the clerical control of education, but in time developed into a general attack on the independence of the Roman Catholic Church – a renewal, in fact, of the indecisive dispute between the Church and the Prussian state which had been broken off in 1840. Bismarck always held that the best foundation for an alliance was to have a common enemy; and he pushed the conflict with the Roman Catholics to extremes largely in order to give the liberals a target for their hostility. The conflict served too the needs of his foreign policy. It won the sympathy of the Tsarist government, itself in conflict with the Roman Catholic Poles; of national Italy, in fierce dispute with the Pope; of the liberal anti-clericalist government in Austria; and even of the French radicals and English Protestants, so that the last public act of Earl (Lord John) Russell was to hail Bismarck as a fellow soldier of liberty. It was a stroke against the aristocratic clericals of the Habsburg court and against the monarchist clericals of France – the two parties who still longed to reverse the verdicts of 1866 and 1870. But most of all, it was a conflict against the enemies of Prussia-Germany inside the Reich – against the traditionalists of western Germany who were at once particularist and Greater German. Though religious in form, the conflict was, in essence, political: Hanoverian Protestants who opposed Prussian rule supported the Roman Catholics; Roman Catholic capitalists on the Rhine or in Bavaria supported Bismarck. The conflict of civilizations brought into being a Roman Catholic political party – the Centre – a party uniting men of all classes in defence of the Church. The Centre was from the first without rigid political principles: it would support any political line and cooperate with any political party so long as the rights of the Roman Catholic Church were secured. It was prepared to be German or anti-German, liberal or anti-liberal, free trade or protectionist, pacific or bellicose; a party of expediency as unscrupulous as Bismarck himself. The Centre had no parallel in any other European country; it was born of the unique religious balance of the sixteenth century which had left Germany strongly, but not predominantly, Roman Catholic. If the Reformation had succeeded, the few remaining Roman Catholics would, in the nineteenth century, have secured religious equality; if the Reformation had failed, the Roman Catholics would have had to take responsibility for Germany. As it was, the Roman Catholic Centre could never be strong enough to govern Germany, but was always strong enough to hamper its government by anyone else.

The conflict with the Roman Catholics, instead of consolidating Bismarck's position of balance, threatened to overthrow it and to force him entirely into the hands of the liberals. The Junkers, despite their Protestantism, could not stomach liberal anti-clericalism and sympathized, absurdly enough, with the particularism of the Centre. Bismarck had to treat the National Liberals as though they were the official government party, and in 1877 invited Bennigsen, the National Liberal leader in the Reichstag, to become a Prussian minister. The liberals thought that their hour had come and that, just as they had achieved without effort the programme of liberal reform, so now they were without a struggle actually to achieve power. They expected Bismarck to abdicate in their favour and demanded that the Prussian ministry should be transformed into a parliamentary government, with the liberals in a majority. This would have ruined Bismarck's system, for it would have been the prelude to an open conflict with the Junkers. The alternative was to compromise with the Junkers and with the Centre, neither of whom disputed the authoritarianism of Bismarck's rule, but only a particular application of it. In any case economic developments were forcing Bismarck away from the liberals. Until the eighteen-seventies the growth of population kept German (like English) agriculture prosperous despite Free Trade. Then the railways of Russia and of the American continent made possible the ruinous competition of cheap grain. Economic forces, if left unchecked, would destroy German, as they destroyed English, agriculture, and would transform Germany, as they transformed England, into a purely industrial country. This Bismarck would not allow: a flourishing agriculture was essential to self-sufficiency in war, and, a more profound reason, a powerful rural community was, he believed, essential for the preservation of the conservative values to which Bismarck just as much as any other Junker was devoted. Agricultural Protection compelled a breach with the academic middle-class liberals.

But it was not only to agricultural protection that Bismarck was converted in 1879. Before 1871 the industrialization of Germany had been proceeding at a rate which seemed rapid to contemporaries, but which was nothing much above the English average. The spiritual exhilaration of unification; the diversion of middle-class talent from politics; and the more material stimulation of the French indemnity produced an industrial expansion unparalleled in history. German industry was 'forced' as vegetables and rhubarb are forced: exposed for centuries to the frost of disunity and absolutist rule, it was brought suddenly into the hothouse of the new Reich and shot up in luxuriant unnatural growth. Germany had few natural claims to be a great industrial country. Her resources of raw materials (except potash) were small, her iron ore of inferior quality, and her true coal so limited that she had to supplement it from the beginning with 'brown coal' or lignite – a substitute which an English miner would refuse to handle. Many of her industrial centres lay far from the sea, and the few great rivers were no real substitute for the sea-borne traffic which contributed so much to British prosperity. The roots of Germany's industrial revolution were psychological, not material – a sudden inspiration of confidence and of unlimited possibilities, in fact a typical 'bubble' period like the period of speculation in England which preceded the crises of 1826 and 1847. Germany had a similar crash in 1873, a crash which completed the ruin of old-fashioned liberalism both in Germany and in German Austria.

The financial crash of 1873 was a normal event of the age of capitalism; not normal was its sequel, a sequel which began the destruction of free capitalism in Europe. In England when the speculative bubble burst, those who had blown it took the consequences – speculative industries were closed down, speculators were ruined, and more sensible forms of industrial activity found. But the German industrialists had not the long tradition of self-help which made British capitalists fend for themselves until long into the twentieth century. Besides, they had made an implicit bargain with Bismarck: they had renounced political power in return for economic wealth, and now they expected Bismarck to keep his bargain. Bismarck distrusted and feared industrial development which made the balance of his system increasingly unworkable. But if he had refused to give industry protection, the result would not have been the arrest of industrialization. As had happened in England, each crisis would have made industry raise its standards and would have bound Germany more deeply to the world market. Without protection, Germany would have had a less grandiose production of iron and steel, would have imported more, and would have concentrated instead on the more profitable finishing industries. She would have had a higher standard of life, a better and more fully developed system of transport, and every step in her economic advance would have promoted the prosperity and peacefulness both of Germany and of other countries. In fact Germany would have been so deeply bound to the world market as to be incapable of war. This was the vital consideration which made Bismarck's conversion to Protection inevitable. Germany must produce both the raw materials of war and the weapons of war herself. Therefore her heavy industries, far from being restrained or cut down by the working of economic forces, must be speeded up and driven on. The price was paid by the mass of German people who did not reap the full benefit of the great industrial advance; but as not even Protection could prevent some benefit to the mass of consumers this was not realized for many years – and then the tariffs were condemned as being too low. With each dose of Protection

German industry became ever more top-heavy and the need for new outlets ever more pressing. In Bismarck's time few thought of finding these outlets by war. The method of the 'eighties was economic conflict; fast on the heels of the tariff came the Kartells, the great trade associations which fixed prices high for the home market, artificially low for export – and which went on from price-fixing to the regulation of production.

The last of the old duties, inherited from the early days of the Zollverein, ended in 1877; new duties were imposed in 1879. Thus, except for two years, Germany missed the era of Free Trade which gave to England her three most prosperous generations, and passed virtually without a break from the age of Colbert to the age of Dr Schacht. Judged by the standards of a later generation, the duties of 1879 were so moderate as to be almost imperceptible – just as German brutality in the war of 1870 was gentle and humane in comparison with their conduct in later wars. But they were the decisive step which led logically and inevitably to autarchy and the 'New Order', to the doctrine of 'guns before butter', and which made the survival of Germany conditional on the conquest of Europe. The tariff of 1879 was not created to protect new struggling industries from established British competition – the colonial tariff pattern. Nor was it invoked, as in France, to save leisurely old-fashioned industries from the challenge of the up-to-date. German industry was the most modern and best established in Europe. The tariffs gave protection in the way that bombing aeroplanes give defence. They were a weapon of war: to destroy competitors by dumping and, ultimately, to enroll consumers by compulsion. Thus was completed the severance of Germany from the western world: political breach by Bismarck's victory over the Prussian constitution in 1866; international breach by the war of 1870; economic breach by the tariff of 1879. As in other spheres, Bismarck tried – not without success – to resist the consequences of his own policy and certainly obscured these consequences during his period of rule; but in the long run they were inescapable. Protection was a further step towards the Greater Germany which it was Bismarck's life-work to resist.

The new economic policy changed both the spirit and the structure of the Bismarckian balance. The balance of the eighteen-seventies had been a balance of ideas – Junker conservatism and middle-class liberalism. The Junkers disliked national Germany; the National Liberals disliked Prussia. Both therefore accepted Bismarck as a *pis aller*: the Junkers preferred him to a government of liberals, and the liberals preferred him to an out-and-out Junker. But neither party dropped its dislike of the other. The balance of the eighteen-eighties became a balance of interests – Junker agrarianism and capitalist industrialism. Until 1879 the conservatives were a party of great landowners, and the prosperous middle peasants were as liberal as the prosperous middle classes of the towns – indeed, the most resolute opponents of Bismarck in the Prussian parliament between 1862 and 1866 came from the rural constituencies of East Prussia. After 1879 the conservatives became agrarians pure and simple, and both rural liberalism and true conservatism vanished. Henceforth the 'national' cause was essential for Junker prosperity. The Germans had to pay more for their bread in order to preserve the allegedly best element in German society and to keep up the supply of officers for the German army; and the Junkers in return had to take seriously their national role. At heart they still hated national Germany, but their prejudices had to be rigorously concealed, and, with infinite distaste, they began to wear the appearance of German enthusiasts. In 1879 Bismarck regarded agrarian protection as primary, and industrial protection as part of the regrettable price to be paid for it. But once the two causes were knit together the Prussian landowners were committed to every further step which was necessary to advance German industry – at first steps to higher tariffs, but ultimately steps to the conquest of Europe. Thus the Junkers, enemies of Greater Germany, could only preserve their anomalous social position and the prosperity of their over-capitalized estates by becoming the agents of a Greater German programme of unlimited expansion.

Equally profound was the effect of Protection on the National Liberals. The liberals of the 'seventies were still a party of principle. They had given up the struggle to achieve a strictly constitutional state, but they worked with Bismarck in order to infuse a liberal spirit into the laws and administration of the Reich. Their Cobdenite training made them oppose Protection in general, and the Imperial constitution made opposition imperative, for tariffs, permanently imposed, would give the Reich a steady and automatically increasing income and so would place it beyond all parliamentary control. These liberals would go with

Bismarck no longer. But they refused to go over to the irreconcilables of 1866, the Progressives led by Richter, who kept up a ceaseless flow of destructive impotent criticism. The majority of liberals washed their hands of public affairs and withdrew into a liberalism of the spirit, as Luther had done three hundred years before. These were the men who in the following fifty years convinced so many foreign observers that Germany was liberal 'at heart'. Their liberalism was indeed buried deep in their hearts: with principles of the deepest liberal purity, none ever raised his voice against the course of German policy, and all silently acquiesced in its consequences. In the Reichstag there was still a National Liberal remnant, but it retained little of liberalism beyond the name; it was a straight interest-group, promoting tariffs and extolling power. Thus the liberal surrender which had taken place in Prussia in 1866 was completed in Germany in 1879. Germany's liberal period had lasted eight years.

The new economic policy changed also the character of the Centre. Bismarck had no reason to continue the conflict with the Roman Catholic Church and every reason to bring it to an end. He had broken with the liberals and needed Junker conservative support in Germany as well as in Prussia. The conflict had outlived too its international purpose. In France the republic, anti-clerical and pacific, was firmly established, the clerical-monarchist policy of revenge defeated. In Austria the fall of the liberal government in 1879 had not prevented the making of the Austro-German alliance. The aristocratic clericals of the Habsburg monarchy, Bismarck's former enemies, had at last come to realize that alliance with Bismarck was their best defence against German radicalism inside Austria and the strongest security for Austria-Hungary's international position; it would make things easier for them to end the attack on the Roman Catholic Church in Germany. The Centre on their side were ready to compromise. They had resisted the Reich so long as it had seemed to be based on liberal principle, but themselves an interest-group (though the interest was spiritual) they were quite at home in the new era of agrarian and capitalist bargaining. Where the others bargained for tariffs, they bargained for Roman Catholic schools; and in any case they owed their votes to the very classes who benefited by protection – Roman Catholic peasants and Roman Catholic industrialists who desired to reconcile their economic and spiritual needs. The Centre had no fixed political principles: they had been Greater German and federalist in the interest of the Roman Catholic Church; they became Little Germans, protectionist, and ultimately advocates of German conquest for the same reason. Each side carried its point: Bismarck dropped the anti-Catholic laws; the Centre accepted Bismarck's Reich and instead of his enemy became his critic. If Bismarck had allowed it – and had paid a sufficient price in the shape of more privileges for the Roman Catholic Church – it would have become his supporter. Only his old-fashioned Protestant prejudices stood in his way. Cynical and realist as he was, he could not rival the freedom from the principles and scruples of this world which is given by devotion to a supernatural cause. With all other parties he could safely apply his maxim, *a corsaire corsaire et demi*; with the Centre he knew that it would be applied to him. Thus throughout the 'eighties Bismarck pursued a course of policy satisfactory to the Centre and yet treated them as a party of opposition. And the Centre made the best of both worlds: they obtained from Bismarck concessions spiritual and economic, and yet continued to win votes as the defenders of democracy and the enemies of militarism. In fact, so long as there was a secure conservative-National Liberal majority for Bismarck in the Reichstag, it paid the Centre better to harass Bismarck in co-operation with the Progressives. If ever the Centre held the balance in the Reichstag, they would have to decide between authoritarianism and democracy; but until the critical moment they deferred their decision.

The new Bismarckian balance needed to be sustained by a new fighting cry, if there was not to be a tariff auction every year. The Social Democrats were the predestined whipping-boy to take the place of the Centre. Probably Bismarck genuinely believed in the turnip-ghost which he conjured up. He was, after all, a pupil of Metternich and, like Metternich, committed to the hopeless defence of a moribund order. The liberal peril had implied for Metternich all the social and national tensions within the Habsburg empire which it was impossible for him to overcome; and so the socialist peril meant for Bismarck all the mounting tensions which made the permanence of his Reich impossible. The Social Democrats had sprung from a coalition of the followers of Marx and of Lassalle in 1875, and they talked in Marxist revolutionary terms. In fact their rejection of the Reich was neither

Marxist nor revolutionary: it was democratic and particularist, the reluctance of the artisans of Baden and other south German states to be forced into an authoritarian industrial Reich. Marx had no patience with this attitude and attacked his south German followers, Bebel and Liebknecht, the leaders of the Marxists inside Germany, for their opposition to the war of 1870; in his view the Social Democrats should welcome any concentration of power which broke down the trad-itional defences of the old order. On the other hand, Marx certainly intended his followers to oppose Bismarck and the new Reich until it actually passed into their hands. Lassalle, who died in 1864, had gone a stage further. Accepting the Marxist view of the class struggle between capitalists and workers, he proposed an alliance between Bismarck and the working-class movement, an alliance to defeat political liberalism and economic *laissez-faire*. Ostensibly Lassalle's view was rejected by the combined Social Democratic party after 1875; in fact its victory was only deferred. Thus Marx's revolutionary authoritarianism was strong enough to remove the democratic outlook of his followers, but it was itself threatened by a social opportunism inherited from Lassalle. Lack-ing the firm basis of democratic principle, the Social Democrats were ultimately, like the Centre, a party with whom a bargain could be struck.

There was no bargain in Bismarck's time. As in his dealings with the Centre, Bismarck treated the Social Democrats in a curiously old-fashioned, high-principled way. Men are bound to their generation, and Bismarck, despite his Realpolitik, had much more resemblance to Gladstone than to Hitler or even to the Social Democratic and Centre tacticians of the nineteen-twenties. Boasting of his freedom from prin-ciple, he yet took seriously both his own principles and those of his opponents. He took the Marxist challenge to society at its face value and believed that there was no political weapon against it but persecu-tion. Hence the anti-Socialist laws enacted in 1878 and renewed until 1890: the Social Democratic party was made illegal and its press for-bidden. Yet this persecution bore the unmistakable stamp of the liberal era: Social Democrats were still allowed to be candidates at elections and to sit in the Reichstag; the number of members of the party increased steadily; and in all about 1,500 persons were imprisoned (an average of a little over a hundred a year). The anti-Socialist laws were little less futile than the Karlsbad decrees, and their only practical effect was to prolong the illusion of the revolutionary character of the movement. Like the Karlsbad decrees, the anti-Socialist laws were primarily for political effect: the decrees to scare the German princes into subservience to Metternich, the laws to scare the electors into subservience to Bismarck.

Bismarck had a more positive method of combatting Socialism, the system of social insurance sometimes absurdly called Bismarckian Socialism. Between 1883 and 1889 Bismarck established compulsory insurance for workers against sickness, accident, incapacity, and old age, contributory schemes organized, but not subsidized, by the state. Liberty and Security, the two basic Rights of Man, are no doubt conflicting principles; and refusal of the one has often implied compensation in the other. Bismarck's method was peculiarly ingenious: he consoled the German workers for their absence of liberty partly by providing security at the expense of the employer, more by making them provide security for themselves out of their own pockets. Social security did not achieve its immediate aim; it did not arrest the growth of the Social Democratic party. In a more profound sense it was successful; it made the German workers value security more than liberty and look to the state rather than to their own resources for any improvement in their condition. The German workers came to feel that they too were receiving Protection and that the Reich was, in some sort, doing their work for them – the very feeling that had been earlier the ruin of German liberalism. If social security had been won by political struggle, it would have strengthened the confidence of the working-class movement to make political claims; as it was, the workers seemed to have received social security as the price of political subservience, and they drew the moral that greater subservience would earn a yet greater reward. In this sphere too Bismarck followed an old-fashioned line: he used social security as a weapon against the Social Democrats, his successors as a means of collaborating with them.

The general election of 1878, the prelude to Bismarck's change of system, was won on the cry of the Social Peril. It gave Bismarck a reliable majority with which to introduce Protection, repeal the anti-Catholic laws, and begin the campaign against the Social Democrats. In the general stir the first septennial renewal of the army grant passed almost unnoticed. But the Social Peril was an emergency weapon, too clumsy for everyday use. In the 'seventies Bismarck had controlled the Reichstag by the prospect of liberal measures; in the 'eighties he had to invoke the 'national' cause, most dangerous of political expedients. To every country there come rare moments of real crisis, when 'the country in danger' demands real national unity – so in France in 1792, so in England in 1940. But when the cry is raised in time of profound peace, it is (as in England in 1931) a confession of the failure of statesmanship. In the 'eighties Germany was not threatened from abroad but by internal disunion; and the foreign peril was the only common cause. In sounding this alarm Bismarck condemned and doomed his own work. He had fought three wars to give Germany security; what had been achieved if Germany was now more menaced than ever? The Germans could not be allowed to conclude that Bismarck's work was wrong; they had to conclude that it was inadequate. The Greater German programme was revived, and security sought in new wars and wider conquest. Bismarck fabricated perils in order to keep himself in power, just as he had artificially prolonged the constitutional peril in the 'sixties in order to keep the support of William I. His unrivalled political genius enabled him to avoid the dangers which he conjured up; but every step he took spelt doom for the modest conservative Reich which it had been his object to establish.

To maintain his hold over the German people, Bismarck had to present himself as the champion of the 'national' cause, but by no means of all that the 'national' cause had implied in 1848. The change of direction is revealed even by the appearance of Bismarck's Reich on the map. 'National' Germany included East and West Prussia and the Grand Duchy of Posen, which had never been within the German borders before, and the *Reichsland* of Alsace and Lorraine which had not been German for two hundred years. It excluded Bohemia, the German and Slovene provinces of Austria, and Trieste, which had been within the Reich from time immemorial. The crusade to promote the German cause in the Polish lands was pressed on in order to conceal the abandonment of the German cause in central Europe. The destruction of Polish nationalism became an essential condition of German unity. In the first days of the Reich the struggle with the Poles was cultural – persecution of the Roman Catholic Church, promotion of German schools, denial to Posen of the local autonomy established elsewhere throughout Germany in 1872. With the ending of the *Kulturkampf*, Bismarck had to find new methods, and in 1886 he embarked on economic war, buying out Polish landowners and seeking to promote German colonization, a campaign waged steadily but with no success for the following twenty years. The Poles organized counter-buying in self-defence and more than held their own. This battle over landownership was a dramatic struggle, but it served to conceal that the great landlords of eastern Germany were the real agents of the Polish advance, importing cheap Polish labour to work their great estates at an increased profit. This was overlooked, and German nationalism once more swallowed the Junkers as national heroes.

The struggle in the *Reichsland* was more directly political, a ceaseless campaign against separatism waged by a semi-military government. Both struggles served the same purpose. In eastern Germany it enabled liberal peasants to vote conservative and yet retain their national self-respect; in western Germany it estranged the liberals and radicals from France, and the reaction from Alsatian separatism developed in them an enthusiasm for the Prussian Reich. Alsace and Lorraine played an essential part in Bismarck's internal policy; and the need for them made his alleged regret at their annexation a meaningless hypocrisy. When he sought to win France for his international combinations he occasionally relaxed the rigours of military rule; but these diversions were rare. Anti-Polish policy never clashed with his international schemes. It was the basis of his friendship with Tsarist Russia, and, as the disputes between Germany and Russia on other issues increased, became in time the essential link between them. Liberal Germany, if it had ever existed, would have been friendly to France and hostile to Russia. Bismarck's 'national' policy enabled him to win the support even of liberals for a policy friendly to Russia and hostile to France – the logical consequence of the reactionary revolution which he had carried through.

The deeper 'national' cause lay in central and south-eastern Europe, but with this Bismarck would have nothing to do. Never since a German Reich existed were the Germans in the lands of the Danube so deserted by the Reich as in the days of Bismarck. Bismarck repudiated the Near East, and so all schemes for Mitteleuropa, in the revealing phrase – they were 'not worth the bones of a Pomeranian grenadier'. And indeed what concern had Pomerania with the Balkans? But for centuries south-eastern Europe had been judged worth the bones of Tyrolese and Styrians, still more the bones of Germans from the Banat or from Transylvania, just as good Germans as the Junker landowners of West Prussia and Posen, and often better. But Bismarck washed his hands of them all. Not merely did he refuse to promote German expansion in the Balkans. He welcomed the Habsburg compromise with Hungary in 1867, by which Hungary became a Magyar national state and the Germans of Hungary an abandoned minority as much subjected to Magyarization as Roumanians or Slovaks. In 1880 the city council of Budapest, hitherto the organ of German traders, at last gave up German and took to Magyar, a consequence of Bismarck's policy which would have shocked Bach or even Metternich. Even in the Austrian half of the Habsburg monarchy the Germans received from Bismarck neither protection nor encouragement. He made no attempt to prevent the setting up of the clerical Taaffe government in 1879, despite its concessions to the Czechs and Slovenes; and was always stonily severe towards the German nationalist agitation which sprang up in Austria during the eighteen-eighties. He was the irreconcilable enemy of Greater Germanism; but he had been the enemy of the Habsburg dynasty only so long as it refused to accept the Hohenzollerns as equals. Conservative aristocratic Austria was the guarantee against Greater Germanism; Magyar domination in Hungary and the recollection of the defeat of 1866 the guarantee against the renewal of dynastic ambitions in Germany.

Bismarck gave the Habsburg monarchy a generation of peace and security, but he had robbed it of all purpose. Lacking German support, it could no longer be the missionary of German enterprise in southeastern Europe; subordinate to Germany, it could not be the protector of the Slavs against German expansion. It could not balance indefinitely between the master and the subject peoples, yet Bismarck prevented it from taking sides. Bismarck never appreciated that the Slavs of southeastern Europe were an altogether different problem from the Poles of Polish Prussia. He thought that the problem could be eliminated in the same way – by partition between Austria-Hungary and Russia. But the Poles were estranged from Russia; the Slavs of Bohemia and the Balkans were not. Therefore nothing short of national liberation from the Magyars and Germans and the break-up of the great estates would reconcile them to the Habsburg monarchy. Bismarck made either reconciliation or subjection impossible. He could not allow an aggressively German policy which might have kept the Slavs in check, since any such policy would have made it impossible to exclude Austria from German affairs. But equally he could not allow the overthrow of the Magyar supremacy in Hungary, which alone curbed dynastic ambitions, still less could he risk an Austrian policy openly anti-German. He repeatedly advised the Austrian statesmen to assert the strength of the dynasty in the Balkans; yet he feared an assertion of strength which would enable the dynasty to escape from his control. In fact, he desired the political and national balance in Austria-Hungary to remain permanently crystallized in the position of 1867; as in Germany, he was committed to perpetuating the accidental compromise of a moment. His devices and counterdevices – support of the Magyars on the one side, refusal to promote the German cause on the other – were meant to preserve the Habsburg monarchy and so to bar the way to a Greater German Mitteleuropa; in the result they made any free development of the Habsburg monarchy impossible and so inevitably imposed upon Bismarck's Reich a Greater German programme. The conservative clerical dynasty was, for the Prussian Junkers, preferable to Greater Germany; but Greater Germany was preferable to a community of free Slav peoples. For the idea of freedom is catching; and once encircled by free peoples, even the Germans might not always remain immune. German supremacy or German withdrawal in the lands of the Danube valley was the greatest question in Germany's future; in this, as in all else, Bismarck's genius lay in postponing the answer.

The last and most casual of Bismarck's 'national' appeals was his apparent surrender to the agitation for colonies overseas. A strange contradiction: Bismarck abandoned the old-standing German colonies in south-eastern Europe, yet risked a quarrel with England for the sake of colonial territory with no German inhabitants and often with no inhabitants at all. The contradiction is not so flagrant as it appears. Bismarck, it is true, always spoke contemptuously of colonies and insisted that Germany was a Continental power. He would have preferred to follow a foreign policy strictly static and unacquisitive. Junker

Germany was truly a 'satiated' power, and any increase of territory would make Junker predominance more difficult. But if German national feeling demanded outlet, colonial ambitions were its least harmful form. The demand for colonies, like the later demand for a navy, was a Little German demand, originating in the Hanseatic towns of north Germany and easily reconcilable with a conservative policy in Europe. Colonial agitation was a red herring to distract German ambitions from eastern and south-eastern Europe, their natural outlet. It was not an effective enough red herring to be worth much trouble, and Bismarck would never have taken up colonial schemes, if they had not in 1884 and 1885 fitted in with his attempt at a Franco-German entente directed against England. Colonial disputes with England gave Bismarck an easy popularity with national feeling in the Reichstag and in Germany; but he dropped them as soon as they ceased to accord with the general current of his foreign policy. In this accidental way Bismarck acquired for Germany great colonial areas in Africa with the exception of a military post in China, the full extent of the German colonial empire – colonies which in 1914 contained in all 5,000 permanent German inhabitants and which cost the German taxpayers in subsidies six times what the German merchants and investors made out of them in profits.

The German colonies were of no economic or social importance, and of military use only in the unlikely event of war with England. They were a profound and revealing symptom of the dilemma of Bismarckian Germany. After the Congress of Berlin in 1878, which came at the end of thirty years of European conflict, all the Great Powers shrank from any new attempt to re-order the balance of Europe. They all accepted the broad lines of the European order which had been established by Bismarck and aspired only to small modifications. Each wished to increase its strength imperceptibly and without fuss, to make gains on the cheap. This was the meaning of the 'age of Imperialism', evidence not that Europe had become unimportant, but that every inch of it was so important as not to be modified without a general war. Each Great Power found at its back door a zone of expansion where it did not immediately run up against determined opposition – France across the Mediterranean in North Africa (until it ran up against England in Egypt), Russia across Asia (until it encountered British opposition in Persia and Japanese opposition in Korea), Austria-Hungary in the Balkans, England in that universal back door to all the world which was given by sea-power. But Germany was surrounded by established powers and had no back door, no zone of easy expansion. To expand into south-eastern Europe, she must absorb Austria-Hungary and ruin the Junker Reich; to acquire new wheat-growing areas, she must conquer the Ukraine from Russia; to acquire new sources of industrial raw materials, she must conquer north-eastern France; to escape from Europe and draw her resources from overseas she must depend on the goodwill of England or else conquer from her the mastery of the seas. For Germany it was all or nothing: either to maintain static and unchanged the Reich created by Bismarck in 1871, or to overthrow the European order in a bid for European domination. Germany could not advance imperceptibly, could not make small gains. The acquisition of colonies cloaked, but did not alter, this dilemma. They were certainly won on the cheap, but they were not gains; they added nothing to Germany's strength. Their only purpose was emotional, an inadequate safety valve for the growing desire that united Germany, as a Great Power, should display all the characteristics of greatness shown by others. Bismarck's Reich was a 'made' state, without tradition of its own. It aped the traditions of others, and 'made' its colonial ambitions, as it had 'made' its constitution, its industrial system, and its mode of thought.

Certainly Bismarck never intended the Reich to advance beyond the frontiers which he had laid down. In colonial affairs what mattered to him was the dispute, not the reward; and he was both astonished and annoyed at British acquiescence in his demands, which at once deprived him of his quarrel and saddled him with unwanted colonies. Still, a quarrel was somehow squeezed out of colonial affairs during the latter half of 1884 and the early months of 1885. As well as serving his designs in foreign affairs, these colonial quarrels gave Bismarck a useful fighting cry during the Reichstag election of 1884. The Social Peril alone was not enough to keep the electors in alarm at succeeding elections; and grievances against England were a welcome 'national' substitute. But not a very effective one. Both Centre and Progressives held their own in the general election, and the Social Democrats increased their vote. This was the more serious in that the time for a new septennate was approaching. The army grant was due for renewal in 1888; but with the breakneck increase of the population, the army chiefs wished both to increase the size of the army and to put the increase into force in 1887. The majority in the Reichstag were ready to agree to the increased grant, but attempted to secure in return increased parliamentary control – to make the grant triennial, instead of septennial; a last echo of the similar demand in Prussia which had brought Bismarck to power in 1862. In 1886 Bismarck used his familiar weapons and befogged the constitutional issue with the 'national' cry. 'The Fatherland in danger' served to conceal the fact that the demands of the Reichstag majority affected not the size of the army, but the autocratic powers of the Emperor and Chancellor; it was the old trick of 1862.

But there was also a profound difference. In 1862 Prussia had really been endangered by the German ambitions of Austria and the ineffective Utopianism of Napoleon III; and Bismarck had passed without regret from alarms of war to war itself. Germany was not seriously endangered in 1886, and the sole aim of Bismarck's foreign policy remained peace. European relations, indeed, were somewhat strained – an incipient crisis between Russia and Austria-Hungary in the Balkans, and a nationalist revival led by Boulanger in France. But Bismarck never intended to strike first, and his alarms were largely spurious: his guns were being loaded to preserve the balance of his political system in Germany, not to be fired. The real danger, if it was real, lay in the conflict between Russia and Austria-Hungary; and the German military plans at this time envisaged an invasion of Russia and a purely defensive war in the west. But Bismarck was too good a Junker, his policy too sharply focused on Poland, ever to project a genuine breach with Russia. In April 1887, at the height of the supposed 'war crisis', he inaugurated negotiations with Russia for a neutrality agreement, the Re-insurance Treaty; and had it come to a real crisis, he probably intended (as he contemplated in 1889) to partition Austria-Hungary with Russia, taking as little as possible for Germany and leaving all the Slav areas, perhaps even Bohemia, to Russia, anything rather than to be caught up in the Greater German plans for German domination in central Europe. Such a policy would have doomed his work, for only open military dictatorship could have forced it on the German people;

and this dictatorship was the proposal to which he was logically led in 1890. In 1886 and 1887 he still tried to bridge the gap between Junker interests and national sentiment by presenting France, not Russia, as the common enemy. With France profoundly pacific and despairing, the risk of a real crisis was remote; and Bismarck had to take the risk. His manœuvre was successful. In January 1887, the Reichstag rejected the new army bill and was dissolved. Bismarck fought the election with the cry of 'the Fatherland in danger' and won a majority for his coalition of agrarian and industrialist supporters. The reconstituted National Liberals, the party of capitalist interest, were for the last time the largest party in the Reichstag.

The army bill was passed without difficulty in March 1887. It was the last triumph of the Bismarckian *tour de force*. With the staggering progress of industrialization and with the increase of the political consciousness of the masses, Germany became ever more unmanageable. How could the German people be persuaded to accept indefinitely the political monopoly of the Junkers and the economic monopoly of the great landowners and capitalists? The way of social and political concession was, by definition, ruled out. Bismarck, after a lifetime of expedients, gave up the problem in despair: he proposed in 1890 to scrap the constitution, to break with German feeling, and to re-establish a reactionary alliance with Tsardom, as it had existed in the days of Frederick William III. This was to invite the fate of Metternich. The capitalist liberals would be driven on to the side of the masses, and, in any case, capitalists and landowners together could not stand against a widespread revolutionary movement. Old Prussia had rested on an army composed of dumb obedient peasants; but the German army was, in large part, the Social Democrats and the Centre in arms. There remained only the 'national' cause, obscuring the conflict of classes in a general hostility to the foreigner. At the beginning of the century, the demand for liberty had been diverted into the War of Liberation against the French; in the middle of the century, the danger of liberalism was overcome by the programme of liberating Germany from Austrian and French interference; by the end of the century, it was becoming necessary to liberate all Europe for German ambitions. Bismarck had fought Greater Germanism in order to preserve the political and social order in Prussia; yet now, as the logical conclusion of his work, only a Greater

German programme could enable this social and political order to survive. In the election campaign of 1887 Bismarck played the great card of fear – fear of France, fear of Russia, fear, even, of England. Fear was to make the Germans cower under the protection of their established leaders. There was an inescapable conclusion: Germany should end these fears by conquering those who threatened her. Too late Bismarck tried in 1888 to undo the effect of his alarms with the last of his perorations: 'We Germans fear God and nothing else in the world' – strange ending to a campaign for increased armaments. Bismarck could not efface his own work. He had taught the Germans that conquest was the only cure for danger; and he had whipped up the dangers in order to maintain his order. In the long run, the Germans would break the bounds which he had imposed and would seek to conquer all Europe – and God too. The Bismarckian system aimed at security and peace; but it left the ruling classes of Germany no alternative – to preserve themselves they had to enter on a path of conquest which would be their ruin. Bismarck, the greatest of political Germans, was for Germany the greatest of disasters.

8

THE GERMANY OF WILLIAM II: THE CONQUEST OF PRUSSIA BY GERMANY, 1890–1906

Bismarck had been a Napoleon in the German political structure. In true Bonapartist fashion he played off against each other conflicting social forces and maintained himself above them at the point of rest. He could not be overthrown either by the Prussian parliament or by the Reichstag, by the militarists or by the liberals, still less by the discontent of the industrial workers. His impregnable position had a single weak spot: he must be regarded by the Emperor as indispensable. In 1890 this weak spot brought him down. The old Emperor, William I, remained unshakeably faithful until his death in 1888: often dizzy at Bismarck's manœuvres and reluctant to accept Bismarck's expedients, he lived always in the memory of the liberal menace which had sent him into exile in 1848 and almost driven him to abdication in 1862, and clung to Bismarck as the saviour of the Prussian monarchy. Frederick, his son and successor, was bound to Bismarck by the memory of the achievements of 1870. Liberal in phrases, he was at best 'national liberal', prototype of all the worthy Germans for whom unification cloaked a multitude of sins; and if he had lived, the Bismarckian system, with a slightly more liberal colouring, might have run on a little longer. But he died within a few months of his accession; and as soon as William II came to the throne the elaborate Bismarckian structure began to tumble down.

William II, still under thirty, was a product, and a characteristic one, of the Germany which Bismarck had made. He had experienced none of the dangers of the 'sixties, knew nothing of the risks which had been run nor of the narrow margin by which success had been achieved. He had been formed in the shadow of Germany's expanding and seemingly limitless might. His character reinforced the effect of his environment. He had none of the modest caution and modest cunning of the usual Hohenzollern, of Frederick William III or of William I; he was of the same mould as his great-uncle, Frederick William IV, hysterical, grandiloquent, craving popularity, pursuing limitless dream-projects and abandoning them unfinished – in short the perfect representative of the Germany of the eighteen-nineties. William II repudiated the precautions which were the essence of Bismarck's system: he thought that the Hohenzollern monarchy was strong enough to stand in Germany, and Germany strong enough to stand in the world, without the support of checks and balances. When Bismarck left office William II announced: 'The ship's course remains the same. "Full steam ahead" is the order' – the first sentence blatantly untrue, the second the profound motto of his reign. The nagging dispute between Bismarck and William II which dragged on from November 1888 to March 1890 was much more than a clash of two personalities: it was the decisive struggle between precautions and 'Full steam ahead'.

William II and Bismarck disputed on almost everything, but their most profound disagreement was over domestic politics. For Bismarck there were only two 'national' parties – the agrarians and the industrialists. With the Roman Catholic Centre he was on terms of armed neutrality; with the radicals in political conflict; with the Social Democrats in open legal war. William II desired an absurdity – to be Emperor of all Germans; just as he desired an absurdity in Europe – for Germany to be loved by all the Powers. The dispute was brought to a head by the Reichstag elections of February 1890. Bismarck had not been able to engineer a new European crisis, nor even to run a new colonial campaign. The Reich was manifestly not 'in danger', and the 'national' parties had no rallying cry. The Bismarckian coalition, principally from National Liberal losses, fell from 220 to 135; the Progressives, the Centre, and the Social Democrats – by no means a coalition, but all opposed to Bismarck – rose from 141 to 207. Bismarck's magical touch had failed: success, the basic condition of his power, had abandoned him. Bismarck himself confessed failure and proposed to scrap his own work: to tear up the constitution, limit the suffrage, establish open voting, and drive the Social Democratic party completely out of existence, to return in fact to the days of Metternich. But ever since the struggle of 1862, indeed ever since his experiences at Frankfurt in the eighteen-fifties, Bismarck had held that the conservative order could be preserved only by increased doses of demagogy and that naked conservatism would be the prelude to revolution. His own past condemned him. William II, dismissing Bismarck and seeking to conciliate the German masses, was merely going further along the path which Bismarck had marked out; not less demagogy but more was the inevitable outcome of the collapse of the Bismarckian balance. Bismarck and William II were not divided on any question of principle; both were determined to preserve the authoritarian monarchy with its military foundation. Their difference was over tactics. Bismarck held that the Roman Catholics and the Socialist workers were, by the principles of their existence, enemies of the Prussian-German Reich, enemies both of its social conservatism and of its static foreign policy. In a curiously old-fashioned way he took the principles of his opponents seriously. William II, rejecting Bismarck's policy of restraint, believed that Roman Catholics and Social Democrats could both be won over if the Reich followed resolutely enough the path of greatness. No doubt in 1890 he underrated the difficulties of this line of policy and thought, like Frederick William IV, that a few rhetorical expressions of Imperial grace would cause opposition to melt away. Still, in the long run, William's calculation proved correct. The worship of power, the acceptance of 'authority', the identifying of Germany with the Prussian army, did not stop short at the Protestant middle class. At a high price, far higher indeed than anyone anticipated in 1890, the two parties of the masses were transformed, as the liberals had been, into agents of the Reich, and the reign of William II ended in 1918 in a situation in which the Centre and the Social Democrats became the political mouthpiece of the army, the defenders of the great estates and of great industry, and the upholders of the 'national' cause.

Once Bismarck quarrelled with William II he had nothing to sustain him; for he was not the leader of a party or the spokesman of a social interest. The parties of the Left were ready to oppose the Emperor but would not support Bismarck; the parties of the Right supported Bismarck but would not oppose the Emperor. The Progressives, the Centre, and the Social Democrats had no illusions about Bismarck; they knew that he was their implacable enemy, and they were implacable in their turn – five years later, in 1895, these parties in the Reichstag defeated a proposal to greet Bismarck on his eightieth birthday. Nor did the 'national' parties care much for Bismarck except as a stick with which to beat their opponents. The Junkers had forgotten the perils from which Bismarck had rescued them in the eighteen-sixties and resented the concessions to liberalism and still more to German nationalism which Bismarck had forced them to make. The industrialists had forgotten their impotent liberal efforts to unite Germany and resented the restrictions which Bismarck imposed on their plans for economic expansion. Only the few who knew the frail foundations of German greatness regretted Bismarck; all the rest of all parties were glad to see him go. In any case it would have helped Bismarck not at all even if the entire Reichstag had been on his side. William II could still have dismissed him without the least trouble. Bismarck indeed recognized this, and his later attempts to whip up political opposition to the Emperor were outbursts of resentful spite, not a serious effort to return to power. In the culminating dispute of March 1890, Bismarck tried to engineer, not a Reichstag majority, but a strike of Prussian ministers; but it was futile to suppose that professional administrators, with a high standard of duty, would sacrifice these standards and their career for a chief who had always treated them with relentless contempt. There was a more decisive factor. Bismarck controlled the civil side of the German authoritarian state; the army was entirely independent of him, and Waldersee, who had succeeded Moltke as Chief of the General Staff, was a general of political tastes, who believed that a more demagogic policy would strengthen the army and so enable Germany to take a more forceful line in foreign affairs. Thus Bismarck was dismissed with the approval, and indeed partly at the prompting, of the army, the institution on which the Reich really rested.

With the fall of Bismarck in March 1890 there began in Germany the four years of the 'New Course', the short period when a few politicians of indisputable goodwill, but no understanding, tried to follow a more democratic line without changing either the social or economic foundations – an attempt as hopeless as the 'New Era' which lasted in Prussia from 1858 to 1862 or as the projects of Turgot to reform the *ancien régime* in France. Caprivi, who succeeded Bismarck as Chancellor, was a general of no military gifts and little political experience; a military administrator with not a scrap of Bismarck's political understanding, he cared nothing for the Junkers and dreamt emptily of a 'People's Army', seeking to win the support of the masses by social concessions. His first act was to refuse to renew the Re-insurance Treaty with Russia, the expression which Bismarck had given in 1887 to the anti-Polish partnership of Russian Tsardom and Prussian Junkers. Instead he sought reconciliation with France and alliance with England – a liberal foreign policy, favoured even by the Social Democrats, so far as they had views on foreign policy at all. In fact the prospect of war with Russia, the old radical programme of 1848, delighted the Social Democrats and led them to welcome the increase in German military power. Engels, the surviving high priest of Marxism, wrote in 1891: 'Rise, therefore, if Russia begins a war – rise against Russia and her allies, whoever they may be!' and Bebel, the Social Democratic leader, said in the Reichstag in 1892: 'Present-day Social Democracy is a sort of preparatory school of militarism.' Moreover, once German foreign policy ceased to conform to Junker needs, Bismarck's repudiation of the German cause in south-eastern Europe, too, could be abandoned – the more so as the Bismarckian substitute of colonial expansion led to conflict with England. Caprivi defended the German cause in the internal affairs of Austria, especially in Bohemia, and this change of German attitude helped on the fall of the clericalist Taaffe ministry in 1893. At the same time he encouraged Habsburg ambitions in the Balkans and, breaking Bismarck's most cardinal principle, pledged German support to Austria-Hungary in case of a Balkan dispute with Russia. In short the 'New Course', so far as it had any sense, was none other than the old course of Greater Germany, against which Bismarck had always fought.

Caprivi's attitude in home affairs was of a piece. He negotiated a series of commercial treaties to the injury of agrarian interests, arguing that Germany was destined to become a great industrial state drawing cheap food from overseas (under the protection of the British navy). He refused to renew the anti-Socialist laws and looked on undismayed at the increase of the Social Democratic and Centre vote. In 1892, as a logical consequence of his attitude, he ceased to be Prime Minister of Prussia; and Prussia, with a separate Prime Minister, became merely a 'sectional' interest of no more importance in the affairs of the Reich than Bavaria or Saxony. But though his tactics were different from Bismarck's, he had the same political concern – to win the consent of the Reichstag to a further increase in the size of the army. A new bait was added, expressive of the discipline and militarism of the German people as a whole: the reduction of the period of service from three years to two. Caprivi's demands were too great for the majority of the Reichstag when they were first presented in May 1892; and Caprivi was driven to Bismarck's usual resort of a dissolution with the slogan, 'the Reich in danger'. But the slogan could not this time work in favour of the 'national' parties of the Right. As Caprivi was trying to win English friendship, the Reich had to be in danger from Russia. Therefore it could not be saved by voting for the parties of the Right, which were friendly to Russia; and the absence of any colonial campaign against England made it even more difficult to gain votes for the anti-democratic parties. The parties which had defeated the Army Law came back little weaker than before. Caprivi escaped from his difficulty by a new burst of demagogy: more social concessions to please the Social Democrats; further lowering of the food tariffs to please the Radicals; reduction of the period of army grant from seven years to five, to please all the parties of the Left;[1]

[1] The democratic parties had long ceased to hope to make the army grant annual. In Bismarck's time their demand had been for a triennial grant, so that each Reichstag should vote on the army once in its three years of life. Caprivi's arrangement was a compromise: the grant was reduced to five years, and the constitutional limit on the life of each Reichstag at the same time extended to five years, so that the democratic demand was in fact met. The quinquennial grants never caused a serious political crisis; they were

and, most striking of all, a pro-Polish administration in the eastern provinces of Prussia, an open challenge both to Tsardom and the Prussian Junkers. This demagogic window-dressing brought its reward: both Centre and Progressives split, and a minority of each voted for the Army Law; so did all the Polish deputies; and though the Social Democrats still voted against it, they did so mildly and with open regret. The trick was turned and the Army Law passed in August 1893.

Caprivi had manœuvred well, as smart a trick in its way as Bismarck's carrying of the previous Army Law in 1887. But in supplementing his majority with Poles, Roman Catholics and Progressives, he was ignoring reality: he was behaving as though there had taken place the transference of power which Bismarck had prevented. In fact nothing had changed in Germany except the personality of the Chancellor. Bismarck had managed to combine the Junker-industrialist partnership with universal suffrage, despite the fact that the majority of Germans opposed this partnership – a *tour de force*, but a possible one, since the fraud was in universal suffrage, not in the reality of power. Caprivi, however, tried to follow a social and political line agreeable to the masses, despite the fact that economic and political power remained in the hands of the old order, an attempt without meaning. With the non-political simplicity of a professional soldier, he imagined that the 'national' parties would carry their patriotism so far as to remain loyal, the Junkers to a government which injured the great estates, and the National Liberals to a government which neglected heavy industry. But patriotism is a luxury which only those without private interests can afford; and Caprivi's policy provoked a resistance so extreme as to lead some of the agrarian leaders even to favour an alliance with the Social Democrats against him. In 1894 he ran into headlong conflict with the Prime Minister of Prussia, who was

---

overshadowed by other events. The grant of 1899 was carried almost unnoticed in the backwash of the navy agitation; the grants of 1905 and 1911 benefited from the atmosphere of international tension, and on both occasions as well from the renewed navy agitation which prepared the way for the fleet increases of 1906 and 1912. It was, in fact, a general complaint of German militarists that 'the new navy' was favoured at the expense of 'the old army'. There were supplementary army grants in 1912 and 1913, the second of which certainly needed a prelude of political agitation.

demanding a renewal of the anti-socialist laws, and discovered, despite his slighting of Prussia, that in the Bismarckian constitution the Reich could not be governed against Prussian opposition. The deadlock could have been broken only by the scrapping of the three-class franchise in Prussia, and the transformation of Prussia into a democratic state, a tardy revolution against Bismarck's greatest success. Caprivi, a Prussian general and the agent of the Hohenzollern monarchy, would have had to become the leader of a Roman Catholic–Marxist coalition and conduct civil war in Germany, when his purpose had been not to overthrow the existing order but merely to reconcile the masses to it by a few gestures. Late in 1894 Caprivi disappeared from office, never an important figure nor even a significant one; merely a reminder that Germany could not become a democratic state by a little goodwill. No doubt a 'good German' of the best intentions, he succeeded only in displaying the impotence of intentions to alter the character of the German political structure.

William II had started out with the high resolve of governing without the conservatism and harshness of Bismarck, just as his ancestor George III of England had intended in 1760 to do things better than the corrupt Whigs. And just as George III, having outdone the old gang in corruption, was within five years imploring them to return, so William II in 1894 tried to resurrect Bismarck's system, though without Bismarck's overwhelming personality. Hohenlohe, the new Chancellor, had only the qualification of being old and conservative, a more or less living memory of the great days of 1870 and 1871. The Reich was once more trying to run on its previous reputation. No more attempts at demagogy; instead verbal violence (the only weapon in which William II excelled) against the Social Democrats. No more encouragement of the Germans in Austria; instead support for the Austrian aristocrats and welcome for an authoritarian and even anti-German government in Vienna in 1896. No more support for the Habsburgs in the Balkans or patronage of the Poles; instead a demonstrative reconciliation with the young Tsar Nicholas II and a revival of Bismarck's land laws against the Poles. No more conciliatory gestures towards England; instead a renewal of colonial ambitions and, at the end of 1895, an open quarrel with England over the Boer republics – the Kruger telegram repeating in a characteristically exaggerated and hysterical form Bismarck's colonial campaign of 1884 and 1885, the Reich rather feebly once more in danger. To credit Hohenlohe with a policy would be to do him too much kindness; in a rather haphazard way he was merely attempting to put things back into the established arrangement as he could rather vaguely remember it before Caprivi embarked on his speculative experiment. Equally William II, who had helped to create the confusion, was now trying to behave as he imagined that his grandfather and Bismarck behaved in some half-legendary past. But this brief period of archaic Bismarckianism, with the Kruger telegram as an absurd parody of the Ems telegram of 1870, was altogether too chaotic and formless to deserve the name of a system. There was one new departure. Hohenlohe, a great Bavarian nobleman and – in a long-distant past – Bavarian Prime Minister, had none of Bismarck's Lutheran reluctance to deal with the Centre. He recognized that they were just as much an interest-group as the agrarians or the industrialists – in fact even more so in that the Junkers cared at least for Prussia and the industrialists a little for Germany, whereas the Roman Catholic Centre were quite indifferent as between German confederation or German Reich, between Habsburg rule, Hohenzollern rule, or even French rule, so long as the influence and privileges of the Roman Catholic Church were safeguarded. Therefore, almost without thinking, Hohenlohe began to treat the Centre as a government party, giving them the religious concessions they desired and receiving their support for his general measures; the beginning of a change quite as great as Bismarck's bargain with the liberals thirty years before. For if the Centre had remained, as it had claimed to be, resolutely federalist and democratic, the Bismarckian Reich could never have been refurbished and kept running. The violent reaction which Bismarck himself had proposed in 1890 would have been inescapable, and the authoritarian state with mass support impossible. Germany and all Europe paid a heavy price for this party of sectarian, but no political, principle.

Still, more was needed than merely to bring the Centre within the limits of Bismarckian manœuvring. It was the fatal essence of Bismarck's juggling that each party to the bargain was perpetually increasing its demands, that each arm of the multiple see-saw was being incessantly drawn out, so that the postures of the figure balancing in the middle had to become ever more intricate. The agrarians were not content with the undoing of Caprivi's commercial treaties; eastern Germany was so unsuited to intensive agriculture that food tariffs at the Bismarckian level were not enough to stave off the competition of the American prairies and the Russian plains. Besides, the Junkers were no longer the modest, hardworking farmers of the early nineteenth century: they had developed aristocratic tastes, sought the expensive life of Potsdam, now at last a real court, and tried to hold their own against the nobility of Austria or England. Their estates had never yielded high profits; now they were oppressed with mortgages, the interest on which had to be provided by the German consumers. Not merely higher tariffs, but preferential railway rates, relief from taxation, and finally direct subsidies were essential in the 'national' interest to preserve the ramshackle estates of eastern Germany. The industrialists, too, demanded from the Reich much more than vague approval of the workings of the Kartells. During the eighteen-nineties heavy industry, stimulated into unhealthy life by the tariffs of 1879, reached monstrous proportions; and by 1900 German production of iron and steel surpassed British. The industrialists, alarmed at their own success, called on the Reich to find an outlet for their mounting production. No outlet could be found within Germany without a social revolution; therefore the Reich had to conquer outlets abroad – extract concessions, acquire colonies, use German power to force German goods on foreigners at unfavourable terms.

But it would be wrong to ascribe this tumultuous demand for 'World Power' merely to the calculations of the leaders of heavy industry. The new generation of every class, but the intellectuals – journalists, writers, university professors – above all, demanded of the Reich a taste of the success which had intoxicated their fathers in the days of Sadova and Sedan. Memories were not enough; they must themselves experience the emotion for which they had sacrificed their conscience, and political liberty. Hence the flowering of the dithyrambic associations which extolled various aspects of German power – the Colonial Society, the Navy League, the Pan-German League – associations partly propagandistic, but still more sensational – to experience the feeling of German strength. None of these bodies received government support. Indeed their activities were embarrassing and irritating to the

Prussian-German bureaucrats who were half-consciously trying to keep Germany within the modest Bismarckian limits; but on the other hand the government did nothing against them and allowed itself to be pushed into temptation without much protest. The Prussianized Reich flirted with Pan-Germanism, somewhat ashamed of doing so and willing to repudiate these mad enthusiasts temporarily for the sake of policy; but willing also to accept the popularity and rewards of a Pan-German attitude if the risk was not too great. A Jekyll and Hyde policy, the bureaucrat Jekylls confident until too late that they could always shake off the Pan-German Hyde at their convenience.[1] Yet these associations were an essential part of the pattern of German political life: an official Germany striving to remain conservative, an ever more violent undercurrent pulling towards limitless expansion. German energies could not be confined within a rigid frame, already old-fashioned when it was made in 1871. The work of Bismarck had made it impossible for these energies to find an outlet in social and political change within Germany; therefore they had to be loosed outwards into 'World Policy', and the rest of the world had to pay the penalty for the political incompetence and timidity of the German middle class. The failure of the 'good Germans', not the ranting of the 'bad' ones, was the real crime of Germany against European civilization.

Bismarck, visiting Hamburg in 1896, saw the vast harbour crowded with ships, heard the deep murmur of German power, sensed the ruin of his system, and turned away in fear; 'It is a new world, a new age.' An age altogether beyond the capacity of the elderly Hohenlohe or of any of the industrious Prussian officials; and altogether beyond the

---

[1] This policy was, at any rate, successful enough to take in foreign observers. Thus, the English liberal historian, Dr G. P. Gooch, in his essay on *Franco-German Relations, 1871–1914* (reprinted without change in 1942 in *Studies in Diplomacy and Statecraft*), dwells at length on the activities of the French League of Patriots, refers repeatedly to French 'chauvinism', and catalogues meticulously the French nationalist writers. Déroulède is called 'the most popular man in France'. German writers are mentioned only by implication: 'The German cause could boast of no champions to counterwork the emotional appeal of Bazin and Barrès.' No German nationalist association is even named. Yet Déroulède was persecuted and driven into exile; the league of Patriots was made illegal and broken up; the Pan-German League had more than a million members; it was constantly consulted, and sometimes stimulated, by the German Chancellor and Secretary of State; and the leading Pan-German writers were favoured generals and university professors.

control of the hysterical gestures of William II. The Imperial authority was responsible, all-powerful, and yet helpless. It could no longer ride above the storm, as in the days of Bismarck, but, at the best, ride with it. In 1897, after the Caprivi attempt to go forward and the Hohenlohe attempt to go back, both rigid, both dogmatic, began a more flexible period of German politics, a period of manœuvring without principle other than the principle of survival, a period of twelve years (until 1909) which was the true 'age of William II'. No single man laid down the pattern of this age as Bismarck consciously devised the balance of his system; all the same, it sprang logically from the deadlock and disputes against which Hohenlohe could make no headway and which threatened to end in a despairing attempt at open autocracy. The man who turned William II from dictatorship and won him for a new effort at popularity was his personal friend, Eulenburg, no statesman indeed, but highly intelligent and himself craving for popularity in private life. The instrument of Eulenburg's policy was Bülow, who became Secretary of State in 1897 and Chancellor in 1901. Policy is, perhaps, too high a word. Eulenburg himself defined it: 'to satisfy Germany without injuring the Emperor'. A renewed demagogy, in fact, but without toppling over, as Caprivi had done, into democracy. William II said to Bülow: 'Bülow, be my Bismarck'; and in Bülow's task there was a Bismarckian echo – the monarchy and the old social order were to be made popular, to be 'sold', to the German masses. But the method was very different. Bismarck proceeded by profound calculation and by acts which, however unscrupulous, were acts of statecraft; Bülow had nothing beyond a talent for manœuvre and intrigue. Kiderlen, a far abler man, christened him perfectly: 'The Eel'; and he characterized himself almost as well by his favourite word – pomadig, like hair oil. Resourceful, self-confident, incapable of any general principle, Bülow was called on to slip and slither through all the mounting difficulties of home and foreign affairs, never solving or achieving anything, except to postpone the explosion. He could 'give' almost without limit and so was pulled in all directions both by the political parties and still more by the fundamental divergence between the Bismarckian doctrine of satiety and the chaotic promptings of Pan-German expansion, an india-rubber man who could perform feats of compromise and adaptation quite beyond the capacity of the Iron Chancellor.

The new line, the underlying theme, of Bülow's plausible speeches was, of course, 'World Policy'. German energies were turned outwards against foreign powers. Every German gain, every advance of German exports, was transformed into a grievance that it was not more; and the stupendous, unparalleled development of German industry served to demonstrate the denial of Germany's 'place in the sun'. Like a rich parvenu, Germany, lacking nothing but self-possession, cried out for the possessions of others; convinced that if she could but ruin and destroy her neighbours she would be at last stable and contented. Bülow could clothe these limitless ambitions in fine phrases – or rather fine phrases were spun for him in his Press Bureau, for he lacked even the capacity for original phrase-making and carried with him to the Reichstag a sheaf of carefully prepared variants for his celebrated impromptus. But Bülow and his technical advisers had no discrimination or concrete plan. They would pick up first one scheme and then another, dropping them when they seemed to threaten a serious conflict with foreign powers and then inevitably picking them up again. World policy on the cheap, world policy without a war or major crisis, was their utopian, contradictory aim; and the German Foreign Office laboured patiently to maintain the standards of Bismarck's non-aggressive policy in an age when German demands were offending every Great Power in turn. So the Reich renewed in 1898 its colonial ambitions in Africa and then, fearing to break with England, half dropped them; so it seized in 1897 a concession in China, offensive both to England and Russia, and then feared to play a serious part as a Far Eastern Power; so – most contradictory of all – it prompted and supported in 1899 the project for a German railway across Turkey-in-Asia, yet shrank from the breach with Russia or the support of Turkey that this railway implied. There was no attempt to discriminate: all these projects were sprung on the German Foreign Office from without, and the imperial bureaucrats, inexperienced in the ways of capitalism, had no means of judging between them. For example, the railway in Asia Minor, with its grandiose title of the 'Baghdad Railway', was enthusiastically welcomed as a manifestation of German power; but little German capital was forthcoming for its construction, and the Germans counted it a bitter grievance against England and France that they would not supply the capital to build a railway to the greater glory of Germany. Had the political power in Germany passed into the hands of the great industrialists who controlled her economic strength, German policy would, no doubt, still have been ruthless and grasping; but it would have grasped with some sense and plan. As it was, the German rulers, still guided, so far as they had any idea at all, by the traditions of agrarian Junker Prussia, held out a motley collection of peace-offerings to heavy industry without understanding in the least what they were doing or which achievements were worth the effort.

Two other men shared with Bülow the responsibility for 'World Policy' and gave it a more practical setting: Miquel, the Prussian Minister of Finance since 1891 and Vice-President of the Prussian Ministry in 1898, and Tirpitz, who became Secretary of State for the Navy in 1897. Miquel was a former radical, once a friend and associate of Karl Marx, now intent on renewing the co-operation between Junker agrarianism and Pan-German industrialism which had been broken in the days of Caprivi. All through the eighteen-nineties the Prussian conservatives had threatened to 'bolt', as they did in 1894 when they brought down Caprivi – to intervene, that is, in the affairs of the Reich and so display too openly the artificial Prussian domination of the Reich which Bismarck had so skilfully draped with national enthusiasm. Miquel's aim was to buy the Junkers for the Reich: not metaphorically, as Bismarck had tried to win them by high considerations of social survival, but, quite literally, to buy them by inflated tariffs on grain and by fiscal favouritism. Both aspects of his policy were given a 'national' excuse: agrarian protection was to make the Reich self-sufficient in time of war; and easy credit for the landowners, tax rebates, and the refusal to extend direct taxation enabled the Junkers to defend the 'national' cause against the advancing Poles – oblivious of the fact that these same Junkers promoted the immigration into eastern Germany of hundreds of thousands of Polish labourers, with their lower standard of life and hence of wages. Miquel's financial policy, culminating in the high and rigid tariff of 1902, won the conservatives anew for the Reich. The Junker gentry might still attempt to maintain their narrow Prussian standards and might still look with contempt and fear at industry and its programme of limitless expansion; but the mortgages which weighed on every big estate east of the Elbe drove them to compound with sin and to become, half-heartedly, and with distaste, Pan-Germans in their turn.

Tirpitz provided the bait to content heavy industry, the other half of the partnership; the bait of a colossal German navy. This project, aired throughout the early 'nineties, given a first modest formulation in 1898, and then openly proclaimed in the second Navy Law of 1900, was the sharpest and most perfect expression of the spirit which made up the Germany of William II and Bülow, the Germany of limitless ambition and internal contradiction. The great navy, with its battle fleet, had no defensive purpose. For that Germany needed coastal forts and vessels, which were not built. It was not designed to defend Germany's (worthless) colonial empire; for though some colonial gains (Kiao-chau and Samoa) were made so as to justify a demand for a navy to defend them, the German battleships, built for speed, had a cruising range which confined them to the North Sea. The navy was therefore purely a weapon of offence; and it is not surprising that the British drew the conclusion that the offence could be directed only against them. Yet the conclusion was not well founded; or, to put it another way, the offensive against England was not consciously intended. Tirpitz, indeed, produced a series of political combinations, each of which proved the need for a great navy; but these schemes, contradictory and ill-balanced as they were, were rationalizations, attempts to provide a reasonable excuse for the great navy which was fundamental. One looks in vain through the ceaseless outpouring of propaganda which preceded the first Navy Bill for any sensible justification of the great building programme. Its advocates, Tirpitz above all, fell back constantly on the argument that a great navy was an essential possession of a Great Power. Tirpitz himself said that a great navy was necessary to show that Germany was *ebenbürtig*, as 'well born' (the parvenu note) as England; and Bethmann Hollweg declared that the navy was necessary 'for the general purposes of imperial greatness'. Nothing could better express the roaring spluttering energy of Germany, like a ship's propeller out of water, than this vast naval force, absorbing great quantities of economic power, engendering disastrous international friction, destined never to be used to any decisive purpose in war, but to perform a role in history only as the match which began the explosion and collapse of the Hohenzollern Reich.

The great navy was primarily a triumph of demagogy: with its implied challenge to England, a grotesque substitute for Bismarck's challenges to Austria and to France. Moreover, unlike the army, the navy was a popular, almost a democratic cause. None of the German states, not even Prussia, had possessed a navy. The navy was essentially German, an affair of the Reich. It revived memories of the first German navy of 1848, distant symbol of German radicalism. The great naval programme was carried through at the prompting of the Navy League (itself subsidized by heavy industry and secretly guided by Tirpitz and the Navy Department) and carried through against the will both of the Foreign Office and of the general staff; a seeming victory of the people's will. But, of course, the navy had a more serious practical political purpose. It was the convincing pledge that the Reich would sustain to the limit the selling policy of the great steel Kartell. With an iron and steel production now surpassing the British the Kartell had steadily to cut their export prices in order to force their way on to foreign markets; and this in turn demanded a larger guaranteed market for their steel at higher prices within Germany. Protection was not enough; the Reich had itself to become a gigantic and steady consumer of Ruhr steel. Hence mere talk of a great navy would not do. The Navy Law of 1900 fixed, once and for all, the building programme for the next twenty years, thus incidentally making futile the later British attempts to secure a reduction of German naval expansion, fixed, that is, a minimum programme, for there was nothing to prevent, as in 1906 and 1912, further concessions to heavy industry. The great steel concerns and shipyards were not merely given assurance of a rigid government demand; they were also given financial guarantees from the Reich, so that the profits from government contracts were actually made on government credit. The political effect of the naval programme was far-reaching. It won the enthusiastic support of the great steel monopolies who were its direct beneficiaries. But beyond that it held out a promise to every capitalistic undertaking that, in case of difficulty, it would not be left to its own devices, but that the full strength of the Reich would be used to promote the relentless advance of German economic power.

Agrarian protection and a great navy were thus essentially the two sides of a single bargain, although they represented contradictory policies: the only sensible use of a German navy was to safeguard the import of foodstuffs in time of war, and agrarian protection was intended to make the import of foodstuffs unnecessary. The landowners agreed to a great navy as the price of keeping their estates solvent; the industrialists acquiesced in high food prices for their workpeople in order to secure industrial expansion. Yet this interest-policy could be presented to the German electors as a 'national' policy with demagogic appeal. The academic enthusiasts for the navy forgot their hostility to the Junker reactionaries; the standard-bearers of the German crusade against the Poles added the great navy to their creed. The cattle-raising peasants of western Germany were injured by high grain prices for their cattle, yet swallowed protection (and so, implicitly, the navy) from general loyalty to conservative principles. The capitalists without armament interests, who were in the great majority, yet welcomed naval expansion (and so agrarian protection) as the proof of the identity of 'national' and capitalist interests. But there was a still more dramatic convert. The Centre, too, finally took the plunge and voted solidly for the second Navy Law, a contradiction of all its political past. The Centre drew its support from inland Germany, especially Germany of the west and south, where maritime interests had no meaning. It was the party of the small man who could benefit neither from agrarian protection nor from naval expansion. Above all, it was by its creed not a party of material power. All this counted as nothing against a simple political calculation. The great navy, with its demagogic appeal, was irresistible. The Centre, if it voted against it, would be discredited, would lose votes, and would obtain no sectarian concessions from the Reich. If it became part of the government coalition, it would continue to obtain privileges for its schools and youth organizations. The Centre advocated 'the peace of God' between nations. But alas! the peace of God did not exist in this wicked world. Therefore the Centre made its peace with Mammon.

One concession the Centre tried to obtain for its adherents: it tried to impose the condition that the cost of the navy should be met by direct taxation, levied either by the Reich or through the states by an increase of the matricular contribution. But shipbuilding and agrarian tariffs were knit up together, so that if the cost of shipbuilding increased agrarian protection would increase automatically with it – the larger the navy the greater the benefit to the landowners. The proposal of the Centre would have ruined this combination, and it was decisively rejected. But the political calculation of the Centre remained, and even without their condition they voted for the great navy, thus completing the reconciliation with the Reich which they had begun in 1879. As a matter of fact, even the inflated food taxes were inadequate to meet the cost of German armaments; and both army and navy were run on credit. The Reich, created in 1871, had started without a national debt; and while the French indemnity came in, it even had a credit on capital account. From 1879 on it allowed a deficit to accumulate, feeling that a national debt, like so much else, was 'necessary for the general purposes of Imperial greatness'; and in the twentieth century this debt grew rapidly. Thus while in England every increase in armaments expenditure involved an increase in direct taxation – culminating in Lloyd George's budget of 1909 – German armaments were built on credit, a concealed inflation which was intended ultimately to show a profit at the expense of the foreigner. German finance was therefore meaningless except on the assumption that German policy would culminate in a new 1871 with new and vaster indemnities levied on the conquered peoples of Europe.

The great navy, and still more, the 'world policy' which it implied, restored to Germany a temporary stability. The circle was once more squared, and the difficulties seemed postponed at any rate until 1916 when the shipbuilding programme would begin to taper off. The conservatives, the industrialists, the Centre, were all happily accommodated under the shadow of the Reich. There remained only the doctrinaire radicals, irreconcilable but unimportant, and the Social Democrats. But a great change was coming over the Social Democrats also. A decade and more of legality, an ever-advancing vote, a share of prosperity for their members, offered an absurd contradiction to their principles of revolutionary Marxism. The young generation of Social Democrats were not revolutionary conspirators, but hardworking trade union leaders, quite without political understanding and asking from capitalism only assured employment for their members. The same change, of course, was coming over the Socialist movements in England and France. But in the democratic countries of western Europe abandonment of the revolutionary creed brought political advantage:

Socialist politicians like Millerand and Briand, working-class representatives like John Burns, found an easy way to high office; and it was
only a matter of time for the French and English political systems to
accommodate themselves to actual Socialist governments. But in
Imperial Germany, where office was not open even to a man of
middle-class origin and where the Chancellor was determined by the
arbitrary will of the Emperor, abandonment of revolutionary doctrine
would bring no political advantage, but merely a weakening of party
enthusiasm. Therefore the Social Democratic party clung to its outworn
creed and sharply condemned the 'revisionists' who advocated co-
operation with middle-class liberals in a policy of social reform. Yet on
the other side it equally condemned the few genuine revolutionaries
who wished to embark on a struggle for power and to prepare for a
great social upheaval. In fact the Social Democrats made the worst of
both worlds. Their revolutionary theory prevented any united movement of the Left for liberal reform; their unrevolutionary practice made
them incapable of action in a revolutionary crisis. Yet, in the last resort,
the Social Democrats only reflected the political incompetence and
incapacity which had spread, as by infection, from the German middle
classes to the German workers. They too were awed by power, dutiful
in the face of authority. Capable of economic discontent, they were
incapable of responsibility. Just as the German liberals had been ready
to believe that Bismarck was doing their work for them, so now the
German Socialists argued that monopolistic capitalism was their St
John the Baptist: industrial concentration, they declared, was 'a step in
the direction of Socialism'. Long before 1914, the Social Democrats,
half-unconsciously, were longing to return to the policy of Lassalle and
to co-operate with the authoritarian Junker state against middle-class
liberalism but this time against the middle-class liberal states of western Europe. They retained their Marxist virtue only because the Reich
did not trouble to seduce them.

In one sphere, and that a sphere of great importance, the apparent
estrangement between the Social Democrats and the Reich was, for the
Reich, of inestimable advantage. The German Social Democrats were
the largest and best-organized party of the Socialist International, the
unquestioned repositories of Marxist theory. They preached the doctrine of the general strike against war and imposed it on the Socialist

parties of every other country. Thus they created the impression that the Reich government, however malignant its intentions, would not be permitted to start on a war of aggression; and so greatly strengthened the opposition to both military and diplomatic precautions against Germany in England and France. The German Social Democrats were incapable of imposing on the Reich a single under-secretary; yet they would, apparently, be able to impose upon it a foreign policy. In their own minds the Social Democratic leaders had evaded this contradiction. Germany, with its great Socialist party and its industrial concentrations, was, they argued, practically a Socialist country already; and a German victory would bring a Socialist victory all the nearer. Therefore, while it was the duty of French and Russian workers to strive for the defeat and overthrow of their governments, it was equally the duty of German workers to strive for a German victory − a comforting conclusion not, however, appreciated by the Socialist comrades in the International who continued, to the last, to rely with confidence on the German general strike.

In the Bülow-Tirpitz era between 1898 and 1905 these calculations seemed pointless, for war seemed remote. As in home affairs, Germany won in foreign relations too a new stability, a 'free hand'. Never had Germany enjoyed so great security. World policy did not lead to an estrangement from England, but instead to a series of British attempts to win German favour. With Russia concentrated on the Far East, all danger had gone out of the Franco-Russian partnership. Moreover, the great navy, though a concession to German ambitions, was a blow against the Pan-Germanism which looked towards south-eastern Europe. If, as William II said, 'the future of Germany lay on the water', this was not the water of the Danube. Once more, as in the days of Bismarck, Germany restrained Austria-Hungary in the Balkans and preached co-operation with Russia; refused to assist the German cause in Bohemia; and, most self-confident of all, between 1903 and 1906 acquiesced in the Habsburg attempt to reduce in Hungary the Magyar supremacy, which had been the basic condition of Bismarck's success. Intoxicated by German Power, the Germans felt the need of no allies and made concessions to no one: this, and this only, is the meaning of the 'encirclement' of Germany. The landowners of eastern Germany were drawn to Tsarist Russia by social sympathy and by the common oppression of Poland, and estranged from England by her democratic constitution; they were drawn to England by lack of economic rivalry and estranged from Russia by the threat of Russian wheat. The industrialists, on the other hand, had a common bond with capitalist England and disliked the open autocracy of Tsardom; but they competed with English industry and were beginning to establish offshoots of German industry throughout European Russia. Therefore agrarians and industrialists came together in hostility, or at least coolness, towards both England and Russia, confident that it was unnecessary to choose. The radical lower-middle class and the Social Democrats would have liked a reconciliation with France; but agrarians and industrialists rejected both the liberal reforms within Germany and the concessions in Alsace and Lorraine which this would have implied. Still, the Bülow-Tirpitz system rested on the assumption that England, France, and Russia could never unite; the reverse of its assumption at home that conflicting class interests could be indefinitely reconciled. Neither assumption proved true. Hence the collapse in 1906 and 1907 of Bülow's jugglery and, far more serious, the final ruin of the system of Bismarck.

9

THE CRISIS OF
HOHENZOLLERN GERMANY,
1906–16

Prussian domination in Germany and German predominance in Europe fell together in 1918; but this destruction of Bismarck's work was merely the open culmination of a process which had been in full swing for twelve years. 1906 marked the opening of the crisis in both home and foreign affairs: the authority of the Reich was challenged abroad, and the authority of the Chancellor was challenged at home. In 1905 the German government, estranged from both Russia and England, decided to seize the opportunity of Russia's defeat in the Far East and of her revolution at home in order to force France under German protection and so deprive both Russia and England of any foothold in western Europe. This was the meaning of the 'first Moroccan crisis', a crisis deliberately provoked by the German government and achieving the dismissal of the French Foreign Minister, Delcassé, at German orders. But thereafter the crisis did not develop according to German plans. Bülow had always reckoned to work with political opinion, but the Moroccan crisis had been devised by the Foreign Office without any propaganda preparation, 'cabinet diplomacy' possible in the days of Bismarck, but ineffective in the age of demagogy and mass agitation.

The French, sustained by British diplomatic support, recovered their nerve, and at the conference of Algeciras early in 1906 it was the German government which had to climb down. For the Bismarckian Reich, founded on the successes of 1866 and 1871, this was a catastrophe. Ever since 1871 the memory of these successes had sustained the Reich at home and Germany abroad. Germany had always got her way by threat of war, and none had dared to threaten Germany in return. Now the threat had not worked; and Germany was driven first to repeat it more raucously and then to put it into practice. From the moment when the Algeciras conference broke up European war was in prospect.

1906 saw, too, the opening of a political conflict within Germany which was an equal menace to Bismarck's work. Ever since 1898 Bülow had been provided with a secure majority not by a coalition but by the separate support of three interest-groups – the agrarians, the National Liberal industrialists, and the Centre. Each steadily pushed up its demands; and in 1906 the Centre pushed up its demands too high. The actual demand which caused the breach was for more Roman Catholic officials and greater privileges for Roman Catholic missionaries in the German colonies; but this was only one aspect of the demand that the Reich, after all a Protestant foundation, should favour the Roman Catholic Church and hamper its opponents, at first, no doubt, only free-thinkers, but later Protestants as well. As a result the Centre voted against the military estimate for suppressing a rebellion in Southwest Africa; and as the Social Democrats always voted against colonial grants the estimate was defeated. Bülow answered by organizing the 'Bülow bloc', a coalition on a 'national' basis, which carried the day at the subsequent general election of 1907. The Bülow bloc was wider than Bismarck's old coalition of agrarians and National Liberals. It included the Progressives, the liberals of principle, who became supporters of the government for the first time since 1862; the quarrel between Bülow and the Centre actually made the Progressives believe that Bülow was going 'left'. The Progressives were small in numbers, but their influence went deep into the non-political middle class and beyond it to the democratic petty bourgeoisie. Their change-over to the government side seemed to guarantee that the 'national' cause would belatedly accommodate itself to democracy; and as a result, though the Centre vote remained unchanged, many who had hitherto protested against the system by voting Social Democratic now refrained, and the Social Democrats declined from 79 to 43.

The Bülow bloc and the general election of 1907 thus seemed evidence that Germany too was following the line of political and social concession which was shown elsewhere, more or less contemporaneously, by the establishment of universal suffrage in Austria, the Clemenceau government in France, the Lloyd George budget in England, and even by the impotent Duma in Russia. It could not be imagined that the Progressives had abandoned their principles after forty-five years of devoted opposition; therefore the Junkers must be willing to abandon some measure of Bismarckian autocracy. This was a false conclusion. The Junkers were indeed increasingly alarmed at the way in which things had worked out. They disliked the demagogy of 'world policy', the prospect of having to fight not a limited war, but a war for world conquest, the megalomania and the instability of Pan-Germanism. They regretted bitterly the quiet and security of the age of Bismarck, and, lacking all political understanding, attributed the repugnant developments of the twentieth century not to the character of the Reich, but to the folly and hysteria of William II. Primitive peoples beat their tribal god when the weather proves unfavourable; and in the same way the Junkers beat William II when the social and political climate ceased to correspond to their wishes. Thus the Bülow bloc carried with it a threat to the Imperial position; but whereas the Progressives criticized William for retaining the powers which had been designed by Bismarck, the Junkers condemned him for abandoning Bismarck's policy. In fact the only unity was provided by Bülow, who in his vanity relished the prospect of taming William II and so accomplishing a job that had been too much for Bismarck.

The explosion came in the autumn of 1908, over the grotesque incident of an interview with William II published in the *Daily Telegraph*. The interview was in the routine Imperial style, rather more restrained and sensible in fact than usual, an emotional, aggrieved plea for English friendship, naïvely voicing the bewilderment which most Germans genuinely felt at English resentment against the German navy and German 'world policy'. In the ordinary way it would have passed unnoticed, as so many of William's outpourings had done. But in the fevered anxious atmosphere of 1908, with isolation apparent abroad and the collapse of stability at home, every party seized on the *Daily Telegraph* interview as evidence of William II's incapacity. He alone was to blame: to blame for weakening Bismarck's system and for maintaining it, to blame for refusing to introduce democracy and for introducing it, to blame for favouring heavy industry and for failing to favour it enough; at any rate to blame. The Reichstag was in revolt; Bülow, ostensibly accepting responsibility, encouraged the uproar; and the Emperor was compelled to announce that he would in future 'respect his constitutional obligations'. Thus autocratic monarchy, the keystone of Bismarck's Prussian-German combination, seemed to have been ended, William II relegated in disgrace to a decorative shelf. But autocracy could be ended only if something else took its place; and of this there was no sign. The crisis of November 1908 had sense only if Bülow became a constitutional Prime Minister, supported by a stable majority and ready to fulfil the wishes of his supporters. Nothing of the kind happened: Bülow remained an Imperial nominee without party connections, apparently absolute in that he had humbled the Emperor without becoming dependent on the Reichstag, in fact a figure in the void representing nothing, and within a few months brought even lower than he had brought William II.

The *Daily Telegraph* incident was Bülow's smart, intriguing attempt to redress the internal confusion. Almost simultaneously, he launched out on a device of external recovery, to restore the prestige lost in 1906. The Moroccan affair had been a defeat for 'world policy', its consequence therefore a strengthening of Continental Pan-Germanism. Moreover the display of German isolation at Algeciras, and the subsequent Anglo-Russian entente in 1907, made the preservation of Austria-Hungary more primary and more vital for German policy. The failure of the last attempts at reform within the Habsburg monarchy had brought into authority men of violence, who believed in forceful methods; and the result was the annexation of Bosnia and Hercegovina, and therewith a diplomatic dispute between Austria-Hungary and Russia, in the autumn of 1908. Bülow, a trained diplomat, understood the cardinal Bismarckian principle of keeping out of any Austro-Russian conflict, as much as he understood anything; and earlier in 1908 he had intensified the measures against the Poles in eastern Germany

partly to win back Russian favour. But with Russia still weak and neither England nor France willing to be involved in a Near Eastern dispute, the opportunity was too good to be missed. Uninvited by
Austria-Hungary, Germany pushed her way into the Bosnian quarrel
and by a thinly disguised threat of war compelled Russia to give way.
The weapon which had failed in 1906 recovered its efficacy; German
prestige seemed again rooted in success. But the sequel was discouraging. In Bismarck's day, or even after, a German threat not merely
brought the opponent's withdrawal, but turned him into a client for
German favours. In 1909 this did not happen: instead the bonds
between England, France, and Russia were drawn tighter. All Bülow had
succeeded in doing was to involve Germany in Austria-Hungary's Balkan difficulties. He condemned his own policy when, on his dismissal,
he said to William II: 'No more Bosnias.'

Bülow, in fact, survived as Chancellor only long enough to bring the
Bosnian crisis to its flashy conclusion. The conservative Junkers were
not long in repenting their co-operation with German liberalism
which they had embarked on to show their spleen against William II.
The King-Emperor, symbol of Junker domination, had been humbled;
but the Junkers had no intention of humbling themselves. Bülow,
whom the *Daily Telegraph* affair had made ostensibly dictator of Germany,
was even less to their taste than William II had been. German policy in
the Bosnian crisis was a worse departure from the principles of Bismarck than anything devised by William II; and even the latest measures of 1908 against the Poles had an alarming demagogic element.
They empowered the government to take over lands in the eastern
provinces by compulsory purchase – a weapon directed against the
Poles, but which might easily be transformed into a general attack on
the great estates. Thus, by a strange contradiction, conservative
spokesmen became defenders of the Poles and opposed as 'liberal' the
measures taken against them. The actual breach in the Bülow bloc came
over the question which had been implicit in the finance of the Reich
ever since 1879 – whether the richer classes ought not to contribute to
the mounting expenditure. A balanced budget, and balanced too by
direct taxation, was the price demanded by the Progressives for their
support, the evidence that Germany had genuinely taken the turn
towards liberalism. Death duties, always the enemy of great estates,

were the symbol chosen – symbol rather than reality, for the yield would have been small – and to prevent death duties the conservatives broke up the bloc, returned to alliance with the Centre, and defeated Bülow by a narrow majority. Nothing could better illustrate the difference between the political foundations of Germany and England than the contrasting fates of the German death duties and the English taxation of land values. Both were political demonstrations, not serious financial measures, and both were violently opposed by the owners of property; but in England the property-owners, though stretching to perversion every device of the constitution, were defeated and accepted their defeat; in Germany the property-owners were victorious without a struggle, and victorious in alliance with a party which drew its support almost entirely from the lower classes.

The defeat of the death duties ended the Indian summer of sham-liberalism in Germany; ended also Bülow as Chancellor. Without a Reichstag majority, Bülow was once more dependent on William II, whom he had humiliated, and William II turned him out without delay. Bülow was the last of the real Chancellors, the last to wield incompetently and without understanding the vast powers created by Bismarck for himself. The events of 1906 to 1909 reduced the Bismarckian constitution to chaos: the *Daily Telegraph* affair had ended the autocratic power of the Emperor; the dissolution of the Bülow bloc ended the independence of the Chancellor. Henceforth there was no one to speak with any semblance of authority. The office and title of Chancellor remained; but it was not the Chancellorship of Bismarck's conception. The Chancellor became merely a superior clerk, the administrator of a vacant estate, pushed hither and thither by conflicting impulses, bewildered, impotent, and industrious. Bismarck, Caprivi, even Bülow, had a 'policy'; but there was no such thing as the 'policy' of Bethmann Hollweg or Michaelis. From 1909 to 1916 there was in Germany an interregnum, 'full steam ahead' no doubt, but no one even attempting to hold the wheel or set a course; it is not surprising that the ship ran on to the rocks. After the fall of Bülow a consistent government of the Reich was impossible. The Prussian conservatives had been strong enough to prevent any step towards parliamentary rule, but they were not strong enough to prevent the advance of 'world policy'; the middle classes had failed politically, but threw their energy all the more into the march of economic power. All that remained of the Bismarckian structure was the army, the force with which Bismarck had won success. But the army leaders, though resolute against political interference in military matters, were without political sense or ability, as aloof and innocent in worldly affairs as any monks. After 1909 they went their own way, laboured constantly to improve the army as a fighting weapon, tried rather fumblingly to pursue their own foreign policy; but only after seven years of intensifying crisis did they realize that they must themselves take over responsibility for the Reich which they alone held together.

Bethmann Hollweg who became Chancellor in 1909 typified in all that he did and failed to do this strange period of interregnum. Unlike his precedessors he had no experience either of politics or of foreign affairs. He had not even the feeling of feet on the ground which comes of being a great landowner: he was a civil servant from Frankfurt, of a family who had supplied the Hohenzollerns with bureaucrats for generations, and would have been far more at home in the dull conscientious administration of Frederick William III than in the feverish atmosphere of 'world policy'. He was, without doubt, of higher private character than any of his predecessors, with none of Bismarck's brutality or Bülow's shiftiness. Cultured, sympathetic, honest, he ran over with good intentions: desired a reconciliation with Russia, good relations with England, fair play even for the south Slavs, co-operation even with the Social Democrats. All he lacked was any sense of power; and so it came about that this 'great gentleman' (a phrase taken from the elegant pages of Dr Gooch) became, through his very irresponsibility, responsible for the Agadir crisis, for the military violence at Saverne, for the violation of Belgian neutrality, for the deportation of conquered peoples, and for the campaign of unrestricted submarine warfare – crimes a good deal beyond Bismarck's record, all extremely distasteful to Bethmann, but all shouldered by his inexhaustible civil servant's conscience. It was useless, one might say dishonest, for him to have a high character: his sin was to belong to a class which had failed in its historic task and had become the blind instrument of Power which it could not itself master. Bismarck had said in 1867: 'Let us put Germany into the saddle. She will ride'; but in reality he had been the rider and Germany the horse. Now Bethmann threw the reins on the horse's back.

A runaway horse or, more truly, an overpowered engine out of control; such was Germany in the last years of apparent peace. Runaway in economic development, with steel production now twice as great as British, German exports passing the British mark, and German national wealth well above that of either Great Britain or France. Runaway in population with the sixty-five million mark passed in 1910 and more than 60 per cent of the population living in towns. Runaway in armaments: in 1883 Great Britain and France together spent three times as much on armaments, and Russia alone twice as much, as Germany; thirty years later England and France together spent only one and a half times as much as, and Russia considerably less than, Germany, and all three had great extra-European empires to defend, Germany, for practical purposes, none. Runaway in political ambitions, all the Pan-German projects now coming to maturity – the Baghdad railway accepted by all the interested powers, the reversion of the Portuguese colonies to Germany agreed to by England, all Germany's neighbours speaking with sympathetic awe of Germany's claim for 'a place in the sun'. In both population and economic power Germany advanced with unparalleled rapidity; and a little time must have brought both France and Russia, as it had already brought Austria-Hungary, into political and economic dependence. But for this Germany needed patience, tact, and political direction. She had none. German pride and German power demanded immediate results.

Blatant symptom of the runaway dominance of Pan-Germanism was the second Moroccan crisis, the crisis of Agadir, in 1911. In diplomatic form it resembled the first – a renewed attempt to force France away from Russia and England into the arms of Germany. But the spirit was so different as to make it inconceivable that only five years separated one crisis from the next. In 1905 hardly anyone in Germany had cared for Morocco, and popular indifference had led to the defeat of Germany at Algeciras. In 1911 the Pan-German league adopted the shady Moroccan claims of the Mannesmann brothers, adventurers in iron and steel. The Agadir crisis, designed by Kiderlen, Bethmann's Secretary of State, as a restrained manœuvre to win over France, became a demonstration of German enthusiasm, a development as unwelcome to the great German industrialists, who had been steadily buying up French iron ore undertakings, as to the German diplomats. Far from having to whip up German feeling, Bethmann – who had invoked German armed strength far more openly than Bülow did in 1905 – was badgered and humiliated in the Reichstag for his timidity, and had to defend himself by claiming that he had given a painstaking imitation of a bully. Ominous for the dissatisfaction which it caused in Germany, the threat of Agadir was even more ominous for the reaction it provoked abroad. Instead of alarm and surrender, there was resistance and a new solidarity between England, France, and Russia. In France the advocates of a Franco-German economic partnership were driven from power, and succeeded by the men of the *réveil national*, first genuine assertion of French confidence for a century. In England Agadir was followed indeed by a new attempt to restore good relations with Germany, but not on the German terms of the exclusion of England from Europe; and the mission of Haldane to Berlin, early in February 1912, designed to reconcile the two countries, began instead a British realization of the extent of German ambitions. The power of the German threat was exhausted; and with it the prestige of the tottering political order within Germany. Futile and empty mechanically to reproduce Bismarck's old manœuvre of an enlarged armaments programme. The Reichstag agreed without demur to Tirpitz's new naval demands and to a supplement to the Army Law; but it agreed also without enthusiasm – the display of German weapons no longer impressed either the Germans or foreign powers.

Clear symptom of the crisis within Germany was the general election of 1912, when the middle-class liberal parties at last abandoned their former prejudices and co-operated belatedly with the Social Democrats. The Social Democrats were returned as the largest single party, at last outstripping the Centre; and had it not been for the antiquated distribution of constituencies, which gave the rural areas, though with only a third of the population, equal representation with the towns, the Social Democratic preponderance would have been even greater. Had the liberal parties been sincere in their new professions, they would have embarked on a fight for constituency reform; but they made no move – they were ready to invoke the threat of the Social Democrats, but determined to keep the threat an empty one. Still, Bismarck's work was clearly in dissolution when, after forty years of unity, the government of the Reich was unable to count on a majority in the Reichstag. Bethmann acted in this crisis of home affairs as he acted with foreign powers: he made impotent and meaningless gestures of appeasement, consulted the Social Democratic leaders – though he did not act on their advice – and even promised to end the three-class franchise in Prussia, basis of Junker power, but took no steps to fulfil his promise. One step, and an important one, taken in 1913, had a demagogic air and revealed by anticipation how the political crisis must end. The general staff, alleging the danger from the increased peace-time levies in Russia and from the change in France from two-year to three-year military service (which would not be effective until 1915), presented a demand for £50 million (1,000 million marks) for 'non-recurring military expenditure'. This sum, incomparably vast for those days, was to be spent within the year and, for once, was to be raised not by loan, but by direct taxation, by means of a capital levy. The capital levy did not challenge the great landowners, as death duties had done, for their capital consisted of mortgaged estates; but being 'Progressive', a concession to the view that expenditure should be met by taxation, it was welcomed by the Reichstag and supported even by the Social Democrats. Germany, internally rent asunder, could still unite on a programme of great armaments, if only they were given a certain demagogic flavour.

This demonstration did nothing to strengthen the position of Bethmann. It served only to underline the contradiction of German wishes: the great majority of Germans wanted a Germany overwhelmingly strong, asserting by means of this strength her claim to 'a place in the sun', and basing her security on Power, not on agreement with her neighbours; at the same time they wanted a constitutional system inside Germany and resented the arrogance and predominance of the military caste. Few Germans felt the absurdity of desiring to dominate all Europe and yet to escape domination themselves; and this blindness was convincingly shown in a great protest against militarism which united almost all Germany in the autumn of 1913. This was the affair of Saverne (Zabern), one of the few districts of Alsace loyal to Germany, but where the arrogance of the officers of the garrison provoked quarrels with the townspeople; the officer in command defied the law and, on his own authority, arrested and imprisoned some of the inhabitants. All Germany was stirred. Bethmann, as usual, thought that the military were wrong and, again as usual, thought it his duty to defend them. The government was challenged in the Reichstag and, deserted by all but a handful of dumb agrarians whose loyalty was inexhaustible, was condemned by a vote of 293 to 54, impressive victory of Liberals, Social Democrats, and Centre. But the vote had no sequel. Bethmann remained as Chancellor; Colonel von Reuter, the commander at Saverne, was acquitted by a court martial; the capital levy continued to pour in and to be at once poured out again to the great steel and armament firms; and the military leaders, recognizing Bethmann's impotence, continued to act on the assumption that no civil government existed. The Saverne affair is sometimes adduced as proof that Germany was on the way to constitutionalism. It is made the basis of a plausible 'if only' of the sort which has so often served to cloak German failings. If only Bismarck had not been superlatively clever, German liberalism would have done the trick; if only William II had not been so wild, German foreign policy would not have been so aggressive; and so, in 1914, if only the Serbs had not defied Austria-Hungary, Germany would have matured into a democracy. In fact, the Saverne affair showed that the Germans were perfectly aware of their political condition and perfectly incapable of remedying it.

Or thought perhaps of remedying it by foreign war? The advocates of constitutional government were unable to overthrow the militarists in time of peace; but they would be reconciled to the militarists in case of war. Even more than in 1870 war held out the only hope of national unity; and indeed had there been in the Reich any planned direction, it would have aimed at war in the summer of 1914. There is much evidence of a conscious German focusing on August 1914: the capital levy would then have been raised and spent; the Kiel Canal would be open for the passage of dreadnoughts; and Germany's gold reserve would be at its highest level. This view cannot be combated by examining the official documents of the German government; for Bethmann's intentions, which are all that these record, were irrelevant to the issue. The German military leaders were confident of their strength, anxious for war, and without any political scruples. But on the other hand they were also without political gifts or understanding. They were professional soldiers, incapable of action or policy until the guns began to fire. In fact to accuse Germany of having consciously planned and provoked the outbreak of war in August 1914 is to credit Germany with more direction than she possessed. Berchtold, the Austrian Foreign Minister, overwhelmed in July 1914 with contradictory telegrams from Bethmann and Moltke, the German Chief of Staff, passed the best verdict on German politics: 'What a joke! Who does rule in Berlin then?' Bethmann did not want a war at all, nor even the advance of German supremacy; the German masses wanted a glorious Germany, but without war or even military domination; the great industrialists wished to advance their economic domination over north-eastern France and southern Russia, but could do it better and more certainly without war; the Junkers wanted a militarist Germany to preserve their social position, but not a war of conquest which would ruin it; the generals wanted a victorious war, but as an academic exercise and without the slightest idea what they would do with their victory when they had won it. It would be absurd to imagine that Bethmann ruled in Berlin, or even William II; but equally absurd to suppose that Moltke, nervous, timid, ill – the man who imposed on the Schlieffen plan of destroying France a defensive spirit – ruled in Berlin either. What a joke! No one ruled in Berlin. The impulses that desired peace added up to nothing; the impulses that aimed at aggression added up irresistibly to war.

The diplomatic crisis of July 1914, which preceded the outbreak of war, was not, as were the two Moroccan crises or even the crisis of 1909, a manufacture of the German Foreign Office; it was imposed on Germany, though it corresponded all the same to her needs. The two Moroccan crises had been crises of 'world policy'; the crisis of 1909 a deliberate stroke for internal popularity. The crisis of 1914 was more fundamental, for it raised anew the question which had always hung over Bismarck's Reich – was Germany to abandon or to extend the advance into south-eastern Europe which had been proceeding without direction for centuries? Bismarck had abandoned this advance, in the interest of the Prussian landowners, or rather had attempted to arrest it; but he was seeking to arrest the deepest force in organized German life. In 1914 the ice which Bismarck had tried to perpetuate on the Danube and the Balkans melted for good. Germany must either jettison Austria-Hungary and go back – abandon, that is, south-eastern Europe and Bohemia to the Slavs, tolerate the overthrow of Magyar supremacy in Great Hungary, and content herself with a Reich that would end at Vienna – or she must support Austria-Hungary and go forward – reassert the German character of Bohemia, second Magyar predominance in Hungary, and carry German power through the Balkans to the gates of Constantinople, and beyond. Germany, in her internal political confusion, no doubt chose her means badly: it was grotesque to leave the decision in the hands of the aristocratic muddlers of Vienna. But even with better political leadership the decision would have remained to be made. The Habsburg monarchy was falling to pieces: was Germany to allow its legacy to pass into the hands of the Slavs, or was she to claim the legacy of the Habsburgs as she had already identified herself with the legacy of the Hohenzollerns? The question answers itself. No German government of whatever political complexion or political capacity could freely abandon all eastern Europe from Bohemia to the Balkans; the most it could do, as Bismarck did, was to postpone the decision by attempting to keep the Habsburg monarchy in being. The Habsburgs were, in fact, the essential condition of 'Little Germany'; and the moment that the Habsburg system broke down – as the breach with Serbia proclaimed that it had done – Greater Germany, the Germany without limits, was the alternative which only a German defeat in war could prevent. Many Germans, Bethmann at the time and most German historians later, condemned the haste and provocation of Austria-Hungary's action; but the difference was one of tactics – none ever doubted that Magyar and German supremacy must be preserved throughout south-eastern Europe. Similarly the difference between Bethmann and Moltke, which has sometimes served to give the civilian German government a sort of acquittal, was tactical: Moltke thought that the superiority of the German and Austro-Hungarian armies was at its greatest; Bethmann, believing that England could be detached from France and Russia, thought the moment ill-chosen. But, as usual, Bethmann conformed to the requirements of the general staff: he condemned, and supported, the Austro-Hungarian ultimatum; condemned, and supported, the German match through Belgium. Thus all the agencies of Bismarck's Reich – not merely the army command, but the Emperor and Chancellor and all the social forces of Junkerdom which it had been Bismarck's aim to preserve – threw themselves into a struggle for German domination of

Europe, a victory in which would make the survival of old Prussia impossible. Such was the conclusion, paradoxical but inevitable, of Bismarck's work: Greater Germany had taken her Prussian conquerors captive. To outward appearance all Germany surrendered to Prussian militarism – in reality it was Prussian militarism which was fighting for an alien German cause. Of this the regrets of the conscientious Prussian official Bethmann were evidence; and even plainer were the protests of Heeringen, the old-fashioned Prussian Minister of War, against the inflation of the German army as the result of the capital levy – for him the object of policy was not to conquer Europe, but to preserve the aristocratic character of the Prussian Officer Corps. But the bargain imposed upon Prussian landowners and German industrialists by Bismarck in 1871 had to be carried to its logical conclusion. The Junkers who desired a conservative static policy agreed to conduct a war of aggression; and the capitalists who desired to master Europe by economic penetration agreed to achieve their aim by military violence.

But it would be wrong to present the First World War as solely the product of a bargain between Junkers and capitalists; the German people counted for something in this bargain too. In fact, if they had not played their part, the bargain would have been meaningless. The cry of 'the Fatherland in danger' had latterly lost some of its force when raised in a purely diplomatic crisis; but with war it once more came into its own. The Social Democrats held out longest, but they too were swept away by the prospect of war with Russia; for this was the old radical programme of war against Tsardom, the war which had been so often preached by Marx and Engels. As a result the Reichstag, without receiving any clear explanation of German policy, agreed unanimously on August 4th, 1914, to the grant of war credits. Nor was this all. The parties went further: they declared Burgfrieden, a civil truce, agreeing neither to criticize each other nor to oppose the government. Nothing had changed in Germany: Bethmann was still feeble; William II still hysterical and erratic; the militarists still arrogant and ruthless. Yet Bethmann, and the system for which he stood – the weakest of Chancellors and a system in dissolution – received a demonstration of national confidence never accorded to Bismarck, still less to the free German government of 1848. This was an abdication of the whole German people, an abdication not, of course, to Bethmann, but to the

High Command. Tsarist troops in East Prussia were the excuse for this abdication, not the cause. How could any German who knew the vast preparations of German militarism suppose that Tsardom was a serious danger to the German army? The Tsarist danger soon proved mythical, the principal enemy France, and still more England. But Social Democratic propaganda accommodated itself as easily to the struggle against 'entente capitalism' as it had done to the defence against 'Tsarist absolutism'. The Social Democrats, in truth, had long been waiting to enter into alliance with the authoritarian Reich as the Centre had done before them; and in August 1914 they returned eagerly to Lassalle's programme of alliance with Prussian militarism against capitalist liberalism, this time on an international stage. The Prussian bureaucrats and the Prussian generals were to accomplish the revolution which the Social Democrats had been unable to achieve themselves. For just as the Prussian liberals of 1866 were confident that Bismarck would establish a liberal Germany, so the Social Democrats of 1914 were confident that the High Command would give them Socialism. Rationing was Socialism; production of armaments at high profits was Socialism; the transportation of Belgian workers to distant ends of the Reich was Socialism; the unification of all the industry and iron fields of western Europe under German control was Socialism. 'Socialism as far as the eye can see,' one of them exclaimed in 1915. The German Socialist leaders knew well that the great expansion of German industry, on which the security of their trade union members was based, had been achieved by methods of economic conquest, and they recognized that military conquest was now necessary to second the economic advance. One of them wrote: 'The ruin of German industry would be the ruin of the German working class.' And as German industry would be ruined by anything less than the conquest of all Europe, the German working class were willing to become the instrument of this conquest.

The German war plan, consciously formed by the general staff, unconsciously assumed by the German people, was a plan for a short war, a repetition of the successes of 1866 and 1870. France was to be defeated within six weeks, Russia within six months; England, internally divided and without a Continental army, would be excluded from Europe. Hence the lack of defined war aims; hence the surrender of all parties to military authority; hence the ominous financing of the war by loans and the issue of paper money – an indemnity would put everything right within a few months. In September 1914, this war plan met disaster at the battle of the Marne, imperishable glory of French arms. The chance of a quick victory faded, disappeared. Yet at the same moment the defeat of the Russians at Tannenberg gave Germany the security which was her ostensible war aim, and at any time between September 1914 and the summer of 1917 Germany could have had peace on the basis of the *status quo*: no doubt the French would have demanded concessions in Alsace and Lorraine, but they would have received little backing from England and would have been helpless without it. But for Germany the *status quo* was impossible: for it would have brought to an explosion within Germany all the problems which had led to the outbreak of war. Peace on the basis of the *status quo* would have ended the myth of Success, on which the Bismarckian system was based, and so have brought the authoritarian Reich to chaos; the German armies could not come home unless victorious. Peace without victory was, moreover, impossible financially, for it would have left Germany overwhelmed with debt; it was impossible economically, for it would have arrested the expansion of German industry; it was impossible in Europe, for it would have left the Slavs free to pursue their campaign for liberation; it was above all impossible spiritually, for it would have implied the abandonment of 'world policy' and the destruction of German self-confidence. Logically and inevitably failure to win a quick victory compelled all Germans – the High Command, Bethmann and William II, the liberals and the Social Democrats – to identify themselves with the Pan-German proposals which before 1914 they would have repudiated in all sincerity. Each group contributed some acquisitive element of its own and in return swallowed with reluctance the demands of the others; but since there was no government or unified direction the various programmes all added up to a project of indiscriminate unlimited conquest.

The great industrialists thought in terms of control of French resources and economic struggle against England: therefore annexation of north-eastern France and a protectorate over Belgium. The Prussian landowners wished to strengthen themselves within Germany by joining forces with the 'Baltic barons', the German landowners in Russia's Baltic provinces: therefore 'freedom' for Lithuania and Courland. These were the war aims of the 'national' parties, Conservatives and National Liberals who in the crisis of 1917 revived in the Fatherland Party the Bismarckian coalition of 1887. They were repudiated – more because they threatened to prolong the war, than from principle – by the parties of the German people, the Centre, the Progressives, and the Social Democrats. But these too had their programme of war aims: the achievement of the Greater Germany of 1848. It was a Progressive, Naumann, subsequently a pillar of the republic, who formulated these demands in a famous book and gave them their classical name: *Mitteleuropa*. In Naumann's 'democratic' vision the severance of Austria from Germany was to be undone and all Austria-Hungary was to become part of the German national state; German cultural and economic supremacy was to extend to Constantinople and perhaps beyond; the Tsarist Empire was to be dismembered for the sake of the Ukraine, so that ultimately the bounds of Greater Germany would extend to the Caucasus and the Persian Gulf. This programme was supported by pacific democratic Germans on the naïve ground that as north-eastern France and Belgium – except of course for Antwerp – would be left untouched, England and France would be prepared to ignore what was afoot on the hither side of Germany and would make peace. It was a programme significant of German aims, but even more significant in that it was not a programme of what is loosely called the 'governing classes' – though they had ceased to govern – the industrialists and the Junkers. For this programme, reuniting to Germany the Roman Catholic Germans of central Europe, was in direct contradiction with Junker interests and, for that matter, did nothing to increase the iron-ore supplies of the industrialists of the Ruhr. As in 1848 Mitteleuropa was the programme of a coalition between Roman Catholic romantics and radical Pan-Germans; and, to complete the likeness, the coalition demanded the freeing of Poland from Russia. In this way the Social Democrats could be assured that, though marching under the standard of the Hohenzollerns, they were faithful to the doctrines of the revolutionary war.

Both programmes, the programme of the 'governing classes' and the programme of popular Pan-Germanism, implied a total German victory, the virtual disappearance of independent states in Europe. But there existed in Germany in the First World War forces which repudiated this programme of conquest and sought for an alternative. The first of these forces came from all those members of the 'governing classes' – intelligent industrialists, sceptical generals, rigid Junkers, competent bureaucrats, Bethmann himself – who believed that Germany could not win the war; but as a peace without victory raised even more terrifying problems than endless war, their opposition counted for nothing. They regretted, they lamented, they complained; but they acquiesced in every step taken to achieve a world conquest which they believed to be impossible. On the other side there grew up within the ranks of the Social Democratic party two separate movements of those who could not stomach the co-operation with the authoritarian Reich to which the party had committed itself in August 1914. The first was the movement of Liebknecht and Rosa Luxemburg, later known as Spartacists; the second the group of Social Democrats who, when expelled from the party, took the name of 'Independents'. The Spartacists were revolutionaries, loyal to the teaching of Marx and Engels which was still the official party programme, and for whom the war mattered only as a way of achieving their revolutionary aim. To this revolution everything else was subordinated; but in fact their national aim, which they would have had to operate if they had ever gained power, was Pan-German – in Rosa Luxemburg's phrase, 'a great united German republic', as Marx had demanded in 1848, including, that is to say, both the Czechs of Bohemia and the other Slav peoples of the Austrian Empire. Thus the Spartacists objected to the programme of Pan-Germanism only that it was being achieved by counts and generals and the Hohenzollern Emperor instead of by Rosa Luxemburg and Karl Liebknecht. The Independent Socialists, however, genuinely repudiated Pan-Germanism as well as its protagonists. They were the last upholders of civil virtues; the last to value freedom and the rights of the individual above conquest and the rights of Germany. Their war programme, so far as they had one, was to end the war by agreement and to establish in Germany a democratic régime. Or rather democratic régimes; for in essence they repudiated the Reich, with its military foundation, and, knowing well the weakness of democratic feeling, desired to make a beginning in the separate states. They were, that is to say, particularists, at any rate by implication; the heirs of the liberals of the early nineteenth century, who had found 'true Germany' in the liberal particularism of Bavaria, Wurtemberg, and Baden. In essence, they found the problem of the Reich insoluble – perhaps rightly – and therefore wished it out of existence; but by doing so they wished themselves out of existence as a German force – they could achieve their aim only if others destroyed German power, and they acquired a temporary importance only in the hour of German defeat. In repudiating Pan-Germanism, they repudiated Germany. Of course, both the Spartacists and the Independents gained a certain fictitious support as the war dragged on and its hardships mounted; for, with no war taxation and less control on war profits than in either France or England, the conditions of life between rich and poor became ever more blatantly contrasted. But the support they received was merely the expression of a grumbling discontent; much as the English working man who finds the public-house out of beer at 7 p.m. proclaims himself a communist. In reality few of the Spartacists were Marxist revolutionaries; and even fewer of the followers of the Independents desired the destruction of the Reich.

The Reich existed in the armies; the government of the Reich had already ceased to exist as a directing force. In the first two years of war first Moltke and then Falkenhayn, his successor as Chief of the General Staff, were overwhelmed with their military tasks and had neither time nor ability to attempt also the task of government. Therefore Bethmann, last remnant of Bismarck's system, was left in nominal control, impotent to influence events, but striving still to hit on a programme which would both end the war and satisfy the demands of the political forces inside Germany – with the exception, of course, of the Spartacists and the Independents. To tempt the Allies he made offers to withdraw from Belgium and northern France; to satisfy the industrialists he made these offers spurious. To satisfy the Social Democrats he held out hopes of the liberation of Poland; to satisfy the Junkers and to keep the door open for a separate peace with Russia he made these hopes spurious also. To satisfy the Greater Germans he encouraged the reestablishment of German supremacy in Bohemia; to remain faithful to the principles of Bismarck's policy he continued to treat Austria-Hungary as an independent and non-German power. Similarly, in home affairs, he promised a reform of the Prussian franchise; and took care never to put his promise into action. This was not government, nor even tactics; it was the helpless lurching of a machine utterly out of control. The government of the Reich had become as shadowy and meaningless as the movement of constitutional liberalism which it had ordered out of existence fifty years before; it would vanish at a word. This word was spoken on August 29th, 1916, when – as the result of the failures on the western front – William II dismissed Falkenhayn and appointed in his place Hindenburg, hitherto commander in the east, with Ludendorff as his Quartermaster-General. On that day the supremacy of the military leaders, which Bismarck and even his successors had resisted, was established; the Chancellor, and for that matter the Emperor, ceased to exist as a separate force; and there began a dictatorship of the High Command, which ended only after the defeated German armies had marched home and dispersed.

10

THE RULE OF THE GERMAN ARMY, 1916–19

In August 1916, the German military leaders became for the first time the undisputed rulers of Germany, no longer subordinated to the Emperor, still less held in check by the Chancellor. The reason for this change was simple: German policy, as represented by Emperor and Chancellor alike, had failed. Success, the key to political authority in Germany, rested with the military leaders alone. The parties of the Reichstag, unimpeded even by the Social Democrats, flung themselves under the leadership of Ludendorff, as, long before, the liberals had flung themselves under the leadership of Bismarck, regardless of the fact that by so doing they were destroying the constitutional structure to which the Reichstag belonged. In October 1916, when Bethmann was vainly trying to hold up the declaration of unrestricted submarine warfare, the Reichstag, on the motion of the Centre, virtually declared that it would support the Chancellor only if he obeyed the orders of the Supreme Command. Thus the dictatorship was in the fullest sense a dictatorship by consent, a logical development from the original jettisoning of liberal principles during the struggles of the nineteenth century.

The Supreme Commander was Hindenburg, legendary figure of

unshakable popularity, but without either political or military gifts; his role was to play William I to Ludendorff's Bismarck. The dictatorship of Ludendorff was very far from being, as is often alleged, a new version of the 'rule of the Junkers'; it was the rule of an independent military machine which had escaped from the control of its authors. Ludendorff himself was of non-Junker origin, his low birth an insuperable barrier to the attainment of nominal supremacy, but not to the possession of real power. The German army was no longer an army of peasants officered by landowners; both peasant soldiers and still more Junker officers had perished in the first battles of 1914. The soldiers were now Social Democrats and Roman Catholic Centrists; the officers were from the professional middle classes – aping the harshness and brutality of their Junker predecessors, but with none of their political caution and restraint. The generals and high staff officers were still of Junker origin, and disliked much of Ludendorff's policy: they were still loyal to William II, the superseded 'supreme war lord', they resented the patronage of Poland, they abhorred Pan-Germanism. But they could do nothing. The Hindenburg legend was the success myth without which the army would cease to fight: therefore, so long as Hindenburg reposed confidence in Ludendorff, the Ludendorff dictatorship was unshakable, a demagogic dictatorship even though wielded by a general. The rank was an accident; the essential thing was the success-myth and the confidence of the mass army which that implied, and a corporal who captured the myth could fill the role quite as well – in fact better, for he would be free of the Junker prejudices which still hampered Ludendorff.

Ludendorff was without political training and, still more, without political ambition. He became dictator unwillingly, solely to preserve Germany, and his political programme was improvised from day to day, according to the needs and standards of the army. Thus, in domestic affairs he had no guiding principle beyond the resentment, felt by every soldier in the front line, that the factory workers should work under easier conditions and for greater rewards than the man in the trenches; a feeling no doubt anti-liberal, but none the less demagogic for all that. Similarly his 'foreign policy' or programme of war aims, absurdly enough, was not a programme for a peace treaty, but solely for the conduct of the next war, and in it he included the most contradictory elements. The industrialists' demand for north-eastern France and Belgium, a Little German demand, would strengthen the German armament industry; Ludendorff espoused it. The unrestricted submarine campaign, anti-English and therefore also Little German, would defeat England; Ludendorff forced it through. The Junker demand for Lithuania and Courland, which would give the Prussian landowners a new lease of political life in Germany, would strengthen Ludendorff's left flank in the next war: he added it to his programme. But at the same time, he added elements from the Greater German creed of democratic tradition, elements which would ruin the last fragments of Junker power. Ever since the beginning of the war, German policy had fumbled with the problem of Poland – anxious on the one hand to fool the Social Democrats by a pro-Polish policy; anxious on the other not to raise an insuperable barrier to a separate peace with Russia; anxious, above all, not to establish in Russian Poland a genuine Polish movement which would demand the return of Prussia's Polish territories as well. In the autumn of 1916 Bethmann thought that he was at last within sight of peace with decaying Tsardom. Ludendorff, concerned only to bring out a Polish army on the German side, overrode Bethmann and insisted on the proclamation of an independent Kingdom of Poland in November 1916. So, too, with the affairs of the Habsburg monarchy, Ludendorff thought only of how to subordinate Austria-Hungary completely to the German High Command. The answer: German supremacy in Austria, the dream of the radicals of 1848 and of the extreme German nationalists of the eighteen-eighties; the 'Austrian mission', that high-sounding will-o'-the-wisp, became nothing more than an organization for compelling the Slav peoples to fight for German domination both of Europe and of themselves, and the Czechs, Slovenes, and Croats were driven irrevocably on to the side of the Allies. Ludendorff went further: he was impatient with the Magyar attempts to preserve their authority and independence in Hungary, and, if he had had time, would have reduced Hungary, a basic part of Bismarck's system, as ruthlessly as any conquered area. Beyond Austria-Hungary, there was German occupation of Roumania, German administration of Serbia, German military direction of Turkey, German power ranging to the Persian Gulf.

Thus, for purely military reasons, Ludendorff became the champion of the old programme of Greater Germany, the programme in 1850 of Schwarzenberg and Bruck, Bismarck's greatest enemies. But Ludendorff did not operate this programme effectively. It was a demagogic programme and needed for its execution a demagogic spirit. Ludendorff's demagogy was unconscious; consciously he was a narrow-minded Prussian general. To make German supremacy in Austria-Hungary effective Ludendorff would have had to co-operate with the Austrian German radicals and the Austrian German traders whose influence extended to the Aegean. Instead he continued to work with generals and politicians drawn from the Habsburg aristocracy, who were still skilful enough to make his policy empty. The German fanatics in Austria were not given power; instead the politicians of the old aristocracy, driven desperate by fear, tried to escape from the war by a separate peace with the Allies and impeded every German proposal for total victory. Still more in Poland, Ludendorff estranged Tsardom and the Prussian Junkers without winning over the Poles; he could not really bring himself to play the Polish game which might have brought Germany speedy victory in the east. There was an enduring moral: the programme of Greater Germany, to which the army had now committed itself, could only be executed by a genuine demagogue, a man risen from the masses, in fact a corporal, not a general.

Still, even with this lack of a real demagogic spirit, Ludendorff's policy marked the end of the Prussian system. The King of Prussia might have the empty name of supreme war lord; in reality Prussia as much as Austria was subordinated to the High Command. Little Germany and Greater Germany, radical hostility to Russia and conservative hostility to England, expansion down the Danube and expansion overseas (or, more correctly, under them) were all amalgamated. The 'national' parties of Junkers and industrialists supported, with a wry face, the Greater German demagogy of the masses; the masses, sincerely convinced that they were engaged in a defensive war, fought for the imperialist demands of the 'national' classes. The Germans found in war the unity which they had failed to find in peace – unity at the expense of the foreigner, of the French, the Belgians, the Russians, the Czechs, the South Slavs, the Roumanians. In all Europe the only willing allies of the Germans were the Magyars, fighting in a more limited sphere for a similar cause: to divert attention from the great estates by a struggle to maintain Magyar supremacy in Greater Hungary. And even the Magyar chauvinists, alarmed at German claims, would have been glad to escape from the alliance, if they could have done so without sacrificing their national predominance. In sum, German war aims, far from being the desire of a limited 'governing class', expressed the demands of the whole people: German domination of Europe was the compensation for the freedom which the Germans had failed to achieve at home. It was a people's war, and Ludendorff, the guarantor of success, the people's leader.

But suppose he did not succeed? This discouraging question raised its head in the winter of 1916–17, the hardest winter of the war years, with transport disorganized and food supplies terribly inadequate. Ludendorff, able strategist as he was, could not work miracles. He had taken over a difficult situation and planned for 1917 a defensive policy, with dispiriting results. More setbacks followed. In March 1917, the first Russian revolution ended all hope of a separate peace with Tsardom and seemed to threaten a greater Russian war effort on a more popular basis; in April 1917, the United States was provoked into war by the unrestricted submarine campaign. As a result there was at last wide support for the Spartacists and Independent Social Democrats, a protest of war weariness which reached its peak with mutinies of the German fleet in July 1917. But these two parties were outside the pale; all the great parties, including the majority of Social Democrats, were committed to the defence of the Reich – all, that is, except the Centre, the party of pure sectarian opportunism. The Centre had tolerated military rule as long as it was successful, but it had no patriotic scruples, only a determination to preserve Roman Catholic privileges, and was quite as ready to gamble with defeat as it had previously gambled with victory. In the spring of 1917 Erzberger, demagogic Centre leader and the smartest of politicians, visited Hoffmann, Ludendorff's successor as chief of staff on the eastern front and his bitter critic, and was convinced by him that the war was lost, Previously the champion of unlimited annexations, Erzberger returned to Berlin the advocate of peace by understanding and the opponent of the High Command; he was concerned not to save Germany, but solely to ensure that in case of defeat the German masses would look to the Centre, and not to the Independent Social Democrats, for leadership. This was the meaning of the attack made by Erzberger on Bethmann on July 6th, when he accused the Chancellor of following a policy of conquest and demanded the enunciation of defensive war aims. Erzberger's line altogether outbid the Social Democrats, who – in order to win the favour of the High Command for the trade unions – had refused to criticize its annexationist programme. But an extraordinary development followed: Erzberger had attacked Bethmann for being too aggressive; Ludendorff objected to Bethmann as too feeble. As a result Ludendorff took the opportunity of the Reichstag attack to get rid of Bethmann and to put in his place a Chancellor who would be utterly subordinate to the High Command; and this move was welcomed by the liberals and Social Democrats, who believed that the Reichstag would capture political importance by getting rid of Bethmann, even though in fact they were attaining their end only with the assistance of the High Command. This attitude was carried furthest by Stresemann, the National Liberal leader, who – believing that democracy was essential for the attainment of the annexationist programme – instituted himself the spokesman of the High Command, in the hope it would give him democracy in return. None dared openly to attack the High Command; even Erzberger had to remember that there were millions of Roman Catholics in the army. The party leaders therefore planned to sap the High Command by intrigue: to accept its co-operation against Bethmann and then to put in his place as the standard-bearer of liberalism and a negotiated peace Bülow, hero of the Bülow bloc, now to be reinforced by the support of the Centre. No one can deny that the German politicians made up for their impotence by an unbounded cunning: they genuinely imagined that they would achieve parliamentary rule in Germany first by playing off the High Command against Bethmann, and then by playing off Bülow against the High Command.

This grotesque 'combination' broke down at the first hurdle. William II had not forgotten the humiliation of the *Daily Telegraph* incident and would not hear Bülow's name mentioned. Ludendorff then produced the first candidate who came to hand, Michaelis, the Prussian Food Controller, and this totally unknown bureaucrat was imposed upon the Reichstag as the mouthpiece of the High Command. Thus ended the great political crisis which was to have won for Germany parliamentary government. Still, the Reichstag parties had to be given some empty consolation: they had failed to make a Chancellor, but they insisted all the more on a declaration of policy. Therefore was produced the 'peace resolution' (passed on July 19th), a string of innocuous phrases about Germany's peaceful intentions, which the Centre, the Social Democrats, and the Progressives regarded as a great victory. But the 'peace resolution' was accepted by Michaelis on behalf of the High Command 'as I understand it'; and this understanding was subsequently found to include the treaties of Brest-Litovsk and Bucharest. Nor was this understanding confined to the High Command. Erzberger, its author, himself said: 'You see, in this way I get the Longwy-Briey line [in north-eastern France] by means of negotiation.' In truth the peace resolution was without significance as a serious declaration of German policy, still less as a renunciation by the Germans of their annexationist plans. It counted only in internal politics and served a double purpose. For the High Command, it was a way of convincing the German masses that they were not fighting a war of conquest and so revived mass enthusiasm for the war; for the Social Democrats and the Centre, it was a gesture against the war, a re-insurance so that in case of defeat they could appear with clean hands before the German people, perhaps even before the Allies. Thus the political move which gave Germany the energy to pursue for fifteen months more a struggle for European supremacy was later used by its authors to prove their freedom from aggressive designs; an example of the 'heads I win, tails you lose' spirit which had so often characterized German policy.

Hardly had the 'peace resolution' been passed than it appeared to become academic; for in the early autumn of 1917 Russia's resistance collapsed. Hoffmann's anticipations seemed to have been proved wrong; and with the prospect of victory there was no need to cajole the German masses by a conciliatory policy, still less to insure against a German defeat. Therefore all parties, except the Independent Social Democrats, once more abandoned the platform of the 'peace resolution' and welcomed the victories of the High Command. Ludendorff, on his side, made a gesture of appeasement. He recognized that Michaelis, the joke Chancellor, was incompetent even to sustain the figleaf of parliamentary pretence which was all that the Reichstag parties asked; therefore Michaelis was ordered out of office, as Bethmann had been, and succeeded by Hertling, aged Bavarian Prime Minister and a leader of the Centre. This was ostensibly a victory for the Reichstag; and it was certainly a strange development for Bismarck's Protestant Prussian Reich to have a Roman Catholic Bavarian as war Chancellor and Prime Minister of Prussia, and quite as strange to have in Payer, the Vice-Chancellor, the only Progressive ever to become an Imperial minister. But Hertling and Payer regarded it as their duty only to keep the Reichstag in a good temper; they did not attempt to carry out its wishes. The threadbare project for a reform of the Prussian franchise was given a fresh airing, exposed in the window but not for sale; and the Prussian parliament was still discussing the abolition of the three-class system when, on November 19th, 1918, events swept both franchise and Prussian monarchy out of existence. So, too, in the more critical sphere of foreign affairs Hertling and Payer acquiesced in and supported all the annexationist projects of the High Command; opposition, solely on grounds of expediency, came from Kühlmann, the Secretary of State, cynical professional diplomat, and a paradox indeed – from General Hoffmann, the chief of staff on the eastern front.

In the winter of 1917–18, with both Russia and Roumania utterly defeated, Germany had a chance of making peace in the east and so of freeing all her forces for the decisive struggle in the west; it was the moment of destiny. But now the High Command was the prisoner of its own demands. A moderate peace with Russia, really ending the eastern war, would have saved Germany from catastrophe in France; and it could always have been denounced in case of victory. But Ludendorff was too deeply committed: the prospect of a German Baltic, of the Ukraine under German control, of German forces on the Caucasus, was too much for him. Such were the terms presented to Trotsky, the Bolshevik representative, at the conference of Brest-Litovsk. The Bolsheviks did not expect to gain anything by negotiation with the German imperialists; but they still harboured illusions about the revolutionary German people and appealed over the heads of the generals and politicians to the German soldiers and workers. In the ranks of the German army this propaganda produced no response; among the German, and still more the Austrian, factory workers, war weariness rather than Bolshevik propaganda produced, in January 1918, an outburst of strikes, conducted on the basis of a muddled programme of democratic demands and containing among the more obscure points the item of 'a speedy peace without annexations' – speed, rather than no annexations, being the serious consideration. These strikes, in any case concerned only with domestic grievances, came to nothing, though they were later to provide the evidence, flimsy enough, of the German 'will to peace'. The German working class, with its solid Social Democratic majority, had claimed to be fighting only to defend Germany from Tsarist invasion; yet they continued to fight when Tsardom had fallen and the Russian army collapsed, and when there was imposed on Russia a peace treaty which deprived her of a territory nearly as large as Austria-Hungary and Turkey combined; of fifty-six million inhabitants; of a third of her railway mileage; of 79 per cent of her iron and 89 per cent of her coal production. Betrayed by the German working class the Bolsheviks signed on March 3rd, 1918, the treaty of Brest-Litovsk.

There was a final stage: the treaty had to be ratified by the Reichstag, written into the records which contained the 'peace resolution'. But the peace resolution was primarily the outcome of the prospect of defeat; it declared, that is, in favour of a peace of conciliation, if Germany was defeated. But Brest-Litovsk was evidence that Germany had won; therefore in the eyes of the Centre and the Progressives, the peace resolution no longer applied. The Social Democrats followed a more elaborate reasoning. They disliked the methods of the High Command and repudiated its pursuit of a purely military purpose; on the other hand, still echoing the radical programme of 1848, they welcomed the 'liberation' of Lithuania, Courland, Poland, and the Ukraine from Russian rule. As a result they protested against the way in which the treaty had been made, but abstained from voting. Only the Independent Social Democrats, with their genuine democratic and pacific principles, voted against the treaty. Their reward was to lose the last by-election fought in Imperial Germany. There remained the Treaty of Bucharest with Roumania: an indefinite occupation (at Roumanian expense); all her oil, all her foodstuffs, all her railways, under the control of German monopolies; a vast indemnity. For this treaty there voted not only the Centre and the Progressives, but the majority of Social Democrats as well.

So was attained in the spring of 1918 the Greater German dream of Mitteleuropa, all the spoils and all the labour of central and eastern

Europe fallen under German control. The longstanding ambition of cultural supremacy, the equally longstanding plan of taking resources from other countries and providing nothing except 'military protection' in return, were accomplished. The new ideas of Pan-Germanism jostled the last echoes of the Holy Roman Empire in the dim haze of war. Crowns were distributed, or rather bickered for: William II wished to be Duke of Courland; the King of Saxony to be King of Lithuania, a dignity for which Erzberger ran a Wurtemberg prince as rival candidate; a prince of Hesse was to be King of Finland; an Austrian archduke aspired, absurdly, to be King of the Ukraine. These royal claimants, and their protector of the High Command, overlooked two things. The war in the west had not been won; and the terms of Brest-Litovsk and Bucharest completed the Allied determination, especially the determination of the United States, for total victory. Moreover, the east had not been subdued: greater forces were needed in 1918 to collect the plunder of Brest-Litovsk than had been needed in 1917 to destroy the Russian armies, and a million German soldiers, scattered from Finland to the Caucasus, were the price paid for Greater Germany – a million soldiers who might have turned the scale in the war in the west. After Brest-Litovsk, as much as before it, Germany had to carry the burden of the 'war on two fronts'.

This burden Germany could no longer sustain. In the spring of 1918 there came the last bid for decisive victory, the 'Emperor's battle', undertaken much against the Emperor's will, which was to prepare the way for a Brest-Litovsk in the west. Victory over the British on March 21st; renewed victory over the British on April 9th; victory over the French at the end of May; a new offensive against the French on July 15th; victories, but no decision. On July 18th the French struck back, on August 8th the British broke through. The war was lost. But Ludendorff was still confident that he could fight a defensive war and, at the end of August, was still talking of a German protectorate over the Flemish parts of Belgium; to tremble for the eastern conquests of Germany never crossed his mind. Then in September came the collapse of Bulgaria, and the collapse of Austria-Hungary was imminent. Germany could not man another front; an immediate armistice was necessary to save the German army. Ludendorff knew that the Allies would not negotiate with a military dictator; therefore a civilian constitutional government must be established. On September 29th Ludendorff issued his last orders as dictator: constitutional monarchy in Germany; peace on the basis of the Fourteen Points. Within forty-eight hours Prince Max of Baden became constitutional Chancellor by grace of the High Command; and on October 2nd the party leaders were told by Ludendorff's representative that the war was lost and that the Reichstag must assume the governing of Germany.

Ludendorff did not in the least understand what constitutional government meant, and he had never read the Fourteen Points. He attempted to dictate to Prince Max as he had previously dictated to Bethmann and Hertling, and when, towards the end of October, he realized what the Fourteen Points implied, he desired to renew the war in desperation. This does not alter the fact that both constitutional government and the confession of total defeat were made on the orders of the High Command. Ludendorff, prodded on by the Allied armies, was sole author of the 'October revolution'. Constitutional monarchy, the highest ambition even of the Social Democrats, was achieved without the effort, almost without the knowledge, of the German people; it was a manœuvre on the battlefield, not an event in domestic history. The parties of the Left were completely satisfied, constitutional changes were carried through, Social Democrats sat in Prince Max's cabinet. In fact for all practical purposes there was set up in October 1918 the system of the Weimar republic: political liberty, but no changes in economic or social power. The sole difference was that in October 1918 the Emperor remained as constitutional figurehead; and to this not even the Social Democrats objected. Indeed they did their best to save his throne and sacrificed him only because of the refusal of the Allies to treat with him. Thus in essence the Weimar republic came into being on Ludendorff's orders.

Negotiations with the Allies dragged on until November, so that the fall of the Emperor, final act of the 'October revolution', the revolution which temporarily succeeded, became entangled with the 'November revolution', the revolution which failed. For, as well as the revolution by numbers carried out at the behest of the High Command, there was an attempt at a genuine revolution, with a real shift of political and economic power. The Reich had been made and held together by victory; now the Germans learnt without warning that the army had

suffered irremediable defeat. What followed was not so much revolution as collapse, collapse of all confidence, collapse of respect. The
soldiers still did their duty, but not even German soldiers would continue to fight indefinitely when they had learnt from their own leaders
that defeat was certain. As for the civilians, and especially for those
quasi-civilians, the sailors, who had been shut away inactive in their
harbours for months or years, they had only one desire: to end the war
at the earliest moment. This universal anti-war sentiment, suddenly
released, turned to the two groups which had notoriously opposed the
war, the Spartacists and the Independent Social Democrats, though
without understanding the principles for which either stood. Berlin,
which could not imagine itself without a Reich, turned mainly to the
Spartacists, who were radical German nationalists; the rest of Germany,
indignant at the failure of the Reich to which everything had been
sacrificed, turned mainly to the Independents. These revolutionary
movements demanded the overthrow of the Emperor as a symbol that
the war was ended; and the Allies would end the war only with the
symbolical overthrow of the Emperor. And as the High Command also
desired the end of the war, it too demanded the Emperor's abdication,
although for very different reasons from those which were agitating
the crowds in the streets of Berlin. Practically the only group to attempt
to preserve the monarchy, if not the monarch, were the liberal and
Social Democrat ministers, the men of principle.

Ludendorff was dismissed on October 26th, after his mad attempt to
renew the war. Hindenburg remained, devoting his prestige to sal-
vaging the German army in defeat; and his new Quartermaster-
General, Gröner, was a hardheaded determined realist, uniquely
devoted to the army of the Reich. He did not take long to realize that
only the Emperor's abdication, perhaps even the overthrow of the
monarchy, would arrest the advance of the Allies and secure an armistice while the German army was still intact; and it was Gröner who
forced through these views at the High Command. At the same time,
while William II was gradually being driven into disappearance, Berlin
became unmanageable. On November 9th Liebknecht, the Spartacist,
prepared to proclaim a Soviet republic. Prince Max's cabinet tried to
meet this threat by proclaiming the abdication of the Emperor; at the
last moment Scheidemann, one of the two Social Democrat members

of the cabinet, saved the day only by himself proclaiming the republic – much to the fury of Ebert, his colleague. Prince Max handed over his office to Ebert, who thus for twenty-four hours became – though in rather an irregular way – the last Imperial Chancellor. But there was no longer an Emperor. The news from Berlin at last decided the High Command; and on November 9th William II was badgered and cajoled until he vanished into Holland. Thus the High Command and the Social Democrats, much against their will, succumbed to the pressure of the Allies and the Berlin streets, and created the German republic.

The republican government needed something more than the posthumous blessing of Prince Max of Baden. On November 10th, the workers' and soldiers' Councils of Berlin were hastily called together – Councils which imitated in name the Russian Soviets, but merely strove without revolutionary purpose to keep some order in the immediate chaos – and this meeting elected a Council of People's Representatives, which governed Germany for the next three months. Naturally they chose the Socialist leaders best known to them; and these leaders were none other than the last constitutional ministers of the Emperor, men who, far from being revolutionaries, had opposed the revolution, thought now only of curbing it and of saving what could be saved of Germany – of its territory, of its social order, above all of its army. No Spartacist was elected to the Council of People's Representatives; there were three Independent Socialists, but they were isolated and inexperienced and within a month were driven to resign; it was more important, and more lasting, that the Council employed as 'ministers' members of the Centre and Progressive parties, Erzberger above all as Secretary of State. In other words, the German 'revolution' had only managed to put into power the parties of the Reichstag which were non-'national' in that they did not represent the great estates or great industry, but which had supported the war at every stage. The revolutionaries and the opponents of the war were left out in the cold. Still more, a formal alliance was at once established by private telephone between Ebert and Gröner, the revolutionary government and the High Command: the government would maintain order and resist 'Bolshevism' – that is, any real social change – the High Command would give the government its support. The High Command sacrificed the dynasties, who tumbled down all over Germany; the Social Democrats sacrificed merely the future of democracy.

The policy of Ebert and Scheidemann followed logically from the line which the Social Democrats had taken unconsciously for more than a generation, consciously since the outbreak of war. They were not revolutionaries, but good trade union leaders, loyal to the interests of their members, and, with the collapse both of the army and the old institutions, controlling in the trade unions the only organizations which still represented the unity of the Reich. They were in the position of a worthy trade union official, who, finding the boss taken ill, bars the door and holds off inquirers until the boss recovers: it were grotesque to ask of him that he should proclaim the expropriation of the factory over the house telephone. That the boss should recover and that meanwhile the machinery should not jam or any competitor steal the business, such was their aim. They refused to take over any great industrial concerns on the ground that they were bankrupt – though, in historical terms, a revolution is precisely the taking over of a bankrupt order by new, more vital, forces. They assisted the affirmation of Hindenburg's authority, in fact sheltered under it; they sought for, and obtained, the services of the imperial bureaucracy; in order to preserve 'national unity' against the Allies they refused to inquire into the inflated profits of the armament industry and made no move against the great estates east of the Elbe. They were Germans first, and would have been Socialists second, if there had been room for a second. They were faithful, after a sort, to the democratic ideas which they had preached in the Reichstag: they established universal suffrage in Prussia and the eight-hour day, the right of association and a system of unemployment relief, steps which might have been revolutionary in 1848, but which now served only to set up a middle-class republic.

For a brief period the 'October revolution', the coalition of Ebert and Gröner, and the 'November revolution' of Liebknecht and the Independent Socialists continued to exist side by side. But the 'November revolution' was purely an upheaval against continuing a lost war; and on November 11th the war ended. The armistice was not an unconditional surrender: the German armies withdrew east of the Rhine and handed over great masses of war equipment; the German navy was interned; but inside Germany the Allies had no other authority than the menace of the blockade. Thus there was in Germany a balance of forces: the revolutionaries, dependent on the dwindling masses in the streets; the Social Democrat government, employing the last flicker of the prestige of the Reich; the High Command, controlling an army still orderly but in dissolution; and, in the distance, the armed force of the Allies which had set all in motion. None could master Germany alone; combination was necessary, and the combination of Ebert and Gröner proved successful both at the expense of German freedom and at the expense of the peoples of Europe. The real menace to the Reich was separatism, the repudiation by the Independent Socialists of the centralized German state; but this was no menace to the Allies. The Allies feared 'Bolshevism', a movement of revolutionary Marxism, which might create a Russo-German alliance, and so enable Germany to renew the war. Ebert and Gröner therefore ignored, for the time being, the setting up of democratic governments in the German states and directed their fire against the Spartacists in Berlin. The Spartacist menace created a common front of Ebert, Gröner, and Marshal Foch.

In actual fact, the conclusion of the armistice had knocked the bottom out of Spartacism so completely that both Liebknecht and Rosa Luxemburg, the only real brain in the movement, came out against any resort to violence. Rosa Luxemburg, indeed, intended to make her peace with the Independent Socialists – a development which would have ruined the plans of Ebert and Gröner. Therefore, in December 1918, the Provisional Government broke the stalemate which had lasted since November, and took the offensive against the Spartacists in Berlin. The High Command, by a refinement of political strategy, took no part in the operation beyond dispatching its blessing. The 'bloodhound' of order was a Social Democrat, Noske, and his instrument the 'Free Corps', organizations of out-of-work officers, who would fight against anyone – at first against the Spartacists and Independents, later against any democratic movement, true condottieri, without any principle or belief other than that of the bullet in the back. These gentlemen, deprived of the pleasures of foreign domination, asked nothing better than to slaughter German workers and liberals; and it was officers of the Guards who murdered Liebknecht and Rosa Luxemburg brutally and without excuse, and also without protest from the Social

Democratic government. The Spartacists were broken; but broken too was the life of the German republic, for it could not exist without a united Socialist movement, and now the blood of Liebknecht and Rosa Luxemburg ran for ever between the associates of Ebert and the men of the Left.

The destruction of the Spartacists improved the standing of Ebert and Noske both with the High Command and the Allies: they were preserving Germany from disorder, from Bolshevism. So was made possible the more difficult operation of February 1919, the destruction of the separatist movements, which alone held out to Germany the chance of a secure civilian future. Here, in the governments of Bavaria, of Saxony and Brunswick, ruled at last the men who saw in Switzerland, and not in the militarist Reich, the true model of German political civilization, and who dreamt of transforming Germany into an association of free Swiss States. These men, Kurt Eisner the ruler of Bavaria above all, were the last and noblest of German liberals, the only Germans to escape from the worship of power. Their very virtue was their undoing. They would not organize force, would not combine, even in defence. The Free Corps, tiny in numbers, but directed from the centre, moved freely across Germany – seconded by the High Command and approved of by the Allies – and crushed the liberties first of Brunswick, then of Saxony, finally of Bavaria. On March 18th Gröner wrote to Noske, now Minister of Defence: 'The High Command has confidence in the Government, limited confidence in the Ministry of War, and unlimited confidence only in the Minister of Defence.' So was accomplished the victory of the Reich, the victory of authoritarianism, over German liberties. A victory, certainly, of brutal, ruthless, military adventurers; but also a victory welcomed by the overwhelming majority of the German people, who had long learnt to interpret liberty as the liberty of the Reich to ride roughshod both over its inhabitants and over foreigners. At the elections for the National Assembly, held on January 19th, 1919, only two million out of thirty million voters supported the Independent Socialists, sole party of liberty and antimilitarism; the great majority of Germans accepted the conquest of the Independent Socialists as the harbinger of German liberation. Only the Allies, blinded by fear of Bolshevism, failed to see that the Independent Socialists could alone secure a free and peaceful Germany; they, too, cheered on the overthrow of Eisner, as, in Hungary, they applauded the fall of Michael Karolyi, solitary spokesman of the Allied cause. Carrying the identification of separatism and Bolshevism a stage further, England and America prevented even the setting up of a republic on the Rhine, though this attempt was made not by Independent Socialists, but by Roman Catholic industrialists.

Thus, in February 1919, the 'November revolution' ended in defeat. There remained the 'October revolution', which had been imposed upon Germany by the military supremacy of the Allies, and this supremacy was still overwhelming. Even though the revolution of the streets had been defeated, the High Command still needed the republic in order to make peace with the Allies; the Allied armies preserved for the Germans the liberties which they had been unable themselves to defend. In the spring of 1919 the Constituent Assembly met at Weimar, home of Goethe and therefore spiritual centre of German political idealism, but in real life an insignificant little town of no geographic, political, or economic importance, true symbol of German liberalism. The Weimar Assembly was a repetition, almost a parody, of the Frankfurt Parliament of 1848. In 1848 the liberals had owed their position, not to their own achievements, but to the breakdown of the old order and the revolutionary threat from the masses; yet they had welcomed the defeat of the radicals by the Prussian and Austrian armies and sat in amiable illusion under the protection of Prussian bayonets, until these same bayonets chased them out of existence. In 1919 too the Weimar liberals owed nothing to their own efforts: they were the creation of Allied victory and were themselves protected from radicalism by the Free Corps, the members of which would have liked nothing better than the chance to massacre these liberal idealists. In 1848 the radical menace was broken within a few months; after 1919 the sapping of Allied supremacy was prolonged for a few years. That was the sole difference between the system of Frankfurt and the system of Weimar. Or, if there was a further difference, it was that in 1848 the liberals still hoped for success and believed in their own system; in 1919 even the men of Weimar despaired of their ideals. In 1848, with the crumbling of the dynasties, the liberal intellectuals represented all the energies of the middle class; in 1919 the great capitalist middle class was tarred with the 'national' disaster, and the intellectuals, impotent and ignored for forty years, were alien to and repudiated by it. By a strange but inevitable paradox, the Weimar constitution was the work of the smallest of the parties in the Assembly, the Democrats; a party without force and almost without backing, but possessing to the full the 'spirit of 1848'.

So there came into being the Weimar constitution, most mechanically perfect of all democratic constitutions, full of admirable devices – parliamentary sovereignty, the referendum, the most elaborate and perfect system of proportional representation ever conceived – a textbook constitution for the Professor of Political Science. This, it was claimed, was a German constitution, not a constitution for Prussian ascendancy in Germany. The claim was true, the motive of the change not appreciated by the idealists of Weimar. With the establishment of universal suffrage in Prussia, which inevitably followed the events of November 1918, Prussia – more industrialized than the rest of the Reich – was no longer solidly Junker, but solidly Social Democrat; and the 'emancipation' of Germany from Prussia was nothing more than a precaution against the continuance of Social Democratic rule, a precaution that proved successful: Prussia continued to have a Social Democratic government until 1932, Germany none after 1919. The relation of the Reich with the states was left in a strange hotch-potch. On the one hand the doctrinaire 'Frankfort liberals' and the Social Democrats desired a unitary German republic; on the other hand the 'national' forces, discredited but still powerful, wished to maintain the states as brakes on democracy, and they were strangely seconded by the Independent Socialists out of dislike to a powerful Reich. The constitution makers were anxious to preserve a united front of all parties in face of the Allies and therefore allowed the states to continue in existence; but they phrased the constitution in such a way as to make them powerless. The result was to be expected: Reich governments of the Left, anxious to avoid constitutional disputes, dared not interfere with state governments of the Right; Reich governments of the Right, caring nothing for the prestige of the constitution, did not hesitate to overthrow state governments of the Left. In other words, the constitution became an instrument for crippling the democratic elements in Germany, if they ever attempted to defend it against its enemies.

But even at the moment of its establishment the Weimar republic had few friends, only the tiny group of Progressives, now called the Democratic party. The Centre was indeed republican, in the sense in which it had previously been Bismarckian: it supported the republic not out of principle, but in order to increase the privileges of the Roman Catholic Church; and it would jettison the republic the moment that a more powerful patron of the Roman Catholic Church presented himself. The Social Democrats were republican, but they lacked all sense of authority: trade union officials, they awaited a boss with whom they could resume the bargaining over wage rates and conditions of employment. Every phrase, every clause of the constitution, presupposed a strong and constitutionally minded middle class, the equivalent of the French radicals who for so long sustained the French republic. A working class, even if politically educated, cannot of itself maintain a political system: every worker has to be at his bench or loom for eight hours a day, which rules him out as the day-to-day instrument of government. The administrators, the professional men, the moulders of opinion, must hold the system together; and in the Weimar republic these men continued to come from the 'national' classes, who saw in the republic only the symbol of their defeat. What hope was there for a middle-class republic which the middle class almost unitedly opposed? Only the hope that it could continue in being, as it had been created, by order of the High Command; and this indeed took place.

The prospect of a peace treaty had almost been forgotten during the constitutional discussions; and so little were the consequences of defeat understood that Hindenburg, moving his headquarters to the east, actually projected a war against the Poles with the aid of the Free Corps, until arrested by an ultimatum from Marshal Foch. Suddenly, at the beginning of May, the Germans were presented with a peace of defeat – admission of responsibility for the war which they had so enthusiastically welcomed; reparations, though not on the scale of Brest-Litovsk; disarmament; and, worst of all, loss of territory to the despised Poles. The discussions of May and June revealed all that was to follow: no German advocated genuine acceptance; the only dispute was whether to reject the treaty at once or to agree to it with the intention of evading, and later undoing, its terms. But to renew the war was impossible: this was the verdict given by the High Command, reluctantly but unmistakably. If Hindenburg had so much as lifted his little finger, war would have blazed out under the restored dictatorship of the High Command; Allied military supremacy forbade it. By their protests the Germans obtained many minor modifications of the original terms; but no modification could remove their essential grievance. For the Treaty of Versailles barred the way against German supremacy in Europe; it confined the Germans to their own national area, compelled them to abandon both Poland and the lands of the Danube, in fact put the Slav peoples of eastern Europe and the Germans on an equality. This was the indelible disgrace. The loss of colonies which had always been an expensive luxury; reparations, which the Germans never supposed they would have to pay; even disarmament, which they knew they could evade – these, perhaps, could have been tolerated; but not the suggestion that Poles and Czechs should rank as 'men'. The suggestion appeared to Germans so fantastic that even the representatives who signed the treaty made no attempt to conceal their attitude: they were signing so much waste paper, signing solely because the High Command was unable to resume the war. And so, too, the Weimar republic was maintained in being as scapegoat.

The Treaty of Versailles (signed June 28th) gave the final blow to the cause of democracy in Germany, not from any fault of the Allies, but through the blunders and national passion of the Social Democrats. These men, Ebert, Scheidemann, Noske, and the rest, were sincerely democratic: that is, they desired a constitutional state and the rule of law. But they were in awe of 'authority' and they shared the national arrogance of every class of German society. Carried to power by no effort of their own, they wished to prove their patriotism – just as the Jacobins had done in France in 1793 and the Bolsheviks in Russia in 1917. But lacking all belief in themselves or conviction in their cause, they took a very different line. Instead of placing the blame for defeat on the old order, instead of guillotining or shooting the Imperial generals and politicians, they helped the old order back into power and bore the burden of its disaster. They would not follow the line of revolutionary war; but still less would they take the line of pacific democratic acceptance. The Social Democrats could claim that, for whatever reason, they had opposed Imperial policy before 1914, and that of all parties, except the Independents, they had been most reluctant to support extreme imperialism, while the war was on. It was not their policy which brought Germany to Versailles. But they swallowed without question the view that the liberation of the peoples of eastern Europe was a victory of 'entente capitalism'. They imagined that the German militarists had become defenders of Socialism; whereas it was the Socialists who had become the advocates of German militarism. Scheidemann, the Social Democrat who had become Chancellor when Ebert was elected President, shouted: 'May the hand wither that signs this treaty!' It was the Social Democrats who signed the treaty and their hand which withered. Ludendorff and Hindenburg, the architects of Germany's defeat, became 'national' heroes; Ebert lost two sons in the First World War and preserved the Reich in the moment of disaster, but in 1933 his remaining son was martyred in a 'national' concentration camp.

The forefront of the 'injustice' of Versailles was the severance of Polish territory from the Reich. Most Germans had denied to the Poles any national existence; and even the friends of the Poles had thought only of a Poland carved out of Russia's share of the partitions. All repudiated the loss of the Polish lands. It was a government with Social Democratic members which maintained the separate identity of the remaining fragments of West Prussia and Posen, instead of merging them into the neighbouring provinces, and gave to these fragments the menacing name of Grenzmark, the frontier march – clear declaration of impermanency. The Germans could not dispute that the lost lands were inhabited by Poles; but they objected that the wedge of Polish territory ruined East Prussia. In reality the 'corridor' was a godsend, for it served to obscure that East Prussia had been equally 'ruined' before 1914 and that the cause of its ruin was the existence of the bankrupt Junker estates. Now the maintenance of these estates became a vital obligation of the 'national' cause, and, with the approval of all parties, tens of millions of pounds were poured into the bottomless pockets of the Junker landlords, a policy culminating in the gigantic Osthilfe of 1927 and that in its turn completing the destruction of the republic. Germans never ceased to rail against the eastern frontier. But, since the lost lands were inhabited by Poles, on what grounds? On the grounds of 1848: the right of the stronger and 'healthy national egoism'. Thus, the Social Democratic resistance to the Treaty of Versailles inevitably committed them to making Germany once more 'the stronger' and so doomed the Weimar republic even before it was born. For the Treaty was signed on June 28th, 1919; the constitution only completed in August.

Even more decisive for the future of Germany was the settlement of Austria, part of the Versailles system, though not of the Treaty. With the dissolution of the Habsburg monarchy into national states, there remained only the rump, the Germanic Alpine lands, sometimes called 'German Austria'. This fragment had no separate existence, no tradition of independence; it was merely the centre of a non-national Empire which had fallen to pieces. The Austrian Social Democrats who were now the predominant party had opposed the war much more resolutely than the Social Democrats in Germany; but they were indisputably German nationalists, and the German Austria which they set up proclaimed itself part of the German republic. The republic they envisaged was the federative democratic republic of the Independent Socialists; and the defeat of the Independents in February, above all in Bavaria, was a defeat too for the Social Democrats in Austria and thus ultimately for the Allies also. For Austria could not be incorporated in a unitary German republic; this would be unwelcome even to the Austrian Social Democrats and impossible for the new Czechoslovakia, which would then be hemmed in by the Reich. The alternative was somehow to renew, on a federative democratic basis, the link with the rest of central Europe which had been broken in October 1918. But this too was impossible. The classes which had formerly sustained the Habsburgs – bureaucrats, clericals, territorial aristocracy – would not work with peasant democracies; the Social Democrats who had rejected the Habsburgs would not work with non-German national states. The Allies could not make Austria independent: they could only order its separation from Germany, in the hope that somehow a way out would be found. No way out but the worst of both worlds followed: the Social Democrats began to turn towards Czechoslovakia just at the moment when they were overturned by the impenitent clericals who would have nothing to do with a democratic state and so delivered Austria into the hands of nationalistic Germany. Of all the states which succeeded the Habsburg monarchy only Hungary retained, thanks to the folly of the Allies, a conservatism which satisfied the clericalist rulers of

Austria – Seipel, Dollfuss, and Schuschnigg – and only with Hungary would these Austrians co-operate. But the Hungarian gentry were also madly revisionist, blaming the treaty settlement for all the evils which were, in fact, the product of the Hungarian social system. Therefore, despite their dislike of the Germans, they were prepared to abet German revisionism and were thus eager to betray their Austrian clericalist allies. The association between Prague and Vienna, sole salvation of central Europe, was never made.

The imposed quasi-independence of Austria completed in Germany the amalgamation, which had been proceeding during the First World War, of the Little German and the Greater German causes – the cause of the 'national' classes and the cause of radical enthusiasm. Before 1914 the struggle against the Poles, waged by the Junkers, and the struggle against the Czechs, waged by demagogues, had been rivals; now they became identified. Before 1914 the Social Democrats would have welcomed the liberation of Poland as realizing the legacy of Marx and Engels; now, irrevocably severed from the German workers of Austria and Bohemia, they denounced the loss of Polish lands as well. Similarly, before 1914 the Prussian landowners regarded the separation of Austria from Germany as Bismarck's greatest achievement, the guarantee of their own position; now, resisting the loss of their Polish lands, they were prepared to resist the loss of Austria also. The Treaty of Versailles was a defeat both for conservative German nationalism and for demagogic German nationalism; therefore it united them as never before and ensured that all parties in Germany would combine to overthrow it the moment that the army leaders gave them permission to do so. The Weimar republic and the settlement of Europe alike reposed solely on the realization by the German generals of Germany's military weakness.

11

REPUBLICAN INTERREGNUM,
1919–30

The republic created by the Constituent Assembly at Weimar lasted in theory for fourteen years, from 1919 to 1933. Its real life was shorter. Its first four years were consumed in the political and economic confusion which followed the First World War, and in its last three years there was a temporary dictatorship, half cloaked in legality, which reduced the republic to a sham long before it was openly overthrown. Only for six years did Germany lead a life ostensibly democratic, ostensibly pacific; but in the eyes of many foreign observers these six years appeared as the normal, the 'true' Germany, from which the preceding centuries and the subsequent decade of German history were an aberration. A deeper investigation might have found for these six years other causes than the beauty of the German character.

Few Germans, perhaps none, had understood the meaning of the armistice; hardly more took in the meaning of the Treaty of Versailles. For more than four years the Germans had believed that they were winning the war; only for a month (from October 2nd, 1918, until November 11th) were they faced with the truth of defeat, and as soon as the fighting was over the impression of the truth began to fade. The fact of defeat was not yet explained away by the intellectual trick of the 'stab in the back', the unfounded allegation of the collapse of the home front; defeat was merely ignored, overlooked. The signing of the treaty was regarded as a gesture of humiliation, brutal but inescapable, which the Allies had imposed upon Germany; but it occurred to no German that the signature would have any consequences. The Germans had not even grasped that, quite apart from the penalties imposed by Versailles, the failure to win the war would compel them to meet at least their own war costs: directly, to deal somehow with the vast national loans by which the war had been exclusively financed; indirectly, to replace the capital equipment which had been worn out during the period of total war. For the Germans, and their sympathizers abroad, never distinguished between the sufferings consequent on defeat and the sufferings consequent on war as such. Germany had fought harder and more completely than any other country; the resultant burden was bound to be greater. Not the Treaty of Versailles, but the delayed strain and exhaustion of four years of military effort produced the economic difficulties of Germany in the post-war years. So little did the Germans grasp this that they blamed the Allies, for instance, for the inadequacy of the German railway services and thought that the victorious Allies ought to reconstruct the railways which had been worn out in conveying German soldiers to the western front.

Thus, immediately after the conclusion of peace, Germans of all classes expected two things: they expected that the Allies, having received their pound of flesh (in the shape of an empty German signature of the Treaty), would now perform out of love for Germany all the services which in other circumstances they would have been compelled to perform by defeat; at the same time the Germans expected to annul, without trouble, the principal enactments of Versailles – enactments which they were sincerely convinced must have been due to some sort of mistake or misunderstanding. In some ways they succeeded almost at once: the trial of war criminals, about which so many promises had been made in Allied countries, turned out the most preposterous farce. The original idea of trial by an international court was soon abandoned – it would be too humiliating for the Germans. Instead the High Court at Leipzig undertook the trials, inflicted a few derisory sentences on non-commissioned officers, gave an even more derisory acquittal to a few generals, until the Allies, become utterly

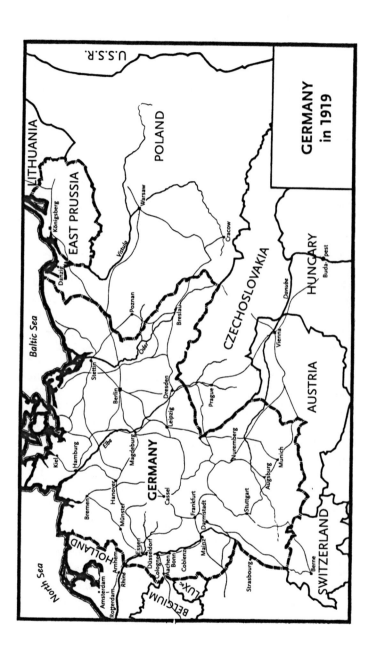

GERMANY
in 1919

ridiculous, called off the trials altogether. But in other ways the Germans took things too easily. The Free Corps, veterans of civil slaughter, were moved over to the eastern frontier, where they fought the Poles and maintained the Baltic as a German sphere of influence until well on in 1920. The war against the Poles and the war against German democracy were, as the history of the Free Corps showed, part of the same struggle, the struggle for the restoration of 'national' Germany. This connection was obvious to the 'national' leaders who arranged the murder of Eisner at one moment and conducted the campaign against the Poles in Upper Silesia the next: it was unfortunately not obvious either to the Allies, who welcomed the defeat of the Independent Socialists, or to the German democrats, who still thought that the 'liberation' of Silesia would somehow be also a victory for liberalism in Germany.

In 1920 the Germans tried to move too fast: they were quite willing to forget that they had lost the war, the Allies not yet altogether forgetful that they had won it. The first German attempts to rub reparations off the slate and to play off England against France were too barefaced; they failed. On the eastern frontier and in the Baltic the Germans were ordered out. By a logical development the Free Corps soldiers and 'national' politicians, deprived of the chance of tyrannizing over the peoples on their eastern frontier, sought compensation in a renewed attack on German liberties. The republican government in Berlin, driven on by the Allies, attempted to disband some of the Free Corps; the Free Corps answered by overthrowing the republic. This was the Kapp putsch, fertile source of historical legends and misconceptions. Kapp himself, who was installed as Chancellor, was an extreme 'national' politician, one of the founders of the Fatherland party in 1917; his programme: the restoration of the authoritarian state and the repudiation of Versailles. This was also the programme of the army leaders, of the German bureaucracy, of the great capitalists, but with this difference: Kapp and his down-at-heel followers wanted to achieve it in March 1920; the more intelligent 'national' Germans, such as General Seeckt, who was now at the head of the armed forces, remembered that Germany had been defeated and were willing to postpone their programme for a few years. The republican government itself had no force and little authority; it fled in disarray to western Germany and

Kapp marched in triumph into Berlin. The German workers answered the Kapp *putsch* with a general strike, and it suited both generals and politicians to make out that this strike defeated the Kapp counter-revolution. In reality Kapp was defeated by Seeckt's refusal to work with him, a refusal which carried with it the refusal of the army, the banks, and the bureaucracy. General Lüttwitz, military leader of the Kapp *putsch*, called Seeckt 'the soul of the resistance to me'. If Seeckt had given the signal the republic would have collapsed in March 1920, just as Versailles would have been rejected in June 1919 at a gesture from Hindenburg: the resistance of the workers would have counted for nothing. Not principle, but only fear of the Allied armies restrained Seeckt, as it had restrained Hindenburg.

This was clearly shown in the sequel. Kapp and his followers were persuaded to withdraw from Berlin; the offending Free Corps was not disbanded; no one who took part in the *putsch* was punished. But when the workers, whose general strike was supposed to have secured the triumph of democracy, demanded a purge of the army and bureau-cracy, they were branded as 'Bolsheviks', and the very forces which had taken part in the *putsch* were sent against them to break their 'red' rebellion with terror and bloodshed. To the Allies the Kapp *putsch* was displayed to prove the strength of German democracy and Germany's determination to operate the treaty. Within Germany it was used to prove the need for greater German strength; and the elections to the first republican Reichstag, which closely followed the *putsch*, showed that this lesson had been taken to heart – the Social Democrats, indeed all the democratic parties together, were returned in a minority, the republic henceforth depending on a majority of anti-republicans. The new republican Reichstag contained parties with new names, but they were the parties of Bismarckian Germany rechristened and with the more moderate element in every case weakened or altogether removed. This was most obvious in the old Bismarckian coalition of agrarians and industrialists, Conservatives and National Liberals. The Conserva-tives, though authoritarian, had certain standards of decent behaviour and of respect for law, to say nothing of their Prussian dislike of Pan-Germanism. They now became the 'national' party, the patrons of the Free Corps and the advocates of excess both at home and abroad. In democratic pacific Germany this party, which identified the 'national'

interest with the interest of the great landowners and great industrialists, ran the Social Democrats close as the largest party in the Reichstag;
in May 1924, for example, they obtained five and a half million votes as
against six million for the Social Democrats. The 'National Liberals',
who tried to combine Pan-Germanism with a certain liberal spirit of
administration, virtually disappeared: the greatest capitalists were
absorbed in the 'national' party *sans phrase*, only a few traditionalists
survived in the remnant rechristened the 'party of the folk' – a party
most remarkable for its lack of 'folk' support. As for the Progressives,
rechristened Democrats, they indeed were more high-principled and
intellectual than ever, and could claim the Weimar constitution as their
handiwork; but though they could devise a perfect system of voting
by proportional representation, they could not devise any method of
winning votes for themselves.

The Democrats were without voters; the Social Democrats were
without ideas. Before 1914 they were still in theory a Marxist party and
they were not compelled to be anything in practice; after 1920 they
had no basis, either practical or theoretical, except to preserve the day-
to-day liberties of the trade unions. To add to the confusion, most of
the Independent Socialists, defeated in February 1919, trickled back
into the official party, so that Noske and his victims sat on the same
party benches. These independents gave to the party which had in
1918 saved the old order and the German army once more an illusory
appearance of pacificism and democracy; the Independents had learnt
from the events of 1919 the lesson that they must shelter under some
power, and of all forms of power that of the trade union officials
seemed the least dangerous. On the other side, even more bewildering,
the more extreme Independent Social Democrats joined with the remnants of the Spartacists to form the Communist party, who attacked the
Social Democrats as their conquerors in 1918 – which they were – and
as the principal enemies of the German people – which they were not.
The German Communists, never strong in leaders after the murder of
Rosa Luxemburg, were further reduced in wisdom by accepting the
leadership of the Communist International; and Moscow, obsessed by
the turnip ghost of a united intervention of capitalist states against
Russian Communism, cared only to drive a wedge between Germany
and the western powers. The German Communists were therefore

ordered to attack Versailles and to pose as the true champions of German nationalism; a refinement of tactics so enthusiastically executed by these aspiring Machiavellians that the 'national' parties complained of 'unfair competition' – in politics as in economics monopoly was the German way. The Communist party, attacking democracy, attacking the settlement of 1919, overbidding the Free Corps in advocacy of violence and brutality, sealed the fate of peaceful, democratic Germany. The middle classes, poisoned by 'national' passions, would not help the republic; but the republic might have been saved by a united and sincerely democratic Socialist working class. This ideal had been betrayed by Ebert in the fateful days of 1918; but the Communists more than repaid the betrayal in the fanatical campaign against 'the slave treaty' and against the principles of democracy which they waged unremittingly until their campaign rebounded on their own heads and destroyed them. The Communists thought to overbid the 'national' classes: they offered a struggle for German supremacy unrestrained by any considerations of private property. But, playing another's game, they forced the tone and merely delivered the working classes into the hands of their enemies; for no one could play the 'national' game as well as the 'national' classes themselves. All that the Communists achieved was to increase the unscrupulousness of German political life, and to prepare the way for the truly ruthless and unprincipled. When, in 1933, the moment came for the Communists to undertake the battle in the streets to which they had so often appealed, it turned out that they were old-style parliamentary talkers like all the rest.

One party survived the revolution without change of name or of character – the Centre. In Imperial Germany, where concessions could only be won by bargaining with the Chancellor, there was perhaps some excuse for a confessional party; in the republic the rights of the churches were stabilized in the constitution, yet, at the moment when the Centre was no longer needed, it remained stronger than ever, still intent only on safeguarding the position of the Roman Catholic Church and without any fixed political principles. Its guiding line was the same as before: to support the existing system, so long as it existed – but not a minute longer; to support it, in fact, only so long as support was unnecessary. As long as Germany was winning the war, the Centre had supported the programme of victory; as soon as Germany began to lose the war the Centre supported the programme of defeat, and a member of the Centre accompanied a Social Democrat to sign the treaty of Versailles. If the republic survived, the Centre would support it; if the republic was overthrown, the Centre would support the forces which overthrew it. Wherever the dominant current of German political forces led, the Centre would go too – on the clear understanding that these forces would, in return, respect the position of the Roman Catholic Church. As a result the Centre occupied an apparently impregnable position throughout the period of the republic, with members in every cabinet whether of Left or Right. But it had a fatal weakness. Long years of exacting concessions by co-operating with the government had sapped its power to oppose. It talked occasionally of the days of the *Kulturkampf*, but when the need arose it could not recapture their spirit, and had to pretend to be exacting concessions for its co-operation when it was receiving them no longer.

The dominant position of the Centre in the governments of the republic showed, more clearly than anything else, that, despite changes of name both in parties and the constitution, the spirit of politics was still the spirit of old Germany. Although the Reichstag now 'ruled', the parties were still interest-groups, concerned not to govern, but to win concessions for the particular interest which they represented. The electoral system, by which votes were cast for a party, not an individual, indeed increased the emphasis on party interests. In Imperial Germany the parties had bargained with the Chancellor; now they bargained with each other inside the Cabinet. To govern Germany was no part of their aim, and the only value of becoming a Cabinet Minister was to be able to threaten to resign. The Germans still respected 'authority', but it never crossed their minds that the republican cabinets were now the 'authority'. One might repeat Berchtold's question of 1914 – who ruled in Berlin? The answer was the same: no one. Germany was administered, not governed. At the head there was a void, an interregnum, an empty chair. The only 'authority' in Germany was the army, but it was too small and too overshadowed still by Allied power to be able to display its power. The civil administration, drawn from the old imperial classes, continued to perform its routine functions, half the time hardly aware who was the nominal Chancellor. So too the business men and bankers went on their way, pursuing their monopolistic designs, occasionally issuing orders to the government of the day, but certainly never subordinate to it. In republican, as in later Imperial Germany, the only serious function of the Chancellor was to keep the Reichstag in a good temper. But now this was done not so much by speeches as by changing the Chancellor whenever the Reichstag was annoyed – and that was often. There was indeed a residuary legatee of the Emperor, not governing any more than he had done, but still acting as some sort of liaison between the civilian administrators and the independent forces of army and economic power. This was the President, the only civilian to possess a fragment of 'authority'. Ebert, the first President, had acknowledged from the beginning that, while ostensibly the creation of democracy, he must also possess the blessing of the army leadership; the second President was to carry the fusion much further.

The failure of the Kapp *putsch* was evidence that the results of 1918 could not yet be openly undone; and the following three years were dominated by the fact that Germany, having failed to plunder Europe, would have to bear the belated burden of the war. The war had cost the Reich 164 milliard marks. Of this sum 93 milliards had been raised by war loans, 29 milliards had been met by treasury bills, the rest by increasing the issue of paper money. Not a penny had been raised by taxation. Republican Germany might have been expected to reform the finances of the Reich and to impose taxation on the rich; but the 'national' classes were ready for this emergency – they alleged that taxes were needed solely to pay reparations to the French. To oppose taxes became a patriotic act; and in 1921 direct taxes were actually reduced. In reality the claims of reparations were trifling compared to the needs of Germany's internal budget; and in 1921–3 hardly any reparations were paid. The inflation which raged at an ever-advancing pace until the end of 1923 was solely due to the failure to balance revenue and expenditure. There was no connection between reparations and inflation, except for purposes of propaganda. Instead of taxing the rich, Germany paid her way and paid off all the costs of the war by destroying the savings of the poor and middle classes. Inflation had a profound political effect: it left Germany in 1924 as free from debt as it had been in 1871, that is to say, in as favourable a financial position at the end of a lost war as it had been at the end of a victorious war. It had a profound economic effect: it enabled German heavy industry to write off all its prior charges and so be free to carry out a new process of rationalizing its procedure almost as sweeping as the original 'industrial revolution' in the eighteen-seventies. Most of all it had a profound social effect: it stripped the middle classes of their savings and made the industrial magnates absolute dictators of German economic life. The saving, investing middle class, everywhere the pillar of stability and respectability, was in any case newer in Germany than in France and England – hence the instability of German policy even before 1914; it was now utterly destroyed, and Germany thus deprived of her solid, cautious keel. The former rentiers, who had lost their all, ceased to impose a brake: they became resentful of the republic, to whom they attributed their disaster; violent and irresponsible; and ready to follow the first demagogic saviour not blatantly from the industrial working class. The inflation, more than any other single factor, doomed the republic; its cause was not the policy of the Allies, but the failure to impose direct taxes on the rich.

But inflation had, too, an effect in foreign affairs. To sustain the connection between inflation and reparations, it was necessary to cheat and defy the French and to conduct a steady campaign against Versailles, a campaign which gradually convinced even its authors. Once more Germans began to lose caution and to believe that the war had been won. There was new agitation on the eastern frontiers; open refusal to reduce the German army to the prescribed size; and in the reparations negotiations an insolent, almost jeering, contempt so long as Versailles could be blamed for all the ills of Germany, no one would demand an account of their stewardship from the old 'governing classes' who had brought Germany to this plight and who even now were exploiting her weakness and confusion to consolidate their power. For once, German policy had counted without the French. Poincaré, the French Prime Minister, actually thought that Versailles ought to be enforced and that the victory of 1918 should be safeguarded. In January 1923, wearied of the refusal to disarm, of the nationalistic agitation, of the failure to pay reparations, Poincaré, backed by the Belgians and Italians, decreed the occupation of the Ruhr, seat of Germany's industrial power. Even now the Germans did not appreciate the position. They still thought there was some mistake, some misunderstanding. Ever since 1870 they had regarded France as decadent and weak, and they could not suppose the French really capable of invading German soil. Moreover, being themselves willing to forget all the abuse and hostility they had directed against England, they supposed, rightly, that this will to forget was reciprocated. Thus, even though the German army could not turn the French out of the Ruhr, the English friends of Germany, anxious to save Germany from 'Bolshevism' and chaos, would do it for them. The German government therefore ordered 'passive resistance', a great demonstration of national unity against the invader. Factories, mines, banks, offices, in the occupied zone, were everywhere closed. The workers starved in patriotic devotion; the capitalist also suffered in their feelings, though they arranged to sell coal and steel to the French at a high profit. The war, suspended by the armistice of 1918, was renewed.

It was renewed, and lost. The occupation of the Ruhr, far more than the last campaign of 1918, brought home to the Germans the fact of defeat. Until then it had passed unnoticed. Even though fighting had ceased, the Germans had expected the 'peril of Bolshevism' to do the trick. Successive German governments had threatened to ruin Germany unless the Treaty of Versailles was torn up. Poincaré called the German bluff: if the Germans wished to ruin Germany rather than acknowledge defeat, they should be allowed to do so. In August 1923, the German industrialists and generals realized that the bluff had not succeeded. Germany had lost the war. A government of fulfilment was formed under Stresemann, leader of the former National Liberals, the 'party of the folk'. The currency was stabilized, as it could have been stabilized at any moment by a government determined to make revenue and expenditure balance; reparations were paid punctually and without difficulty; even the process of rearmament was temporarily slowed down. The occupation of the Ruhr had been the cold douche which brings a hysteric to her senses. It ended, for the moment, the campaign against Versailles.

'Passive resistance' and extreme inflation shook the Reich almost as gravely as it had been shaken by the events of October 1918; and there was once more, as in November 1918, a quasi-revolutionary situation. The competing forces of November 1918 again raised their heads. The Communists, successors of the Spartacists, posed as the true defenders of Germany against the French and actually tried to adopt as their own Leo Schlageter, a pimp and gangster killed during the occupation of the Ruhr. And indeed they served the German cause. Their rising in October 1923 gave some colour to the 'Bolshevik peril' and therefore made even Poincaré willing to compromise; a rising otherwise utterly purposeless and futile. More threatening to the Reich was the revival of separatism, under the inspiration of the Independent Socialists, in Saxony and Thuringia. For these democratic state-governments actually interfered with the process of illegal rearmament and exposed these plans to the French. The manœuvre of 1918 was repeated: the pacific democratic Socialists were equated with the nationalistic Communists, advocates of violence, as Eisner had been equated with Liebknecht, and the governments of Saxony and Thuringia were overthrown by the Reich and with the approval of the French. There remained the Free Corps, also, like the Communists, combining national agitation and the advocacy of internal violence, but, unlike the Communists, hitherto the spoilt darlings of successive Reich governments. In November 1923 there was a nationalist *putsch* in Munich, echo and repetition of the Kapp *putsch* of 1920. The former dictator Ludendorff (who had also chanced to be at the Brandenburg Gate when Kapp entered Berlin) and the future dictator Hitler united – the one on his way down from supreme command of the German army to a programme of extreme demagogy, the other on his way up from a programme of extreme demagogy to supreme command of the German army. But they had chosen the wrong moment. War-weary, economically exhausted, fearful of the French army, the Germans, for once, could not be caught for the nationalist game. The insurrection of Munich exploded and collapsed. The restoration of order added much to the external prestige of the Reich government; and in the general satisfaction no one noticed that the leaders of the insurrection escaped practically without punishment – in republican Germany severe sentences were reserved for those 'traitors' who exposed the breaches of the disarmament clauses of the Treaty of Versailles.

Fulfilment, the programme of 1923, gave Germany six years of peace and prosperity, ushered in the 'golden age' of German liberalism. The foundation of this 'golden age' was the abandonment, or at least postponement, of a policy of war, an abandonment in its turn promoted solely by the French occupation of the Ruhr. Poincaré, and Poincaré alone, was the author of German prosperity. Even now, during the period of fulfilment, Germany spent more on armaments than did Great Britain; and Great Britain was spending the money on keeping an obsolescent organization going, Germany on building a new one. The shadow factories, still in course of erection in England in 1939, were completed in Germany before the death of Stresemann. Even now the Reichswehr or 'defence force', new name for the tamed army, was more than double the prescribed size; even now it possessed samples of all the weapons forbidden by the treaty. Still, in comparison with any other period of history, Germany was a peaceful state, most of her economic resources, still more most of her psychological energy, devoted to peaceful ends. The result was not surprising. Germany had colossal capital equipment, technical skill second to none, unrivalled leadership both in science and business. As soon as she abandoned, temporarily, the pursuit of foreign conquest, the scars of war began to heal, and civilian prosperity spread over Germany to an unparalleled extent. After six years of peace, Germany in 1929 had a higher standard of life than ever before, a production of coal and steel considerably greater than in 1913, and was on the point of ousting England as the leading exporting country in Europe. Far from being impoverished by fulfilling Versailles, Germany was made, by fulfilment, more prosperous than she had ever been in her history. This recovery was achieved by German efforts. The American loans, which are often alleged to have restored German credit, in fact followed its restoration. Far from stabilizing Germany, these loans did German economic life a great harm: they accelerated the immediate recovery and so ultimately produced an exaggerated rebound. Even without American loans Germany would have been orderly and prosperous after 1923; but without them she would not have had so violent an economic crash in 1930–1.

The period of peaceful prosperity, however, bore within itself its own ruin. German industry once more expanded, but it expanded on the old lines. Heavy industry, the industry of Power, was still the predominant activity of German capitalism; the conquest of foreign markets still its goal. The Kartells gave place to vaster monopolies, agencies of economic war; and the financial autocracies created by the inflation carried through a ruthless rationalization, which made

German industry far more efficient than before, but also threatened Germany with a great unemployment if the process of expansion were ever temporarily arrested. There was no attempt to shift over to lighter consumer-goods, no attempt to even out the inequalities between rich and poor and so create in a great domestic market a buffer against world depression. Even now direct taxation was considerably less than in England and the disparity of income between rich and poor considerably greater. Between 1924 and 1929 German heavy industry found prosperity in cutting away dead wood and restoring the ravages of war; that process once completed, it would have to depend, as in the days of Tirpitz, on a great armaments programme.

Fulfilment, a policy imposed upon the Germans, not willingly accepted by them, gave Germany a brief period of stability. The appearance of stability, and perhaps its rewards, were increased by the emergence in Stresemann of the first German statesman since the time of Bismarck. Stresemann's past had not been promising: he had acted during the First World War as the whip of the High Command and had championed an extreme annexationist programme even in 1918. But like the 'mad Junker' Bismarck he had learnt wisdom, or at least expediency, from the pressure of events. In the bitter days of 1923 he realized that someone must accept responsibility for the government of Germany; he overcame his awe of 'authority' and attempted to exercise authority himself. His task was more difficult than that of Bismarck. Bismarck had won the support of the King of Prussia, and that support carried with it the backing, however grudging and obstructive, of the Prussian army and the Prussian administration; moreover in the easy circumstances of the middle of the nineteenth century Bismarck had been able to maintain a constant flow of successes to oil his system. Stresemann had to govern a Germany that had been defeated. He was the leader of a liberal capitalist remnant, estranged from the working-class parties by his capitalism, estranged from the middle-class parties by his liberalism. He was compelled to stand not above the parties, but aside from them. In 1923 he made a brief attempt as Chancellor, an attempt which failed; thereafter, until his death in 1929, he was only Foreign Minister, forced to watch in internal affairs the old methods of bargaining and compromise, nevertheless keeping the republican machine going by the force of his personality for six years, years of terrible effort which exhausted and killed him.

In 1917, at the time of the peace resolution, Stresemann had advocated both constitutional reforms and great annexations, a marriage of democracy and the High Command. This combination remained the basis of his policy after defeat. He demanded concessions in foreign affairs in order to strengthen the prestige of democracy within Germany; he defended democracy in Germany in order to win concessions in foreign affairs. It is unfair to accuse Stresemann of deceit or hypocrisy. If the politicians of England and France were 'taken in', it was by their own wilful blindness: the same politicians were later to accuse Hitler of deceit when he was faithful to the policy stated in *Mein Kampf*. Stresemann never concealed that he asked for concessions in order to win more. Even at the moment of signing the Treaty of Locarno, which recognized the Franco-German frontier, he declared – even to the English and French, had they wished to hear – that his main purpose in signing was to secure revision of Germany's frontiers in the east. Stresemann agreed with the most extreme Pan-German in striving for German supremacy in Europe and beyond; where he differed from the Pan-Germans was in believing that this supremacy could not be won by military power, but must be achieved by the weight of German industry and the preponderance of German organizing power. He regarded German supremacy as not only desirable, but inevitable; and as he came to care increasingly for the standards of western civilization, he was increasingly anxious that this dominating Germany should be herself democratic and civilized. Europe dominated by a civilized Germany, or Europe dominated by an uncivilized Germany – it did not cross his mind that there could be any third possibility; and, considering the course of English and French policy in the 'twenties (to say nothing of the 'thirties), no third possibility could occur to any reasonable person.

Stresemann acted in democratic sincerity; all the same he did German democracy a disservice, inescapable, but none the less mortal. Stresemann's republic, like Bismarck's Empire, was kept going by foreign success; and, as those who came after Bismarck discovered, the dose of success had constantly to be increased. To base the republic on foreign success was to try to outbid the 'national' parties: the republic was committed to gaining more by negotiation than the 'national' elements could achieve by violence, an absurd and impossible task. Far from consolidating the republic therefore, Stresemann, with the best of intentions, gave the Germans a taste for blood which the enemies of the republic could more easily satisfy. But there was no alternative, or rather the alternative had been rejected in 1918. The alternative to foreign success was achievement at home: not merely the building of swimming baths and municipal libraries, but the breaking up of the great estates, the destruction of the hold of the great monopolies, and the diversion of German economic power from foreign conquest to the service of the German people, in short, social revolution. But social revolution had failed in the revolutionary days of 1918; it could not be revived in the period of stability, and Stresemann was the last man to do it. His aim was to restore liberal capitalism, an antiquarian policy as disastrous as Bismarck's aim of preserving Prussian Junkerdom had been sixty years before.

In foreign affairs Stresemann achieved his aim: he added success to success. In 1924 the Dawes Plan put reparations on a businesslike basis; in 1925 the Treaty of Locarno substituted for French military power a neutral zone in the Rhineland, guaranteed by Great Britain and Italy; in 1926 Germany was admitted to the League of Nations, ranking equally with the victorious great powers; in 1929 the Young Plan, further reducing reparations, carried with it also the final evacuation of the Rhineland, years before its time. Yet Stresemann's accomplishment did not serve his purpose. At every compromise, every withdrawal by the Allies, the German militarists, far from being satisfied, raised their heads a little further. Stresemann had to jeopardize his standing with British and French statesmen by brazen denial of rearmament, lies which these statesmen, however, accepted, since they too had committed their political reputation to a policy of 'fulfilment'. The Reichswehr leaders cared nothing for the string of legalistic concessions: they desired an alliance with Soviet Russia, openly defying the settlement of Versailles; and Stresemann had to go part of the way with them. Most serious of all, Stresemann's achievements did not shake the hostility of the 'national' parties to the republic; instead they increased their impatience to overthrow it. Already, on the death of Ebert in 1925, there had been a warning sign: the new president, elected by direct vote, was Hindenburg, co-founder with Ebert of the republic, and now bringing his prestige as commander-in-chief perhaps to sustain the republic – perhaps not. What life was there in a republic which could find as President only a senile field-marshal of reactionary views? The Third Republic in France had, in its initial stages of confusion and defeat, taken Marshal MacMahon as President; but almost the first act of the consolidated republic was to drive him from office – at precisely the moment when Hindenburg was put there. The Young Plan, liberating all Germany's territory, was the greatest of Stresemann's achievements; yet it encountered in Germany wider and deeper opposition than any of his previous steps, and the strenuous exertions needed to carry it through the Reichstag caused Stresemann's death. The Social Democrats, who did not need to be reconciled to the republic, remained faithful: the 'national' parties now thought that the republic had served its turn. This time they had not made a mistake: not they, but the Allies, had forgotten the events of 1918.

Here was the decisive cause of Stresemann's failure and so of the collapse of the republic. The lesson of the occupation of the Ruhr was not learnt. Stresemann had been carried to office solely by fear of French arms; yet, to strengthen Stresemann's position, one concession followed another. The victories of 1918 were undone. In 1925, by the Treaty of Locarno, Great Britain guaranteed France against Germany and Germany against France. But a guarantee has value in modern times only if followed by military convention; and Great Britain, since she could not conclude military conventions with both France and Germany, concluded them with neither. French security, which had previously rested on the rewards of victory, now rested solely on a German promise of good behaviour. But if Germany's word could be relied on, why were any precautions necessary? Why the occupation of the Rhineland? Why German disarmament? Why the French alliances in eastern Europe? Every one of these would have to be abandoned in order to prove that the Allies did not doubt Germany's sincerity. In 1930 the last French troops left the Rhineland and so signed the death-warrant of the Weimar republic. The death of Stresemann, late in 1929, was merely an incident. The victory of the Allied armies had brought the republic to birth; the occupation of the Ruhr had given the republic life; the evacuation of the Rhineland killed it. From start to finish the

German republic, and the entire structure of German democracy, owed its existence to the supremacy of Allied arms.

The collapse of the republic was accelerated, but not caused, by the economic crisis which swept the entire world between 1929 and 1933. The crisis was not due to the First World War, still less to reparations: in the six years of stability, the Germans paid 1.7 per cent of their national income in reparations and received in foreign loans (never repaid) two and a half times what they paid out in reparations. The crisis sprang from general defects in the prevailing economic system, and the most successful and prosperous capitalist countries were the most seriously struck. England was worse hit than France, Germany worse than England, the United States far worse than Germany. The crisis inevitably produced unemployment, poverty, demands for economy; there was no reason at all why it should justify a nationalistic policy and rearmament, still less an aggressive war. In the United States it produced the New Deal, in England a successful economy campaign against such armaments as existed. In Germany the crisis merely revealed that there was no one to exercise 'authority'. The Social Democrats, reasonably enough, would not attack the standard of life of their trade union supporters; the 'national' parties were delighted to see the republic in difficulties. The only 'authority' remaining in Germany was once more the army; and on the advice of the army leaders Hindenburg called in Brüning, machine-gun captain of the last war and now a leader of the Centre party. All other parties had certain principles: the Social Democrats to defend the republic, the 'national' parties to destroy it. The Centre alone had none and was willing to make a pact with the military leaders, as it had always struck a bargain with whatever force happened to be controlling Germany. Just as Hertling, the war Chancellor, and Erzberger, the author of the armistice, had sat side by side during the First World War so now Brüning could emerge from the ranks of the party which had helped to found the republic and which had ostensibly espoused democracy. If the army was to rule once more, the Centre would be its instrument.

The appointment of Brüning as Chancellor in March, 1930, marked the end of the German republic. Germany had slipped back without effort to the days before defeat when, too, a Roman Catholic Chancellor had carried out the orders of Hindenburg. Then it had been the ultimatum from Supreme Headquarters, now it was the 'emergency decree', by which Germany was ruled; both were signed by the same hand. The 'crisis' of March 1930, which brought Brüning into power, was the deliberate manufacture of the army leaders, and especially of General Schleicher, the army specialist for political intrigue. The decline in world trade, the increase in unemployment, had hardly begun; the only crisis was that even in the years of prosperity the budget had failed to balance. The 'national' classes still drew the line at direct taxation; and it was to impose direct taxes that Müller, Social Democratic Chancellor of a coalition government, proposed to use emergency decrees. But Schleicher and his associates would not put Hindenburg's prestige behind a democratic government; for while the Social Democrats did not impede German rearmament they would not actively promote it. On the other hand, the 'national' party leaders were too wild: if called to office, they would at once denounce the Young Plan and overthrow the shell of the constitution. The Reichswehr leaders were not driven on by a demagogic demand: quite the reverse, their action provoked the demagogic demand. When Brüning became Chancellor there were only twelve National Socialists in the Reichstag; it was owing to his policy that in the general election of September 1930, 108 National Socialists were returned. The National Socialist victory, abhorrent to Brüning, unwelcome to the Reichswehr, was the inevitable outcome of Brüning's dictatorship.

The 'crisis' of March 1930 was provoked by the Reichswehr, and Brüning chosen as Chancellor, for the sole purpose of speeding up German rearmament. The economic crisis was an afterthought, an accident, which took the Reichswehr by surprise. The Reichswehr leaders stood behind Brüning, gave him assurance against disorder, enabled him to disregard, as Imperial Chancellors had done, defeat in the Reichstag. Brüning, in return, pushed on rearmament, redoubled the campaign against the remnants of Versailles, yet, being a member of the Centre, served as window-dressing both to Germans of the Left and to the Allies, who, forgetting his activities during the First World War, failed to see in the pious Roman Catholic the spokesman of German militarism. Yet Brüning's position was sincere enough: wishing to serve Germany, he could serve only the army. Moreover in promoting rearmament he was pursuing a policy in which he himself believed;

thus being in a superior position to all other Centre politicians, whether under the Empire or of the republic, who were indifferent to the policies which they executed. The army was the sole 'authority': that was the key to Brüning's position. The republic had failed to develop a 'governing class'. The middle classes, themselves in awe of authority, had never forgiven the republic for the defeat of 1918; the working classes, with no social revolution to inspire them, were loyal, devoted, but ineffective. The economic crisis of 1929–33 did not give the deathblow to the republic; at most it drew attention to the fact that the republic was dead. Any system can stand in fair weather; it is tested when the storm begins to blow. This test the German republic could not pass: with few supporters and no roots, it fell at the first rumble of thunder.

12

DEMAGOGIC DICTATORSHIP AND THE COMPLETION OF GERMAN UNITY AFTER 1930

In 1930 parliamentary rule ceased in Germany. There followed, first, temporary dictatorship, then permanent dictatorship. Technically the Reichstag remained sovereign (as it did until 1945); actually Germany was ruled by emergency decrees, which the democratic parties tolerated as the 'lesser evil' – the greater evil being to provoke a civil conflict in defence of democracy. Unemployment, the result of the economic crisis, sapped the spirit of the skilled workers, who were the only reliable republicans. Their skill had been the one secure possession to survive the inflation; unemployment made it as worthless as the paper savings of the middle classes. Therefore, though still loyal to the republic, they became half-hearted, indifferent to events, feeling that they stood for a cause which was already lost, ready to respond, though with shame, to a 'national' appeal. The depression, too, completed the demoralization of the respectable middle class. The brief period of prosperity had stimulated a tendency, or its beginning, to postpone 'revenge' to a distant future – just as French pacificism after 1871 began as a very temporary affair. Of course Versailles had to be destroyed, but not while profits were mounting, not while salaries were good, not while more and more bureaucratic posts were being created; the German bourgeoisie felt that their generation had done enough for Germany. But in 1930, with the ending of prosperity, the distant future of 'revenge' arrived: the crisis seemed almost a punishment for the wickedness of neglecting the restoration of German honour and power. As for the great capitalists, they welcomed the depression, for it enabled them to carry still further the process of rationalization, which had been its cause. As one of them exclaimed: 'This is the crisis we need!' They could shake off both the remnants of Allied control and the weak ineffective brake of the republic, could make their monopolies still bigger, could compel even the Allies to welcome German rearmament as the only alternative to social revolution.

The republic had been an empty shell; still its open supersession in 1930 created a revolutionary atmosphere, in which projects of universal upheaval could flourish. Now, if ever, was the time of the Communists, who saw their prophecies of capitalist collapse come true. But the Communists made nothing of their opportunity: they still regarded the Social Democrats as their chief enemy, still strove to increase confusion and disorder in the belief that a revolutionary situation would carry them automatically into power. The German Communists, with their pseudo-revolutionary jargon, were silly enough to evolve this theory themselves; but they were prompted on their way by the orders of the Comintern, which was still obsessed with the fear of a capitalist intervention against the Soviet Union and so desired above everything else to break the democratic link between Germany and Western Europe. The Soviet leaders, with their old-fashioned Marxist outlook, thought that the German army leaders were still drawn exclusively from the Prussian Junkers and therefore counted confidently on a renewal of the old Russo-Prussian friendship. In 1930 German democracy was probably too far gone to have been saved by any change of policy; still the Communist line prevented the united front of Communist and Social Democratic workers which was the last hope of the republic. The Communists were not very effective; so far as they had an effect at all it was to add to the political demoralization, to act as the pioneers for violence and dishonesty, to prepare the way for a party which had in very truth freed itself from the shackles of 'bourgeois morality', even from the morality devised by the German bourgeois thinker, Karl Marx.

To talk of a 'party', however, is to echo the misunderstandings of those lamentable years. The National Socialists were not a party in any political sense, but a movement: they were action without thought, the union of all those who had lost their bearings and asked only a change of circumstances no matter what. At the heart of the National Socialists were the Free Corps, the wild mercenaries of the post-war years, whose 'patriotism' had taken the form of shooting German workers. The Munich rising in November 1923 had been the last splutter of their Free Corps days. Since then they had been taught discipline by a ruthless gangster leader, Hitler, a man bent on destruction, 'the unknown soldier of the last war', but unfortunately not buried, expressing in every turn of his personality the bitter disillusionment of the trenches; and a greater master of hysteric oratory than either Frederick William IV or William II. The National Socialists had no programme, still less a defined class interest; they stood simply for destruction and action, not contradictory but complementary. They united in their ranks the disillusioned of every class: the army officer who had failed to find a place in civil life; the ruined capitalist; the unemployed worker; but, most of all, the 'white collar' worker of the lower middle class, on whom the greatest burden of the post-war years had fallen. The unemployed clerk; the university student who had failed in his examinations; the incompetent lawyer and the blundering doctor: all these could exchange their shabby threadbare suits for the smart uniforms of the National Socialist army and could find in Hitler's promise of action new hope for themselves. In England they would have been shipped off to the colonies as remittance men: their presence in Germany was the high price which the victors of 1918 paid for the worthless tracts of German colonial territory.

The failure of the Munich rising in 1923 had taught Hitler a bitter lesson: he must not run head on against the army and the possessing classes. From that moment until September 1933 he used the method of intrigue, of terror and persuasion, not the method of open assault. Just as the Communists had tried to outbid the 'national' parties in whipping up nationalist passion, so now Hitler outbid the Communists, but with the added attraction, for the upper classes, that this nationalist passion would be turned against the German working classes as well. He was at once everyone's enemy and everyone's friend: his programme of contradictory principles could succeed only in a community which had already lost all unity and self-confidence. To the workers he offered employment; to the lower-middle classes a new self-respect and importance; to the capitalists vaster profits and freedom from trade union restraints; to the army leaders a great army; to all Germans German supremacy; to all the world peace. In reality it mattered little what he offered: to a Germany still bewildered by defeat he offered action, success, undefined achievement, all the sensations of a revolution without the pains. In September 1930, when the economic crisis had hardly begun, but when the French had evacuated the Rhineland, the National Socialists were already hot on the heels of the Social Democrats as the largest party in the Reichstag; the 'national' card was irresistible.

This moral was drawn too by Brüning, who, in his hatred of National Socialist paganism, adopted in succession almost every item of the National Socialist creed. Called in to save German capitalism and to promote German rearmament, Brüning went further on the path already marked out by Stresemann. Stresemann had tried to make the republic popular by winning concessions in foreign affairs. Brüning demanded concessions in foreign affairs in order to win support for his system of presidential dictatorship. If Germany was allowed to rearm, the Germans might not notice the reductions in their wages. More than that, if Germans were brought together in a campaign of hatred against Poland, the disparities between rich and poor would be overlooked. Where Stresemann had tried to conciliate the Allies, Brüning blackmailed them: if they did not make concessions to him, they would have to deal with Hitler and the National Socialists. Brüning knew that the economic crisis was due to deflation, the decline of prices and wages; still, far from attempting to arrest or even alleviate this deflation, he drove it on – forced wages and, less effectively, prices, still lower – perhaps to get the crisis over all the sooner, perhaps to threaten the Allies with the prospect of German ruin. For the Brüning Cabinet was primarily a cabinet of 'front-line fighters', officers of the First World War, who were dominated by the resolve to reverse the verdict of 1918. Stresemann too had desired to liquidate Versailles, but he had cared also for democracy; Brüning was for the undoing of Versailles pure and simple, hoping, no doubt, to win popularity with the German people, satisfying still more his own deepest feelings. For him, as much as for the great capitalists, the crisis was welcome, the crisis he needed. His most ambitious effort was the customs union with Austria in March 1931, ostensibly a measure against the depression, though it is difficult to see the use of a customs union between two countries both suffering from unemployment and impoverishment. In reality the purpose of the customs union was not economic, but demagogic, an evocation of the programme of Greater Germany, and, so far as it had any sense, a move of economic war against Czechoslovakia, exposed outpost of the system of Versailles. France and her central European allies protested and, almost for the last time, got their way: the separation of Austria from Germany was the only remaining guarantee against an over-whelming German power, and this last fragment of victory was shored up for a few more years.

The Brüning policy of combating evil by taking homoeopathic doses of the same medicine, far from checking the National Socialists, aided their advance. If the Allies trembled before Brüning's blackmail, they would collapse altogether before the blackmail of Hitler. Brüning made everyone in Germany talk once more of rearmament, of union with Austria, of the injustice of the eastern frontier; and every sentence of their talk made them turn, not to Brüning, but to the movement of radical revision. Above all, Brüning had overlooked the lesson of the First World War which Ludendorff had learnt too late – that a pro-gramme of German power must rest on a demagogic basis. Austria, Poland, Bohemia, could not be conquered, and Versailles defied, by a Chancellor supported only by a section of the Centre party; for that, a united German will was needed. Captain Brüning was half-way between General Ludendorff and Corporal Hitler, with the weaknesses of both, the advantages of neither. Brüning, the defender of the Roman Catholic Church, shared the error of Stresemann, the defender of the republic: both thought to draw the sting of nationalism by going with it, to silence demagogy by trying to capture its tone. Neither grasped that his every step strengthened his enemy; neither understood that the only security for German democracy, or for German Christian civiliza-tion, lay in a full and sincere acceptance of the Treaty of Versailles. Only if Germany made reparation; only if Germany remained disarmed; only if the German frontiers were final; only, above all, if the Germans accepted the Slav peoples as their equals, was there any chance of a stable, peaceful, civilized Germany. No man did more than Brüning to make this Germany impossible.

The decay, disappearance indeed, of peaceful Germany was openly revealed in 1932 when the time came to elect a new President. The candidate of upheaval and violence was Hitler; the candidate of the peaceful constitutional Left was Hindenburg, hero of the First World War and candidate in 1925 of the 'national' parties. The 'left' had moved immeasurably to the 'right' in the last seven years: what was then a defeat would now rank as a dazzling victory – for it could not be supposed that a senile soldier of over eighty and never mentally flexible had changed his outlook since 1925, or for that matter since 1918. The German people had accepted militarism: the only dispute was between the orderly militarism of a field-marshal and the unrestrained militarism of a hysterical corporal. Hindenburg carried the day, evidence that the Germans still craved to reconcile decency and power, militarism and the rule of law. Yet Hindenburg's victory, strangely enough, was the prelude to National Socialist success. Brüning drew from the presidential election the moral that his government must win greater popularity by some demagogic stroke; and, as a stroke in foreign policy was delayed, he sought for achievement in home affairs. His solution was his undoing. He planned to satisfy Social Democratic workers and Roman Catholic peasants by an attack on the great estates of eastern Germany, breaking them up for the benefit of ex-servicemen; and as a first step he began to investigate the affairs of the Osthilfe, the scheme of agrarian relief inaugurated in 1927 by which tens of millions of pounds had been lavished on the Junker landowners. This was a programme of social revolution, and it could be carried out only with the backing of enthusiastic and united democratic parties. But Brüning's solution of Germany's ills was the restoration of the monarchy, and he would not condescend to democracy by a single gesture; he relied solely on Hindenburg, and this reliance was his undoing. For Hindenburg, once himself the patron of land settlement for ex-servicemen, had been long won over by the Junker landowners, who in 1927 had launched a plan for presenting Hindenburg with an estate at Neudeck, once a Hindenburg property, but long alienated. It was characteristic of the Junkers that even for their own cause they would not pay: all the estate owners of eastern Germany only subscribed 60,000 marks, the rest of the required million was provided by the capitalists of the Ruhr – principally by Duisberg, manufacturer of paints and cosmetics. But thereafter Hindenburg counted himself a Junker landowner; and he turned against Brüning the moment that he was persuaded that Brüning's plans threatened the great estates. On May 29th, 1932, Brüning was summarily dismissed.

With the dismissal of Brüning there began eight months of intrigue and confusion, in which the old order in Germany, which had now come into its own, struggled to escape from the conclusion that, to achieve its ends, it must strike a bargain with the gangsters of National Socialism. Fragments of past policies were resurrected haphazard, as a dying man recalls chance echoes of his life. First device was the Roman Catholic cavalry officer, Papen, and his 'cabinet of barons', a collection of antiquarian conservatism unparalleled since the days of Frederick William IV, the sort of government which might have existed for a day if a few romantic officers had refused to acknowledge the abdication of William II in 1918. Papen's great achievement in the eyes of the Prussian landowners was to end constitutional government in Prussia: the Socialist ministers were turned out without a murmur. It was both curious and appropriate that Prussian constitutionalism, which had originated in the Junkers' selfish interest in the Ostbahn, should owe its death to the Junkers' selfish interest in the Osthilfe. Papen, in his daring, blundering way, continued, too, Brüning's undoing of Versailles, and accomplished the two decisive steps: reparations were scrapped in September 1932; German equality of armaments recognized in December. But it was impossible for a government of frivolous aristocrats, which would have been hard put to it to survive in 1858, to keep Germany going in 1932. Even the Centre, with its readiness to support any government, dared not offend its members by supporting Papen and expelled him from the party. The Germans, divided in all else, were united against the 'cabinet of barons'.

The army was forced to the last expedient of all: it took over the government itself. In December, Papen in his turn was ordered out of office and succeeded by General Schleicher, forced into office by his own intrigues. Schleicher, too, intended to do without the National Socialists, though he had often flirted with them in the past. He was the first professional soldier to rule Germany without an intermediary since Caprivi. Like Caprivi he was a 'social general', intelligent enough to see the advantages of an alliance between the army and the Left, not intelligent enough to see its impossibility. Schleicher imagined that the leaders of the trade unions would display on his behalf the resolution which they had failed to display on their own; even more extraordinary, he imagined that the more socialistic of the National Socialists would follow his lead instead of Hitler's. Neither expectation was fulfilled. On the other hand, the conservative advisers round Hindenburg began to feel that, if they were to do a deal with the National Socialists, they would rather enlist Hitler than one of his underlings. The agent of reconciliation between Hitler and the old order was none other than Papen, who now hoped somehow to manœuvre himself into the key position of power. Papen not only swung the Junkers behind Hitler. Early in January 1933 he negotiated an alliance between Hitler and the great industrialists of the Ruhr: Hitler was to be made Chancellor; the debts of the National Socialists were to be paid; and in return Hitler promised not to do anything of which Papen or the Ruhr capitalists disapproved. Papen's sublime self-confidence had already landed him in many disasters; but even he never made a more fantastic mistake than to suppose that Hitler's treachery and dishonesty, immutable as the laws of God, would be specially suspended for Franz von Papen.[1] Against this combination Schleicher was helpless.

The Reichstag was due to meet on January 31st. Three days before, Schleicher had to confess to Hindenburg that he could not stave off discussion of the Osthilfe; he could not even give assurance against a censure on the Junkers, carried by an alliance of National Socialists and the Left. Schleicher asked for a decree dissolving the Reichstag – the very policy of governing Germany by the armed force of the Reichswehr which he himself had overruled when Papen had proposed it in December. Hindenburg refused the decree. Thanks to Papen, he saw at last a way out, a democratic solution: Hitler, in alliance with the

---

[1] Or perhaps not so great a mistake. Personally, though not politically, they were suspended – at any rate until the present moment.

Nationalists, would not need to rely on presidential power – he would control a Reichstag majority, and thus restore constitutional rectitude. On January 30th, President Hindenburg, field marshal and Prussian landowner, appointed Corporal Hitler chancellor.

It was a symbolic act. The privileged classes of old Germany – the landowners, the generals, the great industrialists – made their peace with demagogy: unable themselves to give 'authority' a popular colour, they hoped to turn to their own purposes the man of the people. In January 1933 the 'man from the gutter' grasped the 'crown from the gutter' which Frederick William IV had refused in April 1849. The great weakness of the Bismarckian order, the weakness which caused its final liquidation in January 1933, was that the interests of the 'national' classes could never correspond to the deepest wishes of the German people. It was the Centre and the Social Democrats, not the Conservatives and still less the National Liberals, who had gained mass support. There was no need for a new party or a new leader to carry out the wishes of the landowners and the industrialists; but there was need for a new party and a new leader who would capture the mass enthusiasm, formerly possessed by the Centre and the Social Democrats, for the 'national' programme. This was Hitler's achievement, which made him indispensable to the 'national' classes, and so ultimately their master. He stole the thunder of the two parties which even Bismarck had never been able to master. The sham Socialism of his programme captured the disillusioned followers of the Social Democrats; the real paganism of his programme rotted the religious basis of the Centre.

There was nothing mysterious in Hitler's victory; the mystery is rather that it had been so long delayed. The delay was caused by the tragic incompatibility of German wishes. The rootless and irresponsible, the young and the violent embraced the opportunity of licensed gangsterdom on a heroic scale; but most Germans wanted the recovery of German power, yet disliked the brutality and lawlessness of the National Socialists, by which alone they could attain their wish. Thus Brüning was the nominee of the Reichswehr and the enemy of the republic, the harbinger both of dictatorship and of German rearmament. Yet he hated the paganism and barbarity of the National Socialists and would have done anything against them except breaking with the generals. Schleicher, in control of the Reichswehr, was obsessed with

German military recovery; yet he contemplated an alliance with the trade unions against the National Socialists and, subsequently, paid for his opposition with his life. The generals, the judges, the civil servants, the professional classes, wanted what only Hitler could offer – German mastery of Europe. But they did not want to pay the price. Hence the delay in the National Socialist rise to power; hence their failure to win a clear majority of votes even at the general election in March 1933. The great majority of German people wanted German domination abroad and the rule of law at home, irreconcilables which they had sought to reconcile ever since 1871, or rather ever since the struggles against Poles, Czechs, and Danes in 1848.

In January 1933 the German upper classes imagined that they had taken Hitler prisoner. They were mistaken. They soon found that they were in the position of a factory owner who employs a gang of roughs to break up a strike: he deplores the violence, is sorry for his work-people who are being beaten up, and intensely dislikes the bad manners of the gangster leader whom he has called in. All the same, he pays the price and discovers, soon enough, that if he does not pay the price (later, even if he does) he will be shot in the back. The gangster chief sits in the managing director's office, smokes his cigars, finally takes over the concern himself. Such was the experience of the owning classes in Germany after 1933. The first act of the new dictators won the game. On February 27th a young Dutch Socialist set fire to the Reichstag as a gesture of idealistic defiance against the Nazis. Hitler seized this heaven-sent opportunity to proclaim a Communist plot and to suspend the rule of law in Germany. The Reichstag fire, burning away the pretentious home of German sham-constitutionalism, was the unexpected push by which the old order in Germany, hesitating on the brink, was induced to take the plunge into gangster rule. The new Reichstag, still, despite the outlawing of the Communists, with no clear National Socialist majority, met under open terror. Hitler asked for an Enabling Bill, to make him legal dictator. He was supported by the 'national' parties, and the Centre, faithful to its lack of principles to the last, also voted for Hitler's dictatorship, in the hope of protecting the position of the Roman Catholic Church; impotent to oppose, they deceived themselves with the prospect of a promise from Hitler, which was in fact never given. Only the Social Democrats were loyal to the republic which they had failed to defend and by a final gesture, impotent but noble, voted unitedly against the bill. But even the Social Democrats went on to show the fatal weakness which had destroyed German liberties. When in May 1933 the Reichstag was recalled to approve Hitler's foreign policy, the Social Democrats did not repeat their brave act: some abstained, most voted with the National Socialists. This was an absurdity. If Germany intended to undo the system of Versailles, she must organize for war, and she could organize for war only on a totalitarian basis. Only by renouncing foreign ambitions could Germany become a democracy; and as even the Social Democrats refused to make this renunciation the victory of the National Socialists was inevitable.

This is the explanation of the paradox of the 'Third Reich'. It was a system founded on terror, unworkable without the secret police and the concentration camp; but it was also a system which represented the deepest wishes of the German people. In fact it was the only system of German government ever created by popular initiative. The old empire had been imposed by the arms of Austria and France; the German Confederation by the armies of Austria and Prussia. The Hohenzollern empire was made by the victories of Prussia, the Weimar republic by the victories of the Allies. But the 'Third Reich' rested solely on German force and German impulse; it owed nothing to alien forces. It was a tyranny imposed upon the German people by themselves. Every class disliked the barbarism or the tension of National Socialism; yet it was essential to the attainment of their ends. This is most obvious in the case of the old 'governing classes'. The Junker landowners wished to prevent the expropriation of the great estates and the exposure of the scandals of the *Osthilfe*; the army officers wanted a mass army, heavily equipped; the industrialists needed an economic monopoly of all Europe if their great concerns were to survive. Yet many Junkers had an old-fashioned Lutheran respectability; many army officers knew that world conquest was beyond Germany's strength; many industrialists, such as Thyssen, who had financed the National Socialists, were pious and simple in their private lives. But all were prisoners of the inescapable fact that if the expansion of German power were for a moment arrested, their position would be destroyed.

But the National Socialist dictatorship had a deeper foundation.

Many, perhaps most, Germans were reluctant to make the sacrifices demanded by rearmament and total war; but they desired the prize which only total war would give. They desired to undo the verdict of 1918; not merely to end reparations or to cancel the 'war guilt' clause, but to repudiate the equality with the peoples of eastern Europe which had then been forced upon them. During the preceding eighty years the Germans had sacrificed to the Reich all their liberties; they demanded as reward the enslavement of others. No German recognized the Czechs or Poles as equals. Therefore every German desired the achievement which only total war could give. By no other means could the Reich be held together. It had been made by conquest and for conquest; if it ever gave up its career of conquest, it would dissolve. Patriotic duty compelled even the best of Germans to support a policy which was leading Germany to disaster.

This implacable logic of circumstance doomed to failure every attempt to arrest the advance of National Socialist 'totalitarianism'. The institutions which had been too much for Bismarck, the conflicting political forces which had for so long pulled Germany this way and that, were all overborne. The political parties were abolished in the summer of 1933; the trade unions were taken over without the semblance of a struggle; the states, last relics of particularism, were wiped out of existence. Nuremberg, proudest of Free Cities, became the meeting-place of the annual National Socialist demonstration; and Bavaria, most separatist of states, the very heart of the National Socialist movement. Only the Roman Catholic Church attempted to resist; and, though it was defeated, yet its defeat was perhaps a little less thorough than that of every other organization in Germany. Roman Catholics accepted Hitler's course of policy, and none ever protested against any of the barbarities of German conquest; but they were allowed to remain Roman Catholics. In this record of subjection, the National Socialist programme was no exception. Where it clashed with the claims of total war, it too was disregarded. The destruction of 'interest slavery', liberation from 'monopoly capitalism', a new social order, these turned out to mean nothing at all; and even when war raged, the profits of the German capitalists were less controlled than in any other belligerent country. Still a Socialist element, in the German sense, remained. What German Socialists and German workers had objected to in capitalism was not so much inequality of incomes, as freedom of enterprise and the freedom of action which comes with the secure ownership of property. This freedom the German capitalists lost as completely as if they had been expropriated: they could not conduct their undertakings ('enterprises' no longer) according to their own wishes and were no more free to choose their course than the most degraded worker driven into the factory by hunger. Capitalism had deprived the industrial workers of their freedom, or so they thought. National Socialism was their revenge: it deprived the capitalists of freedom also.

The strain and tension of National Socialist rule was always great; and at no moment was their 'total' rule complete. A vague grumbling, sometimes more, remained as the last protest of the human spirit. But only on one occasion was there any serious attempt to turn this protest to account and to retard the process of totalitarian advance. The organizer of this attempt was again Papen, the irrepressible conspirator: swindled by Hitler, who speedily deprived him of any real power, he planned in 1934 to undo the effects of his own cunning and to make himself the mouthpiece of German decency. Behind him, vaguely coordinated, was a strange coalition: Reichswehr generals who still hoped to combine a great army and civilized government; great industrialists who still hoped to combine great armament contracts and the rule of law; and on the other side, Hitler's more radical followers, led by Röhm, sexual pervert and organizer of the gangster bands, who still hoped for a social revolution. Figures from the last days of the republic – Schleicher, even Brüning – moved somewhere in the shadows; but it was typical of all 'decent' Germans that they should look to the man who had intrigued them into their difficulties to intrigue them out again. And equally typical that Papen should make the mistake of William II, of the Weimar republic, of Brüning, and of Schleicher, and rely on Hindenburg, now eighty-six, as the saviour of Germany. On June 17th, 1934, Papen delivered the only speech against the régime ever made in National Socialist Germany. As usual Papen's plan misfired: in fact, putting Hitler into power was the only plan of Papen's which ever succeeded, to Papen's bitterest regret. Hindenburg did not respond. Perhaps, tottering into the grave, he was beyond action; perhaps he was carried away by Hitler's threadbare device of a Communist plot. On Hindenburg's orders Papen was spared to continue his irrepressible career of unsuccessful intrigues. All the other elements of opposition were wiped out – Schleicher, Röhm, and the Brown Shirt extremists, old enemies of Hitler from the time of the 1923 failure, anyone who might impede the dictatorship or its workings. The 'blood bath' of June 30th, 1934, washed away the last scruples: it was the clear assertion that there could be no turning back.

Within a month Hindenburg died; and Hitler succeeded him as President and Commander-in-Chief. But his proudest title was Führer, the leader. At last someone ruled in Berlin. The amalgamation of demagogy and the old order was complete. The gangster sat in the managing director's chair. But with a strange, though inevitable, result. Once in the director's chair, the gangster was faced with the problems which had faced his predecessor and attempted to solve them in the same way. Hitler became Ludendorff, and Göring became Thyssen – no doubt a very painful change for Thyssen, but of no moment to anyone else. Just as Bismarck had balanced between agrarians and industrialists, so Hitler balanced between the possessing classes and the masses, keeping the confidence of both by his simultaneous pursuit of Little German and Greater German aims. Hitler had one great advantage over Bismarck, which enabled him to weather greater crises. Bismarck had no 'Bismarck class', apart from a few family friends, who would stand by him through thick and thin; therefore he could not put up a fight when he was turned out in 1890. Hitler discovered a 'Hitler class', his unshakable resource in extremity, the class which he organized into the well-paid, well-dressed Black Guards, the S.S. – the middle class of education but no property. Their education estranged them from the masses, their lack of property from the possessing classes; they were the élite, the 'managers' of the National Socialist system, under whose leadership Germans were united as never before.

Germany was united against the foreigner: this alone justified the suppression of sectional interests, the 'mobilization', in fact, of Germany. From January 1933, or without reserve from June 30th, 1934, Germany was mobilizing for total war. This was the meaning of the planned economy and of the conquest of unemployment, once so admired by English and American observers: England and America too have now discovered that war conquers unemployment. The difference is only that Germany had the foresight to mobilize before declaring war and so enjoyed a great initial advantage. One part of the emotional mobilization, a relic of the discarded National Socialist programme, was anti-Semitism, stock-in-trade of every nationalistic movement. In the beginning, anti-Semitism was an easy outlet for the vague socialism of the National Socialist rank-and-file, the destruction of Jewish shops a showy substitute for social change. As always, anti-Semitism was the socialism of fools. But it soon came to serve a more sinister purpose. The Jews became the helpless objects on which millions of Germans first exercised the brutality essential if Germany was to dominate all Europe. They were the practising ground, the battle-training school, for the Nordic virtues, which were later to find their full expression in Poland, in France, and in occupied Russia. The great pogrom of November 1938, following hard on the victory of Munich, was the test mobilization of German morale. If the Germans could stomach that, they could stomach anything. No voice of protest was raised, in not one instance did a Christian Church, whether Roman Catholic or Protestant, open its doors to the Jews in refuge, no German bishop put on the star of David. The Germans had passed the test with flying colours: they were indeed united.

In one sphere, and one only, Hitler's unification of Germany was surprisingly delayed, a delay which was to recall once more all the conflicting elements of the 'German question'. Hitler was himself an Austrian German by birth, and the National Socialist programme came almost entirely from Habsburg Austria: the nationalism from Schönerer, German leader in the Czech-German struggle in Bohemia, the sham socialism and the anti-Semitism from Lueger, demagogic leader of the Vienna lower-middle class. Hitler's Reich could have no meaning unless Austria was included, nor could the achievement of the Greater German programme be begun without the encirclement of Czechoslovakia. Independent Austria was, in fact, the keystone of the settlement of Versailles. But nothing had been done to make the keystone secure. Austria was supposed to be economically unworkable; but that was one of the myths, a *fable convenue* of the age. Of course, rump Austria, once the centre of an empire of fifty million people, was heavily over-capitalized: not only too many great buildings, too many banks, too many railway stations, but still more over-capitalized in persons – too many bureaucrats, too many generals, too many bankers, too many professional men. The process of adjustment was painful for these classes, but it was accomplished; and by the middle of the nineteen-thirties Austrian economic life had reached a balance. Austria was not so hard hit as Germany by the economic crisis, and she emerged from it without relying on unlimited production of armaments. What Austria lacked was not economic existence, but spiritual belief, a 'way of life'. Only the order of the Allies had made Austria independent, and only the veto of the Allies kept her so. Unlike the other 'succession states', Austria had no sentiment of nationality – except German. No 'Austrian idea', divorced from the vanished empire of the Habsburgs, was discovered. The National Socialist dictatorship gave Austria her last, and great, opportunity. With the submerging of the Centre and the Social Democrats in Germany, Austria could have held out a German alternative: a true version, not a perversion, of the Greater German vision of 1848 – a free federal Germany, not worshipping power, founded on Christian civilization and on democratic Socialist principles.

The opportunity was thrown away. The Christian Socialists, Austrian equivalent of the Centre, who ruled in Austria, wished to preserve Austrian independence, but they attempted to fight without allies, or rather with the wrong ones. Instead of seeking for a common democratic front with the Social Democrats, they strove, even in the nineteen-twenties, to destroy both the Social Democrats and democracy. Seipel, the priest who then led the Christian Socialist party, replied to the Social Democratic attempts at reconciliation: 'No mildness!' With the rise of the National Socialists, Dollfuss, Seipel's successor, faced supreme peril. But he was still obsessed with the struggle against 'Marxism'. He rejected co-operation with democratic Czechoslovakia, and relied instead on the support of Fascist Italy, a support which enabled him to break openly with democracy and in February 1934 to destroy the Austrian Social Democrats in civil war. Artillery breached the working-class flats in Vienna; and those shots breached, too, Austrian independence, last hope both of German civilization and of European peace. In July 1934 Hitler engineered a National Socialist putsch in Vienna. Dollfuss was murdered, but the German army was not yet strong enough to challenge the Italian forces which were moved to the Austrian frontier. The *putsch* was disavowed, and for nearly four years Austria maintained a posthumous existence under the protection of Italian bayonets. Schuschnigg, who took the place of Dollfuss, did nothing to heal the quarrel with the Social Democrats, who represented almost half the Austrian population; nothing, that is, until five days before the entry of Hitler into Vienna in March 1938. The Austrian clerical government made, instead, a revisionist bloc with Hungary and Italy. Hungary could demand 'revision' at the expense of Czechoslovakia, Roumania, and Yugoslavia; Italy at the expense of Yugoslavia, France, and the British Empire. But at whose expense could the Austrian clericals demand revision? Only at their own. Like Brüning in Germany, Dollfuss and Schuschnigg repudiated democracy and so cleared the way for a more ruthless and effective dictatorship.

Without a reconciliation between Roman Catholics and Socialists, Austria could not be a challenge to National Socialist Germany; and after February 1934, reconciliation was almost impossible. Austria's fate was sealed: the few people in England and France who cared for Austria were estranged by the suppression of the Social Democrats, and the moment that Italy ceased to be strong enough to oppose Germany the last prop would be withdrawn – a moment not difficult to attain. Vienna could no longer offer a German alternative; therefore, even before the absorption of Austria, the unification of Germany was complete. Hitler had united Germany, had bound together all the contradictory elements of German ambition. With the same logic of Ludendorff, coherently though not consciously, he abandoned the 'either . . . or' for the 'both . . . and . . .'. Demagogic Pan-Germanism could not succeed without the backing of the Junkers and the great industrialists; the Junkers and great industrialists could not maintain themselves without the backing of demagogic Pan-Germanism. By origin, Hitler was a Greater German, concerned with Austria, with Bohemia, and the Danube route to the Near East; but by adoption, as head of the Reich, he was also a Little German, concerned with Poland and, to a lesser extent, with overseas colonies. The two programmes were amalgamated, emphasis laid first on one, then on the other, as a matter of tactics, solely to divide his opponents. Little German ambitions were directed against England and France, and, being anti-Polish, were by implication friendly to Russia; Greater German ambitions, directed against the Slavs and the Ukraine, were anti-Russian and, indifferent to colonies, were by implication friendly to the western powers. Both were being pursued; but it was essential for their attainment that Russia and the western powers, both vitally menaced, should not unite against them. To keep Russia and the western powers divided was the great achievement of German policy between 1934 and 1941, and the key to German success. Anti-Bolshevism in England and France, suspicion of the capitalist powers in Russia, did the trick and almost gave Germany the mastery of the world.

Translated into practical terms, the Little German policy threatened Poland, the Greater German policy Czechoslovakia, the two limits to German power. Had Poland and Czechoslovakia ever joined forces, the great powers of east and west would have joined forces too; their disunion was the basis of German success. The Poles were Slavs, but ever since the Slav Congress of 1848 they had opposed Slav unity: in part because they were a 'historic nation' with a living aristocracy and so could not co-operate with peasant peoples, in part because Slav unity could only be achieved under Russian leadership, which the Poles would never accept. Recent events had added new causes of dis-union. The Poles would not forget their failure to take Teschen from the Czechs in 1919. Still more, the Poles were irrevocably estranged from Russia by the Treaty of Riga of 1921, by which Poland took advantage of Russia's weakness to annex great stretches of Ukrainian and White Russian land. The Treaty of Riga made a Russo-Polish alliance impossible, for, while the Russians would not take the initia-tive in recovering their territory, they could not be expected to fight for the maintenance of Polish rule over peoples of Russian stock. The Treaty of Riga, not the Treaty of Versailles, made possible the second German war. The Poles, whether convinced or not, had to take Hitler seriously as a Greater German and to imagine that he would neglect Poland for the valley of the Danube; hence the neutrality agreement between Poland and Germany in 1934, which gave Hitler a free hand to attack the Czechs in Bohemia. German policy was turned decisively towards the attainment of Greater German goals; and the succeeding steps of German power – the establishment of a conscript army in 1935, the militarization of the Rhineland and the war of intervention in Spain in 1936 which gave France a third hostile frontier – were in relation to the western powers genuinely defensive. Hitler wished to be left alone while he carried out the Greater German programme.

It appears at first sight paradoxical that the Greater German programme should come first, that Germany should concentrate on the Austrian lands, which had been severed from the Reich in 1866, to the neglect of the Polish lands, which had been lost only in 1918, that the attack on Austria (March 1938) or on Czechoslovakia (September 1938) should have preceded the attack on Poland. The explanation was simple: the greater includes the less. In 1848 the Greater Germans of the Frankfurt parliament soon jettisoned their sympathy with Poland at the call of 'healthy national egoism', even though this committed them to an alliance with the Prussian army; and in 1914 the Social Democrats, who ostensibly supported only the war against Tsardom, were soon persuaded to direct their hostility against 'entente capitalism' as well. On the other hand, the Little German programme, as Bismarck had shown, could become a positive barrier against Greater Germany; and the old Russo-Prussian friendship had been newly reinforced by Russian assistance to German rearmament in the nineteen-twenties. If Germany had first reconquered the lands lost at Versailles, so many powerful elements would have been satisfied, the army leaders above all, that it would have been difficult to go further. As it was, the continued humiliation of the 'corridor' actually made Prussian Junkers desire the inclusion of Vienna in the Reich, although this reversal of the verdict of 1866 would destroy the last remnants of Junker independence.

This calculation was in itself decisive, but it was reinforced by international considerations. The Poles, as the neutrality agreement of 1934 showed, would not go to the assistance of the Czechs; in fact they participated in the attack on Czechoslovakia in 1938. The Czechs, however, would go to the assistance of the Poles: recognizing the nature of the German menace, President Benes refused in 1936 a neutrality agreement such as Pilsudski had accepted in 1934 – unless Poland were included in it. Further, England and France would go to the assistance of Poland even without the co-operation of Russia – and Russia might then be drawn in. Russia would not go to the assistance of

Czechoslovakia without the co-operation of England and France.[1] The greater programme was therefore not merely the more attractive, but actually the easier to accomplish: and, on any reasonable calculation, its attainment would make the attaining of the lesser programme so easy as to be automatic. It was naïve of the British and French to suppose that the sacrifice of Austria and Bohemia would satisfy the German craving for 'world power'; but even more naïve of the Russians to suppose that Russo-German friendship could be renewed in 1939 on the Little German basis of a partition of Poland, when the most cardinal elements in the Greater German programme had already been achieved. Above all it was naïve of anyone to suppose that compromise with National Socialist Germany was ever possible on any point. Economically, politically, spiritually, Germany had to keep up a ceaseless process of expansion. Victories on an ever greater scale were its life-blood; and without this increasing flow of victories, not merely the National Socialist dictatorship, but the entire German order would have collapsed. A sane diplomacy, proceeding one step at a time, could have established German mastery imperceptibly and without war. Still more, the weight of German economic power would soon have forced all

[1] To explain these two sentences would need a long excursion into international policies. England and France having a common frontier with Germany (England only by sea) could threaten Germany without Russian permission. Russia, having no such common frontier, could threaten Germany only if England and France induced Poland to enter the war (the 1938 project of Russia; attacking Germany through Roumania and sub-Carpathian Russia was obviously impracticable in the long run). Anglo-French aid to Poland could not tar Poland more thoroughly with the character of an agent of 'entente capitalism' than she was tarred already; Russian aid to Czechoslovakia would tar Czecho-slovakia with the character of an agent of 'Bolshevism' and expose her to the fate of the Spanish republic. Anglo-French policy was based on the hope that, if the Germans must go somewhere, they would go east; a German attack on Czechoslovakia would be the welcome news that the *Drang nach Osten* was being renewed. But Poland is not the route to the Balkans, and an attack on Poland, with its inevitable consequence of a partition with Russia, would be evidence that the Germans were turning west. Poland belongs to eastern Europe only geographically; politically she belongs to the west. She owed her resurrection both in 1807 and in 1919 to the victories of western arms; and if Russia had remained in the victorious coalition until 1919, there would have been no great Poland. But Czechoslovskia would have come into existence in 1919 with a victorious Russia quite as much as without: she belongs to the eastern system, though to the western system as well.

eastern Europe, and later western Europe too, into dependence on Germany; and in fact the representatives of British industry were in Düsseldorf in March 1939, arranging to become junior partners in a trade war against the United States in South America, when German violence spoilt the game. Like the Agadir *coup* in 1911, the occupation of Prague in 1939 was the shock which brought Germany's prey out of their hypnotic trance just before they were devoured, in 1911 in time to resist more or less effectively, in 1939 too late to save anything on the European continent.

March 15th, 1939, saw the resurrection of the traditional frontiers of the old Reich, Bohemia once more a protectorate, though now a sham one. So complete was now the amalgamation of Little German and Greater German aims that the same day saw the beginnings of the campaign for the recovery of the frontiers of Bismarck's Reich, though these frontiers had no meaning except as a barrier against Greater Germanism. The decisive sign that Germany had postponed further pursuit of the Greater German programme and had turned instead against Poland was the handing over of the republic of 'Carpatho-Ukraine', after twenty-four hours of independent existence, to Hungary. Therewith Germany renounced the project of detaching the Ukraine from Russia in co-operation with Poland. For, in fact, Poland would not co-operate. Poland was compelled by her geographical situation, and still more by the circumstances of her rebirth after the First World War, to be genuinely neutral between Russia and Germany. The territories which she had rightly acquired from Germany in 1919 made her reject an alliance with Germany as decisively as the territories which she had wrongfully acquired from Russia in 1921 made her reject an alliance with Russia.

The German encouragement of Hungarian 'revisionism' had deeper motives: in fact there is nothing in German political psychology deeper than the attachment, even respect, felt by all sections of German opinion for the Hungarian 'political nation'. On everything else Little Germans and Greater Germans might disagree. Greater Germans favoured the conquest of eastern Europe and the defeat of Russia; Little Germans expansion overseas and the defeat of the liberal western powers. But Greater German democrats rose at Vienna in October 1848, in defence of Hungarian independence; and Bismarck, greatest of Little Germans, imposed Hungarian freedom on the Habsburgs and guaranteed it. In the First World War, as for the matter of that in Hitler's war, all other 'allies' of Germany soon became helpless dependants; Hungary alone retained an arrogant independence, and refused to treat her Germans as a privileged minority. In Hungary, and nowhere else in Europe, the Germans ceased to feel themselves the 'master race'. Many elements produced this strange modesty: gratitude for the Hungarian 'revisionist' campaign against the treaty of Trianon in the nineteen-twenties which paved the way for the German 'revisionist' campaign against Versailles in the nineteen-thirties; the awe of a 'master race', still imperfectly sure of itself for a 'master race', which in far more difficult circumstances never lost its confidence and arrogance; but above all, common fear of the rising Slav tide. For on the continent of Europe, beyond the limits of Latin civilization, only Germans and Magyars stood out above the ocean of Slav peoples. German arrogance and brutality, like Magyar arrogance and brutality, were in the last resort the expression of an overmastering fear. In earlier centuries, great landed estates, and serfdom, absolutism or aristocratic government, had obscured this great Slav preponderance. Land reform, universal education, political democracy, and − above all − the industrialization of eastern Europe, at last began to give to the Slav masses their true weight. Sooner or later, the Slav peoples, with their deep sense of equality, their love of freedom, and their devotion to humanity, would end the artificial lordship of both Germans and Magyars. The tide was mounting; and Hitler's war was, in its deepest meaning, an attempt to sweep this Slav flood from the crumbling bastions of Greater Germany and Great Hungary. It is not surprising that the two 'master races' clung together; they were venturing out into a storm which would be their ruin.

The change of German policy on March 16th, 1939, was a confession that the Slav problem was becoming too big for Germany, and an assertion that it would be easier to turn against the western world. Just as the moves against France in 1936 had been defensive − to win a free hand for expansion in the east − so the moves against Poland in 1939 were defensive − to win a free hand for expansion in the west. Poland could have bought herself off, as Czechoslovakia could not, with small concessions, with little more in fact than the cancelling of her alliance with France. But this alliance was her sole guarantee against partition between Germany and Russia; and, refusing to abandon it, she became the means by which instead Russia was bought off and the old Junker-Tsarist partnership renewed in strangely changed form. As in 1938 the western powers had rubbed their hands at the promise of the *Drang nach Osten*, so in August 1939 the Russians folded their hands, if not rubbed them, at the *Drang nach Westen*. The German oscillation between east and west, Greater German and Little German, was still effective. Hitler had achieved Ludendorff's ambition: one army (and one emotional appeal) could win victories on two fronts, his enemies accepting battle only at his time-table. In June 1940, the defeat of France made Germany master of the European continent as far as the frontiers of Russia. The ambition of the generals for total victory, the ambition of the industrialists for the destruction of their competitors, the Socialists' projects for a united Europe, the idealists' dream of Europe at peace under the protection of the German sword, were all fulfilled in the National Socialist 'New Order'. Throughout Germany the bells rang for three days.

They rang too soon. The British were excluded from Europe; they could not be driven to confess defeat. To sustain the dizzy momentum of German industry and German psychology, new employment was needed for her armies and new victories to make the church bells ring. With the Little German programme still uncompleted, Germany swung back to the east, into the Balkans, and at last, on June 22nd, 1941, took the great plunge against Russia. It was the climax, the logical conclusion, of German history, the moment at which all the forces which had contended against each other within Germany for so long, joined in a common struggle against all the world. Germany was at last united. Anti-Bolshevism, anti-capitalism, the conquest of the west, the conquest of the east, German conservatism and German demagogy, were merged in a single cause. This cause was the supremacy everywhere of German arms, of German industry, of German culture, of the German people. It was a cause which carried German power to the Pyrenees and the English Channel; to the Arctic Circle and the gates of Leningrad; to Crete and the gates of Alexandria; to the gates of Stalingrad and the foothills of the Caucasus. This was the cause for which the German people had sacrificed liberty, religion, prosperity, law.

But June 22nd, 1941, was not only the climax of German history, it was also its turning point. Ostensibly the beginning of a new chapter of victories, it was in reality the day of Germany's doom. For on that day, by the greatest act of statesmanship of the century – say rather, of modern times – Winston Churchill proclaimed the alliance of England and Russia. There were no folded hands in England for the renewed *Drang nach Osten.*

German arms could boast of a last year of victories, but the victories were empty: the British Isles were not invaded, the Soviet Union was not subdued. In the autumn of 1942 the tide of German success was halted at Stalingrad by Russians and at Alamein by British arms; the two Great Powers had paid the debt which they had owed to Europe since 1864. Not a halt, but destruction, now threatened the German Reich: and the Germans had made their destruction sure by forcing war upon the United States. England and Russia had ended the period of German victories; but without the help of the United States, remote, secure, and prosperous, they might not have been able to remove Germany from the ranks of the Great Powers. Faced with war on two fronts, unable to hold up the Russians, still less knock them out, before the west was invaded, the German Empire was doomed. In failure, as in success, the German leaders had one trick, and one only: to promote disunion among their neighbours. Never was the turnip-ghost of Bolshevism more persistently displayed than in the death agony of the Nazi Reich. For the last time, too, the Germans of high character and weak politics attempted to take the centre of the stage. Heirs of Bethmann Hollweg and of Stresemann, they had supported German militarism, had denounced the frontiers of Versailles, but had disliked the barbarism, and still more the mistakes of the National Socialists. They were a motley coalition: Field Marshals and religious leaders, business men and Trade Unionists, aristocrats and men of education, united in impotent disapproval, 'great gentlemen' who had once peddled the cause of German power in civilized countries and who now attempted, but with less success, to restore civilization in a Germany from which power was vanishing. This coalition of the highminded had discussed and projected the overthrow of the Nazi gangsters ever since 1939 and perhaps even earlier; but they took the resolve to put their fine principles into action only when the Anglo-American armies had

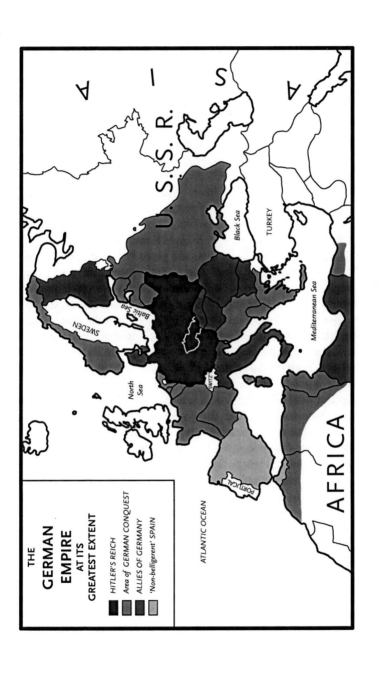

THE
GERMAN
EMPIRE
AT ITS
GREATEST EXTENT

■ HITLER'S REICH
▓ Area of GERMAN CONQUEST
▒ ALLIES OF GERMANY
░ 'Non-belligerent' SPAIN

ATLANTIC OCEAN

PORTUGAL

AFRICA

North
Sea

Baltic Sea

SWEDEN

SWITZ.

Mediterranean Sea

Black Sea

TURKEY

U.S.S.R.

established themselves in Normandy and the Red Army was at the gates of Warsaw. In July 1944 they conspired to assassinate Hitler and to establish a decent, harmless-looking German government with which the Western allies, at any rate, would make peace; even now they were more anxious to save Germany from the Russians than to save Europe from the Germans. They conspired, but, true to form to the last, their conspiracy was a failure. Even at the moment of disaster, Goebbels and Himmler were more than a match for the good Germans. The achievement of Prince Max of Baden was not repeated.

And now in Germany there was nothing, nothing except the grinding relentless pressure of the allied armies from East and West. Unsuccessful in total war, the Nazis accomplished a miracle of total destruction: in their ruin they brought down with them a Reich which had lasted for more than a thousand years. The spring of 1945 saw in Germany a process of dissolution without parallel in history, a catastrophe often unwelcome to the victors but the inevitable outcome of Germany's record. In May 1945 the armies of western civilization and of the Slav world met on the Elbe. Hitler, a will o'the wisp to the last, vanished into thin air; Goebbels, last great manipulator of the language of Goethe, perished miserably with his family in the ruins of Berlin; Himmler, greatest terrorist and policeman of history, perished still more miserably in the hands of his enemies; the rest, deflated and shabby, were left to face trial as war criminals. The German army broke into pieces and dissolved; the government of the Reich disappeared; even local administration fell to pieces. The only reality remaining was the armies of the occupying Powers; and these Powers now discovered the true problem which Germany presented to Europe – not how to resist German strength, but how to promote in Germany a sensible balanced way of life. Once more, as in the days of Napoleon, others would have to carry through for the Germans the liberation which they had been unable to achieve for themselves. In July 1945 the leaders of the three Great victorious Powers met at Potsdam to plan the future of Germany. The 'many great nations', whom Bismarck had dismissed with scorn, now sat in the seats of Frederick the Great, of Hitler, and of Bismarck himself. German history had run its course.

Some books on German history

K. S. Pinson: *Modern Germany: its history and civilization.* 1954.
Ralph Flenley: *Modern German History.* 1953.
E. J. Passant: *Germany 1815–1945.* 1959.
J. H. Clapham: *The economic development of France and Germany 1815–1914.* 1936.
L. B. Namier: *1848, the revolution of the intellectuals.* 1944.
H. Friedjung: *The struggle for supremacy in Germany.* 1934.
A. J. P. Taylor: *Bismarck, the man and the statesman.* 1955.
A. Rosenberg: *The birth of the German republic.* 1930.
C. E. Schorske: *German social democracy 1905–1917.* 1955.
J. W. Wheeler-Bennett: *Hindenburg: the Wooden Titan.* 1936.
Alan Bullock: *Hitler: a study in tyranny.* 1952.
H. R. Trevor-Roper: *The last days of Hitler.* 3rd edition. 1956.

INDEX